DATE DUE

DEMCO 38-296

THE HERITAGE OF OMAN

Peter Vine

IMMEL
Publishing

The maps in this book are not authoritative on international borders.

Photographs, unless otherwise credited are by the author.

Additional Contributors:
    Text:
    Gigi Crocker Jones

Additional photographs:
    German Mining Museum, Bochum, by G. Weisgerber
    German Archaeological Mission to Sultanate of Oman, by Paul Yule
    Ministry of Information, Sultanate of Oman
    Ministry of Petroleum & Minerals
    Petroleum Development Oman L.L.C..
    Chester Beatty Library, Dublin
    Hanne and Jens Eriksen
    Ranulph Fiennes
    Yves Gellie
    Shirley Kay
    Rodney Salm
    Andrew Spalton
    G. Thompson
    Christian Vioujard

Design, graphics & typesetting:
    Johan Hofsteenge

ISBN 1 898162 40 9

Immel Publishing Ltd.,
20 Berkeley Street,
Berkeley Square,
London W1X5AE

Tel. 0171 491 1799
Fax. 0171 493 5524

CONTENTS

Ancient History   9

The Islamic Era   63

Modern Oman   113

Natural History   141

Traditions   213

Further Reading   226

Acknowledgements   227

Index   228

Beehive tombs at Wadi al-Ayn.

ANCIENT HISTORY

EARLIEST SETTLERS

The hunting party

The storm had brought them inland in search of food. Sometimes such storms brought good luck, casting live fish up on the beach, an offering from the spirits perhaps, but this storm was different. Salt spray lashed the shoreline expressing the sea-spirit's anger, but it was still possible to collect shells from the sheltered mangrove creek behind the headland, so they had left the women and young children behind while they came in search of fresh meat. They had never explored this area before. For years they had been moving along the coastline, sometimes remaining in the same place for several moons, but always eventually moving on in search of new lands. Their fathers and grandfathers had done the same - as children they had been on similar hunts, acquiring the skills of tracking from their elders, learning to smell danger, to respect the agility and cunning of the spotted cat, and to savour the victory of trapping the white-horned beast.

The tracks had led them to this strange place. For two days they had been stalking a large herd of white-horns. At times they had been able to see the animals in the distance, their brilliant white skins reflecting the sun and their bodies seeming to float in the sky as the day's warmth caused the horizon to shimmer. It was not as if there was any shortage of wild animals to hunt; they had rarely seen such an abundance. Herds of fleet-footed gazelle danced before their eyes, scattering at their approach; large birds raced across the ground before taking off; the really big ones were unable to fly but could outpace a white-horn. They had large eggs: good to eat and to make into drinking cups. No, there was no shortage of food here, but it was not that easy to catch. Fortunately, they had

come across a solution to this problem.

The gradually rising plain across which they had been walking suddenly dropped into a dramatic, plunging ravine. The group had never seen anything like this before. It had been so difficult to trap the large animals when they were free to run wherever they wished across the grassy plain, but now they had the makings of a natural trap, every bit as good as the narrow mountain ravines where they had hunted three moons ago. Even as they stood there, gazing over the precipice and across the wide floor of the great rift, they heard a clatter of stones and the rhythmic beat of hooves as a family of curve-horns clambered up from the rocks beneath them and emerged on the crest, running along the edge with the big horned male leading and twin calves chasing behind. They had seen similar beasts on one or two previous hunts but had not expected to find them here. The omens were good and their leader motioned for them to sit while he drew pictures on the sand, explaining his plan.

Opposite:
A natural waterfall in mountainous region of the Al Hajr Ash-Sharqi.

Below:
Stone Age arrow and spearheads date back to Oman's earliest settlers.

The Huqf is a remote wilderness area where little has changed since Man first hunted here. Ibex are still found here, clinging to the crest of the precipitous cliffs.

Distribution of blade-arrowhead sites. (After Potts, 1990)

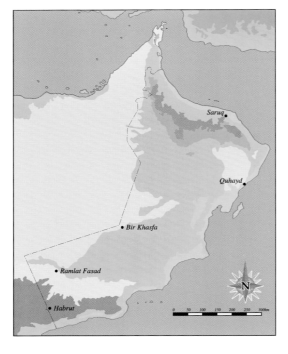

remains of the meat back with them so that their families could join in the feast. Life was good.

By the time they returned the storm had abated and their women had gathered a big pile of the tasty shells from among

For the next two days the best bowmen hid in the narrow ravines as their comrades pushed the game towards them. Their traps were designed to disable prey just long enough for them to move in for the kill. It was not easy, but neither did they need to kill many animals to feed their whole group. By the second evening they had three beasts, one white-horn and two of the smaller cliff-dwelling curve-horns. The animals were skinned and meat burned over an open fire. They carried the skins and

the mangroves. Two women were busy shaping fish-hooks from old shells, chipping at the fragments with sharp-edged flint stones. A fire had been lit on the beach and there was much talk that evening about the men's exploits and the things they had seen. When the men had finished their tale it was the women's turn to talk. One of the older girls spoke about what she had observed the previous day. As she was fishing from the headland two men in a strange craft paddled past her, along the shoreline. They were not of the group's tribe and the girl had not seen a boat like theirs before. It was not the first time the men had heard stories about these people. Only last moon a group had met fishermen from two such boats when they landed in a small bay. They had been impressed by the foreigners' fish-hooks, their strange woven clothes, their water jars and by the boats which were sea-worthy craft made from bundles of reeds. Communicating through signs, it seemed that the strangers had come from a long distance and had been paddling for many moons.

Had they been able to speak the same language the strangers would have explained that they came from a region near the great cities of Ur, Eridu and al-Ubaid in southern Mesopotamia at the head of the Gulf. They had never intended to sail so far south but strong currents off towering cliffs swept

them around the rocky promonotory of the straits and they just kept going, liking what they found and fearing to turn back the way they had come. They were not the first to have made this trip and would certainly not be the last. For the Sumerians, inhabitants of ancient Mesopotamia, the sea was primarily an important source of food and as fishermen ventured further and further afield they improved the sea-worthiness of their boats and honed their seamanship skills. Much later it became clear that these sea-going vessels provided a valuable means of transporting both people and goods. Fishermen who sailed south for fish discovered other treasures in the form of dates, pearls, aromatic substances like frankincense, and eventually also rare and valuable copper, essential for the manufacture in Sumeria of much-prized tools.

Before pottery: Oman's Stone Age

The hunting expedition described above is, of course, entirely speculative, since there are no written accounts of the life led by Oman's early settlers. However, the story is based on a careful evaluation of artefacts which have been found by archaeologists working in the Oman region. The oldest man-made objects that have survived through the millennia, rendering the exciting feel of being in touch with the past, are stone implements. Quantities of stone arrowheads, scrapers, axes and other tools, discarded by those hunters who roamed the area that is now Oman in search of game, have been discovered. Unlike later finds that can be carbon-dated, unless the stone tools are located in definite association with remains that lend themselves to an ageing method, the only way to estimate their age is to compare them with other tools of similar form for which an age estimate has been confidently determined.

In eastern and southern Arabia aceramic sites (lacking pottery) where stone tools

HANNE & JENS ERIKSEN

A mountain gazelle, Gazella gazella, *photographed at Yalooni, is now protected from hunting but in the past provided a vital source of meat for Oman's desert dwelling people.*

have been discovered are relatively numerous and there has been considerable debate as to whether any of these sites can be attributed to the palaeolithic era or early Stone Age. In a recent discussion of this

HANNE & JENS ERIKSEN

*A dramatic view of the
beehive tombs in Wadi
al-Ayn*

14

'palaeolithic' from the vocabulary of Arabian Gulf archaeology, rejecting the palaeolithic identification of those finds catalogued above from Kuwait, eastern Saudi Arabia, Bahrain and Oman". (He confirms however that palaeolithic sites do exist in western Arabia).

The early stone tools referred to above have their contemporary counterparts in Oman. Dating from c7600-5000 BC, they provide us with the earliest solid evidence for Man's presence in Oman. The typical form emanating from the stone industry of the period is a slender, finely retouched blade-arrowhead that may or may not be tanged. Neolithic sites attributable to the this period have been located in a number of places in Oman, including Ramlat Fasad in northern Dhofar; Bir Khasfa and Habarut in southern Dhofar; in the Wahiba Sands, and at Saruq near Muscat. One of the remarkable aspects about flint sites attributable to this early southern Arabian stone-age is that they are so sparsely distributed. This may reflect the fact that the climate during this period in southern Arabia was relatively warmer and drier, and that the game populations that were so prolific during the fifth and early fourth millennia were not nearly so abundant in this preceding era.

Although the number of hunters who depended upon blade arrowheads appears to have been small, this does not mean, however, that these were the only people living in Oman. Whereas the drought ridden interior may have been less than ideal for the hunter-gatherers of the time, life at the coast was a different matter. Much later the Greeks referred to the 'Ichthyophagi' or 'fish-eaters' who clung to the shores of Arabia. The ancestors of these Arabian fishermen were well established during the period from c.7600 to 5000 BC.

As we shall see in the section dealing with the late fourth and third millennia, the

Arabian oryx (Oryx leucoryx) roam freely across the Jidat Al Harasis. They were an important source of food for early settlers who hunted them with cleverly designed desert traps ('kites') and with bows and arrows.

problem, it was pointed out that sites that had previously been regarded as palaeolithic are in fact around 9500 years old, or part of the neolithic. Studies carried out by a French archaeological mission, working elsewhere in south-eastern Arabia, adamantly refuted earlier age interpretations of finds made there. They showed that scrapers previously thought to belong to the mesolithic were of the fifth or possibly fourth millennia BC. Commenting on this work in his excellent two-part treatise, *The Arabian Gulf in Antiquity*, D.T. Potts writes: "J. Tixier and M.L. Inizan have effectively eliminated

HANNE & JENS ERIKSEN

Sunsets at Yalooni are often as dramatic as this one. It is a magical place where nature has been lovingly preserved. It is a place where one steps back into the past and gains hope for the future.

fishing community favoured a number of prominent headlands along the coast of Oman from where they could keep watch for schools of fish and where they tended to the daily tasks of caring for their fishing gear. The site at Ra's al-Hamra, west of Muscat, near the present location of the Intercontinental Hotel, was used by fishermen around 6000 BC and thereafter. The area looked somewhat different in ancient times since the creek beneath the headland was thickly wooded by mangroves and must have been a prime collecting place for the molluscs that formed an important part of the community's diet. Among a series of sites excavated on the Ra's al-Hamra headland one, labelled RH 10, has provided the earliest evidence of these fishing communities having been established in Oman. Carbon 14 dating was applied to bits of charcoal, shells and earth burnt by ancient fires. Graves also contained charred remains of humans. The oldest time frame identified from the C14 testing was 5975 - 5475 BC, whilst a second collection of material gave a date of 5800 - 5390 BC, placing the site firmly in the sixth millennium BC.

Studies on stone implements found in eastern and southern Arabia, dated to the fifth millennium BC, have confirmed a widespread similar tradition in manufacturing techniques for an extensive region,

from the eastern province of Saudi Arabia to Dhofar in southern Oman. Radio-carbon dating confirms that the site at Ra's al-Hamra continued to be occupied throughout the fifth millennium. In addition to remains of meals, evidence of Man's presence comes in the form of net-sinkers and fish-hooks made from the pearl-oyster (*Pinctada radiata*) and bone. The find of sorghum in a layer dated to 4800 BC confirms early use in Oman of a plant that later became a major cultivated crop in south Asia and Africa. It remains uncertain however whether this sorghum was imported or locally grown. A polished greenstone axe, possibly a tool used in wooden boat building, and a large hoard of shell fish-hooks further confirm the essentially seaward outlook of these people.

In his book *The Arabian Gulf in Antiquity*, Potts draws attention to the writings of Baron R. C. Keun de Hoogerwoerd. The Baron was writing in 1886 about the maritime situation in the Gulf and Indian Ocean, and Potts suggests that things might not have been so different in the ancient world. He comments as follows:

Speaking of the inhabitants of coastal Oman, the Baron called them 'true nomads of the sea'. Theirs was a hybrid society composed of Arabs, Persians, Baluchis, Socotris, Mahris and even natives of the Hadhramaut. These men moved about according to the season, spending no less than three months of each year on the coast of Baluchistan, where they salted and dried their catch, before returning to Oman to sell a portion of it.

LATE FOURTH AND THIRD MILLENNIA

Fishing settlements

Throughout the fourth millennium BC fishermen were living in small temporary settlements along the coast of the Batinah. One of their main bases was at Ra's al-Hamra where evidence for their presence at this time has come from carbon dating of remains found there. Fragments of food items indicate that the fishing community's diet comprised molluscs, fish, turtles, dolphin or whales, and land game such as gazelle, all of which were cooked over wood-fires. From remains of post-holes and circles of stones, it is also evident that the inhabitants of this site built huts near the shore. They buried their dead in graves and associated finds include a black burnished ware that represents the earliest pottery known from the Oman peninsula. The graveyard at Ra's al-Hamra is the only fourth millennium grave complex so far discovered in the entire Arabian peninsula.

It is interesting to note that the deceased were buried in two positions, i.e. on their right side facing the north-west (position of the setting sun in late summer and early autumn) or on their left side facing the south-east (position of the rising sun in winter). This has been suggested as evidence for the fact that the Ra's al-Hamra site was probably occupied on a seasonal basis. Another interesting aspect of these early Arabian graves is that, after covering the dead with earth and stones, food items were often placed in the grave, presumably

A green turtle returns to the sea at Ras al Junayz, in a ritual that has taken place here for many thousands of years.

HANNE & JENS ERIKSEN

The cliffs at Ras al Junayz provided a prominent landmark for both nesting turtles and for early fishermen.

as some form of offering. Turtle and fish were common items; others could include molluscs or the remains of gazelle, oryx or marine mammals. Shells of green turtles seem to have had a special significance and were frequently incorporated into the graves. As for the people who died, they were not found with weapons or any elaborate grave goods other than occasional beads made from shell, bone or steatite. The fact that the bead collections ranged from very small quantities to ones with considerable numbers (152 were found in one single grave) suggests that their society was probably ranked.

Fishing methods

Fishermen used several techniques including traps, bone fish-hooks and netting. The early settlement site at R'as al-Hamra, like many other early sites along the Omani coastline, yielded net weights made from stones. For a fascinating picture of ancient fishing methods that survived right up to the recent past, one can do no better than read H.J. Carter's account published in 1851. Commenting on his observations at Ra's Jibsh where fishermen went out to sea in buoyancy aids made from inflated animal skins called *kirbah* (not unlike those made from truck inner-tubes) he wrote:

Fishermen work their nets in the surf zone.

So soon as a shoal of fish, to wit "sardines", is viewed from the heights by those who are watching for them, the whole assemble and seizing their skins and castingnets rush to the water's edge. Here the skin is quickly soaked and inflated, after which the hind and fore legs are tied together with a string. Thus prepared they step into the ring and slipping the skin up towards the lower part of the stomach, throw their castingnets across the left shoulder and wading into the water up to their necks, sit upon the string which rests against the back part of their thighs, and thus paddle away with the hands to where the fish are. In this way I have seen as many as twenty at a time enter the water and swim out to a distance of two miles. When they have arrived among the fish they throw their castingnets, and gathering them up return to the shore with what they contain, having no means of securing the fish on the spot. To give some idea of the poverty of these people I may mention that their castingnets were made of cotton twisted into the coarsest cord, and the sinkers attached to their circumference, instead of being composed of small pieces of lead, consisted of stones half as large as a man's fist with holes in them.

Hauling in sardines, which are especially plentiful along Oman's coastline.

Lasail copper mine.

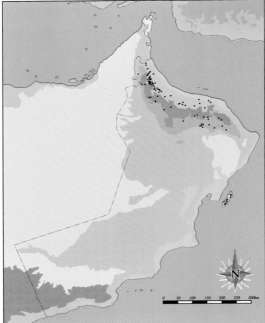

Principal copper mines and copper sources in northern Oman. (After Potts, 1990)

Mining

Whilst fishermen lived at the coast, pastoralist farmers occupied the interior where they raised cattle, goats and a breed of sheep. One of the main settlements at Bat in the Omani mountains commanded control over a major land-route by which copper was exported and was close to copper rich veins that were being mined by increasing hordes of people. The work required organization and the establishment of a social structure. First there was the task of digging the shafts to get at the ore; then there was the problem of protecting the mines and the whole question of ownership and control; next came the work of transporting rock to smelting sites and the stoking of oven-fires to melt the copper; finally, the copper had to be worked into products or poured into moulds of standard size ingots so that it could be sold. The main influence for this new social structure came from the client state of Sumeria from where many goods were imported and to which the precious copper finally found its way.

Burials

Ancient ceremonies and the new order intermixed, especially in death. Large bee-hive shaped burial cairns were built from slabs of locally occurring brown limestone. At first these graves were constructed with thick walls and a small irregular oval chamber, but later the design was modified to larger cairns with thicker walls faced by white limestone and a developed chamber system within. Inside, together with deceased comrades were placed cups, goblets and jars containing water and food to sustain the dead in the after-life. The earlier single chambered graves with two concentric rings of stone heaped into a dome protecting the burial chamber have been found in the UAE and Oman at a number of sites, including Umm an-Nar, Wadi Suq, Wadi Jizzi, 'Ibri, Bat, Siya, Wadi Samad, Tawi Silaim and Jabal Hafit. They are all known to archaeologists as 'Hafit' graves. During the same period other graves were built to the 'beehive' plan. These contained a single chamber and comprised 'two or three curtain walls with hand-sized stones between...built of...brownish limestone' with 'a low plinth, about half a metre wide' around the base (Frifelt, 1976). Although the over-all beehive may reach a height of 8 or 9 metres, the inner chamber is relatively small, 1 to 2.5 metres in diameter.

Settlements & cultivation skills

By far the predominant sign of Man's presence in Oman during the late fourth and early third millennium BC is in the form of burial structures. Remains of settlements have proved extremely elusive and this may be due to the fact that they were located on low ground where there was access to water and where heavy silting will have occurred, covering them with sand. Settlements from this period that have been excavated take on a special significance therefore. One such is the third millennium

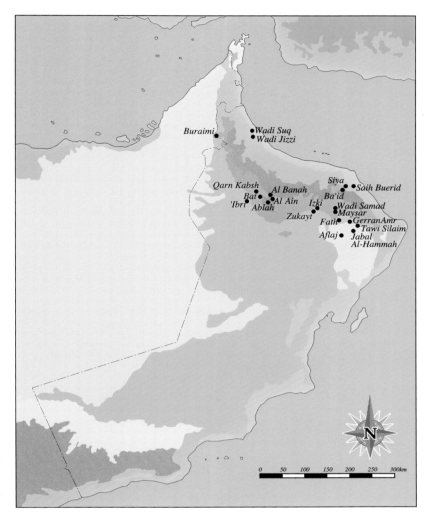

site at Hili in Abu Dhabi. Archaeologists working there have helped to answer a number of questions about how people lived in the region during this period. Analysis of plant material found at this site indicated use of several domesticated crops including emmer (*Triticum dicoccum*), bread wheat (*T. aestivum*), two-row barley (*Hordeum distichon*), six-row hulled barley (*H.vulgare* var. *nudum*), and sorghum (*Sorghum bicolor*). Apart from cereal crops, settlers grew melons and dates and harvested a number of wild plants, including wild oats and jujube seeds. Dates were an increasingly important dietary constituent following cultivation of the date tree. This led to a shift away from an earlier dependence on fish and meat and brought about

Hafit- and beehive-type grave sites in northern Oman (3500-2500 BC). (After Potts, 1990)

Above: View of an excavated Umm an-Nar Period tomb, showing the underground galleries.

Above right: A hoard of copper ingots in the process of being excavated from an industrial site in the smelting village of Maysar.

a noticeable deterioration in dental health.

Whilst sorghum has already been commented on in relation to finds at the fishermens' settlements at Ra's al Hamra, near Muscat, which were active a thousand or more years before, the Hili discoveries are the first clear evidence of local cultivation rather than importation of the important crop. Commenting on these and other observations, Potts concludes: "It now appears that the Arabian peninsula may have served as a bridge in the diffusion of the species from one continent to the other, particularly since it is found here over a thousand years earlier than in the Indian sub-continent" (Potts Vol I, 1990).

Settlements & graves at Bat

At least 60 Hafit graves from the Jamdat Nasr period, around 3000 BC, have been excavated. A characteristic form of pottery, known as Jamdat Nasr ware, has been unearthed from many of the graves at Bat, confirming that their occupants lived around 3200 BC to 2700 BC. In addition to impressive graves the 'Battites' built large towers: structures with recessed ring-walls and raised floors, providing a conveniently elevated base for look-outs as well as protection for freshwater wells. The village of Bat is today a shadow of its former self, an essentially pastoral and agricultural settlement which gives little evidence of the hive

Opposite: Part of an excavated 3rd millenium tower tomb at Bat.

Right: Excavated tomb at Bat.

S. KAY

of activity it must have been more than 5000 years ago. In addition to biconical funerary vessels of fine green or cream colour and 'small egg-shaped cases and jars with perforated necks' thrown on the potter's wheel, copper was worked into implements such as pins, needles and rivets which were sold along with other goods sent to Umm an-Nar (off Abu Dhabi), and onwards via Dilmun (probably eastern Saudi Arabia) to the ports of southern Mesopotamia.

Trade & foreign influences

For thousands of years Oman had been little influenced by happenings in the rest of the world. To the ancient fishermen and hunters who roamed from Musandam to Dhofar, and inland across the game-rich plains and among the leopard-inhabited mountains, it mattered little that great civilizations were developing in Egypt and the Near East, in Mesopotamia, and in Asia. The absence of any written record of dealings between Magan and Mesopotamia

Early trade routes in the 3rd and early 2nd millennia B.C.

23

G. WEISGERBER, GERMAN MINING MUSEUM, BOCHUM

The Umm an-Nar period tower fort Maysar 25. Under attack, the settlers could take refuge here.

during the Late Uruk, Jamdat Nasr and Early Dynastic periods also suggests that there were no links between Oman and the northern Gulf during this time. The northern world was well developed however. The city of Jericho was already 4000 years old! Upper and Lower Egypt were in the throes of coming together under the rule of the first pharaohs. Between Egypt and Meso-potamia lay the great Fertile Crescent that had been nurturing the ascent of Man for millennia. Once contact between the northern and southern Gulf was firmly established, the inhabitants of the richly endowed part of southern Arabia which is now Oman were no longer able to ignore events in the great cultural and economic centres of the globe.

Exchanges between these two worlds were very far from one-way: 6000 years ago regular contact had already been estab-

lished between Oman and neighbouring countries, particularly Baluchistan, Iran, Turkestan and indirectly Mesopotamia via Dilmun. When Sumeria's interest in Oman's copper intensified Oman's links with the northern Gulf shifted to a new level. For all its wealth Mesopotamia lacked many essential raw materials. It had little or no building stone, no wood, no aromatics and no metals. Much of this deficit was made up by trade with Oman, but the copper trade was of particular significance. Just how big the copper trade was is attested by the slag heap at Lasail which has been estimated to contain at least 100,000 tons of ancient workings. Not all of this emanates from the early period under discussion of course since, once it was established, copper mining continued for over a thousand years before it went into decline.

UMM AN-NAR PERIOD
c2500 to c2000 BC

Settlement and grave sites

Trade between Magan and the 'land between the two great rivers', Mesopotamia, increased dramatically at this time, especially the export of copper to the northern Gulf. Most of this valuable metal mined in the mountains of Oman was transported on recently domesticated camels down to the shores of the Gulf, where the island of Umm an-Nar provided a suitable anchorage and loading site. The cultural revolution triggered by the lucrative trading relationship is known after this site as the Umm an-Nar period. In addition to the impressive settlement site and ancient grave remains that have been located at Umm an-Nar itself, other remnants from the period include graves in the Wadi Jizzi and sites at Wadi Bahla, Wadi Far, Wadi Halfayn, Wadi Andam, Wadi Samad, Wadi Ithli, Wadi Ibra, and Wadi Batha; i.e. most of the wadi systems in the Sharqiyah. Discovery of an inscribed Harappan (from the Indus Valley region) fragment of pottery that could be dated to the Umm an-Nar period at the famous turtle nesting coastline of Ra's al-Junayz, 11 kilometres south of Ra's al-Hadd, provides further evidence for the distribution of the culture in Oman.

Sargon and the Akkadian empire

The burgeoning trade between Magan and Mesopotamia naturally drew the attention of powerful interest groups, including local rulers, priests of the temples and foreign forces, not to mention local entrepreneurs and others who were actively engaged in the trade itself. The rival cities and squabbling fiefdoms of Mesopotamia were united by the conquests of Sargon of Akkad who established the Akkadian Empire, an event that caused an acceleration of development through the creation of a period of relative stability and calm.

Sargon was born around 2400 BC and is

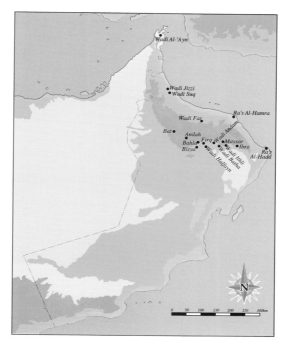

Sites of the Umm an-Nar period. (After Potts, 1990)

Below: Stone jar with lid from the settlement Maysar 1. Most of these jars are funerary offerings.

renowned for building what amounted to the world's first empire. He was not born into nobility or wealth however, having risen from the relatively menial role of cup-bearer to the king of Kish (a city state of Sumer). He is credited with overthrowing a bunch of quarrelsome kings and uniting the whole region under his banner. His own language, Akkadian, then became the official language, replacing Sumerian. During this Early Dynastic I period, ships from Magan docked in Mesopotamian ports alongside other vessels that had sailed from Meluhha (the Indus Valley region) and from nearby Dilmun.

The surge in mining in Oman coupled with its increased availability in the northern Gulf trans-

G. WEISGERBER, GERMAN MINING MUSEUM, BOCHUM

formed copper from a precious metal to an every day commodity used for industrial purposes. Although Mesopotamia was not totally dependent upon Magan for its supplies (copper could also be bought from Anatolia), the copper from Magan was favoured for its competitive value. Akkadian influence spread to Oman where we are told that the people paid a certain amount of respect and possibly allegiance to their northern trading partner. Details of the trading relationship between the two countries can be gleaned from cuneiform texts on stone tablets uncovered in Mesopotamia. One such text reads:

The lands of Magan and Dilmun looked up at me, Enki, moored the Dilmun boats to the ground, loaded the Magan boats sky-high, the Magallan boats of Meluhha transport silver and gold, bring men to Nippur for Enlil.

It is clear from this and other texts from this period that ships from Magan brought more than just local produce to the people of Mesopotamia. They also shipped produce from the eastern civilization of Meluhha, including gold, silver, ivory, precious stones, rare wood, perfumes and even perhaps labourers. Such texts also confirm that Magan was south of Dilmun, and had high mountains (Kur-Maganna) from which a desirable black stone, good for making statues, was quarried. The latter was probably diorite or gabbro.

A rebellion in Mesopotamia, triggered by the accession of Naram-Sin to the throne of the Sumero-Akkadian Empire, caused rumblings in its supplying countries, including Magan. Naram-Sin is reported to have sent an army to quell the unrest and they had a certain amount of success, subjugating King Mannium of Magan and hauling back with them a load of war booty, including a collection of alabaster vessels that have since been recovered by archaeologists. The sub-

jugation must have been a qualified affair however, for King Mannium of Magan was honoured by having a city named after him in Sumeria. The spoils of Naram-Sin's Oman campaign that were discovered in southern Iraq have not all survived into current collections. An alabaster vessel bearing an inscription was lost when the barge on which it was travelling down the Tigris in the mid-nineteenth century was set upon by hostile tribesmen, causing it to sink. Fortunately, someone had made an impression of the inscription which reads:

Naram-Sin, king of the four world corners, vessel (from the) booty of Magan.

Guti upheaval in Mesopotamia

The cities of Ur and Lagash, recently part of the Akkadian Empire, now fell to foreign invaders, the Guti, who dominated the entire region. The governor of Lagash, Gudea (c2144-2124 BC), had a passion for glorifying his reign with decorated statues and cylinders, many bearing inscriptions. He went to extreme lengths to bring the finest building materials for construction of various buildings, including a temple to his god, Ningirsu.

May the land of Magan bring you mighty copper, diorite, u-stone, shuman-stone.

One text also refers to a payment of 241 items of clothing to a local merchant who was bound for Magan. Whereas studies have shown that the black stone used to make Manistusu's statues was olivine gabbro and therefore highly likely to have emanated from Oman, the Gudea statues are actually made from diorite which "does not occur on the Oman peninsula in blocks of any appreciable size" (Potts, Vol I, 1990), although it is found in southern Iran. This suggests that the area known as Magan included part of southern Iran, together with Oman, and was probably a fairly flexible term describing the lands surrounding the entrance to the Gulf.

The Guti dominated period was characterized by an attitude of aggression towards traditional trading partners such as Magan. Inscriptions from Gudea's reign twice mention that he forced compliance on Magan, Meluhha, and Dilmun. Eventually local forces ousted the Guti invaders from southern Babylon. The local wars that brought about the change, between Guti and Utu-hengal, and separately between Utu-hengal and Ur-Nammu, caused a temporary halt to the Gulf trade and a consequent 'recession' in Magan.

Ur-Nammu & trade with Magan

The victor of all these upheavals, Ur-Nammu (2112-2095 BC), wasted little time in re-establishing the lucrative copper trade with Oman. A dedicatory inscription from this early phase of the Third Dynasty of Ur records the achievement:

For Nanna, the first born son of Enlil, his master, did Ur-Nammu, the mighty male, king of Ur, king of Sumer and of Akkad, the man who built the temple of Nanna, return conditions to their previous state. On the sea-shore, in the registry place, he saw the sea-traders safely home and returned the Magan ships to his [i.e. to Nanna's] hand.

Similarly the Code of Ur-Nammu includes the statement:

By the might of Nanna, the lord of the city [of Ur] he returned the Magan-boat of Nanna to the registry [?] place.

During this time the trade was carried out by the buyers from the north actually sailing all the way down to Umm an-Nar in order to strike their deals on behalf of Omani copper merchants. In return for the copper, together with a few other commodities such as onions and fine stones, the Magan traders received wool, garments, silver, leather goods and cooking oil. Among the most prominent of these enterprising sea-traders was Lu-Enlilla an agent to the temple of Nanna during the reign of Ibi-Sin, last king of the Third Dynasty in Ur (2026-2006 BC). He received trading goods (approximately 1.8 tons of wool, (60 talents); 300kgs of an edible plant or plant product; 600kgs of small fish from the storehouse; 70 usbar-garments; 1515 litres of good sesame oil from Lugal-gab and 180 hides from Ur-Sulpae) from the temple of Nanna and local business people in order to buy copper from Magan. A tablet, certified by a courier named Libur-beli, was enclosed in the container of goods and the whole placed on a ship bound for Magan. A record of copper arriving from Magan, perhaps in return for the above goods, is provided on another tablet which records that Lu-Enlilla was in receipt of 154kgs of copper (5 talents and 8 minas) together with ivory, semi-precious stones, and red ochre. The same text records that Lu-Enlilla presented the temple with 10 litres of onions and 20 litres of a certain drug.

Ur-Nammu's good relations with Magan are confirmed by a number of texts that refer to rations for Magan shipbuilders and bitumen being provided for caulking of Magan-ships. Goods sent from Ur to Magan included barley and textiles. There are indications that trade between the northern and southern Gulf followed a seasonal pattern with vessels sailing south in spring time, around March or early April, helped by good following winds.

Despite the success of certain traders such as Lu-Enlilla, such trading was a very risky and fairly expensive business. By the time a trader had sailed down the Gulf and returned against the prevailing winds all

Copper ore from Lasail.

sorts of political upheavals, struggles between rival cities or natural disasters could have occurred in Ur and the other cities. The Gulf could also be a very unkind sea, throwing up steep waves and the reefs off Dilmun were treacherous if approached at night or in bad weather. Added to all of these risks was the threat of robbery on the high seas by rival vessels or of disease due to poor nutrition on board the boats.

Rise of Dilmun

From Magan's viewpoint however, these were relatively good times since it enjoyed direct access to the market for its goods. Some copper had been trans-shipped through Dilmun, whose cultural and economic centre had shifted to Bahrain, but much had travelled direct to Mesopotamia, avoiding middle-men. Unfortunately for Magan, the turmoil caused by fighting to bring down Ibi Sin left a temporary administrative vacuum that was quickly filled by Dilmun. Over recent years copper merchants from Ur had found it more convenient to establish a staging post there. Now they saw their chance to cooperate with the Dilmunites in controlling the trade so that everything passed through their hands on

Bahrain. Although the copper continued to be mined in Oman, it was lugged by camel and donkey across the mountains and desert to the coast, and transported in local vessels as far as Bahrain. From now on the traders of Ur ceased to record purchases of copper from Magan, instead referring to buying from Dilmun which was emerging as the key trading power of the Gulf. Over the ensuing years Dilmun consolidated its position further, gaining great wealth from its effective control of the north-south trade in the Gulf.

A seafaring nation

Despite difficulties in direct trade between Magan and Mesopotamia, Magan was in close touch with countries to the east and south-east, including present day Iran, Pakistan and India. Graves in Oman constructed during this era often contained goods that were imported from these countries. In particular, small rectangular boxes deposited with the dead have close affinities with similar boxes found in Baluchistan. Commenting on the great surge in cross-cultural activity and its influences in Oman, the author William Facey stated in his book, *Oman: A Seafaring Nation:*

The seafarers and traders of Magan thus lived in a milieu of cultural and technological firsts. Long distance sailing vessels, writing, banking, shareholding - all these were in the process of transforming the world, and characterised the period during which man developed a fully urbanised civilisation for the first time.

End of third millennium

Whereas the beginning of the third millennium BC found Oman or Magan in a relatively uncoordinated state, with limited social organization; by its close things had changed dramatically. The country was remarkably stable and at ease with itself. A relatively tall people lived in villages of stone and barasti houses that were built alongside natural water sources. Sorghum, wheat, barley and the date palm were cultivated and their lives were eased by domesticated camels, zebu cattle, sheep and goat. Game in the form of gazelle, oryx and birds were hunted, whilst fishermen worked inshore waters and took advantage of the large numbers of turtles that climbed (and still climb) the beaches of Oman to lay their eggs. Copper was mined and exported in exchange for a variety of useful commodities. Public buildings included large stone-walled enclosures and fortified watch-towers, of which the remains of the towers at Bat are prime examples. Their walls still stand prominently above ground level and their overall dimensions suggest that they were capable of protecting a considerable number of people and animals.

Seals of Umm an-Nar period

Only three seals dating to the Umm an-Nar period have been discovered so far on the Oman peninsula. All three were found at the Maysar site in Wadi Samad. The first is an oval shaped piece of lead bearing a stick figure on the face and a hole drilled through the centre. The second is a triangular prism seal, with three engraved faces, made of grey stone. Side one has a crude illustration of a dog and what appears to be a sheep; side two shows a zebu bull and a scorpion; side three depicts an ibex and another wild sheep. Such prism seals were not uncommon in certain parts of the 'developing world' at that time, although no similar examples are known from Oman. They are known from the latter part of the third millennium in Crete, Syria and Egypt as well as in central Asia. A prism seal found at Hajjar grave site in Bahrain is clearly attributable to the Indus Valley culture. The third seal is a pear-shaped stamp seal, the face of which appears to bear a stick figure of a person with outstretched arms but which may in fact be a character in the Indus script. The low number of seal finds and the complete absence of any seal impressions has been interpreted to suggest that the seals were objects of decoration or status symbols rather than tools of business.

Umm an-Nar funerary ware

The craft of pottery had also developed with fine vessels being created on the wheel and some even painted. Other vessels were skilfully carved from soft stone and alabaster. Typical soft-stone (chlorite) vessels are decorated by geometric shapes such as circles with dots. A considerable number of such vessels have been recovered from Umm an-Nar grave sites in Oman. They have also been found in the settlement excavated at Maysar where it has been established they were also made; most likely specifically as funerary ware. Omani manufactured chlorite vessels have also turned up in graves from this period on Bahrain, Tarut and Failaka.

By the end of the third millennium people in Oman spun their own cloth, made and wore jewellery, rode donkeys and had extended their capabilities for overland travel through domesticating the camel.

COP

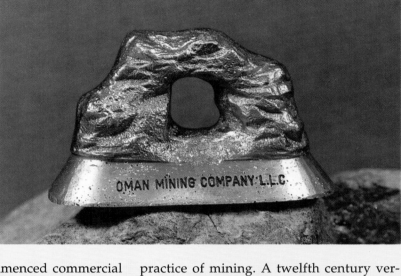

Right: Copper replica of ancient copper mine at Lasail forms the Oman Mining Company logo.

Far right: Remains of ancient copper mine at Lasail (c. 3000 BC).

There is no shortage of evidence for ancient copper mining in Oman and present mining operations further attest to the richness of the country's metallurgical resources. Almost 5000 years after copper mining began in what was then known as Magan, the Oman Mining Company commenced commercial copper mining in the same areas where the ancient mines were established in Wadi Jizzi. By 1986 they were exporting 15,000 tons of high grade copper cathodes to new client states such as Britain, as well as to some of its ancient trading partners among the Gulf countries. However, apart from references to copper from Magan on ancient tablets, we must turn to the tenth century AD for definite written comment on historical aspects of copper mining in Oman.

The industry is first referred to by the Omani writer Ibn Ja'far who reports, in *Jami'*, on several dictates regarding the

A hoard of so-called copper ingots from al 'Agir, near Bahla.

G. WEISGERBER, GERMAN MINING MUSEUM, BOCHUM

practice of mining. A twelfth century version of this text, included within Abdulla al-Kindi's volume, *Kitab al-Musannaf*, writes of a mine owned by the residents of Izki and mentions that copper mines, presumably at Wadi Jizzi, owned by the residents of Sohar, were sublet for 10 percent of the mines' profit. The Arabic author, al-Mas'udi (c943 AD) also writes of copper from Oman. Carsten Niebuhr, the last surviving member of the Danish Arabia Felix Expedition, was one of the first western scientific writers to visit Oman, and he was told of copper mining activities at that time (1765) at Goaber, not far fom Quriyat. The Omani historian Humayd ibn Muhammad ibn Ruzayq, who died in 1873, recorded in his book: *al-Sahifat al-Qahtaniyah*, that an attempt was indeed made to revive Oman's copper industry during this period. A British army officer and author, Lt J.R.Wellstead, wrote in his book *Travels in Arabia*, published in 1838:

Arabia has been pronounced to be wholly destitute of precious metals, but in this province we meet with silver associated as is usual with lead. Copper is also found: at a small hamlet on the road from Semed [Samad] to Neswah [Nizwa] there is a mine which the Arabs at present work, but the others are wholly neglected.

P E R

S. KAY

copper was a common commodity in central Oman; and Col S. B. Miles, who visited Nizwa in 1885 and commented that, while the copper manufacturing trade was still buoyant, the raw material was by then imported in sheets from Bombay. By the early part of the twentieth century it was clear that, while copper was no longer mined in Oman, there had been considerable copper mining there in the past. Interest in the various reports of old copper mines in Oman prompted the establishment of a special investigation in 1924 by the British Association for the Advancement of Science 'to report on probable sources of copper used by the Sumerians'. Meanwhile a geological survey of Oman was undertaken

Additional nineteenth century reports on Oman's copper mining include those by H.J. Carter, who found old open cast mines and smelting sites on Masira island; Palgrave, whose claimed observations that copper was exported from Mattrah in 1863 have been described as fraudulent, and so can perhaps not be relied upon; A. Germain, a French hydrographic engineer who wrote in 1868 that there were old copper mines in the interior of Oman and that

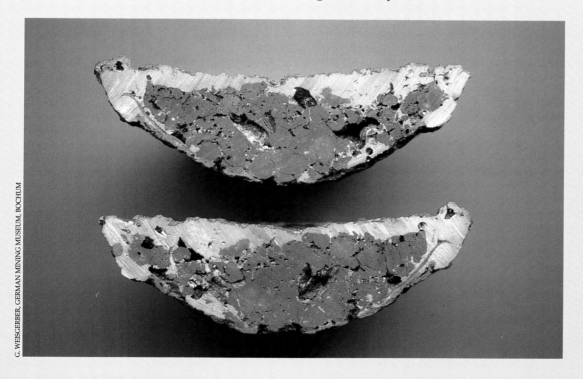

G. WEISGERBER, GERMAN MINING MUSEUM, BOCHUM

A "dirty-trick" ingot from the al 'Agir hoard. The core consists of slag covered by a mantle of copper.

Above: Renovated copper smelting furnace in the upper Wadi Jizzi.

Below: Copper slag.

Below right: A tomb dating to the end of the Wadi Suq period was discovered by children at al Wasit. It was used as a communal burial site.

with the aid of sponsorship by William Knox-D'Arcy, who founded the Anglo-Persian Oil Company. One of the team's geologists, G. S. Lees, took time out from searching for oil to investigate old copper mines and collected samples of ore and slag from one such area inland from Sohar. Studies by the British Association team, together with results from analysis of the collected ores led to the announcement, at the Seventeeth International Congress of Orientalists, held in Oxford on August 29th 1928, that 'the place from which the Sumerians obtained their copper' was Oman. The basis for that conclusion rested on analysis of nickel content in the Omani ore and in copper artefacts associated with Mesopotamia. However, since then it has been shown that similar levels of nickel are found in association with copper at many sites throughout the world. The basis for the conclusion was flawed but the conclusion itself was not necessarily invalidated.

Approximately 50 major deposits of copper have now been discovered in Oman. In addition over 150 smelting sites have been documented, ranging in size from small mounds containing perhaps only one ton of slag to massive heaps in which the estimated slag is around 150,000 tons! Studies on many of these smelting and mining sites have thrown up evidence that some of them were worked in the third millennium BC. The site known as Maysar 1, in Wadi Samad, has yielded a large number of anvil and crushing stones. The conclusions from these studies, including also a survey of ancient mining sites undertaken by a French team in the mid-1970's, has enabled us to gain a fairly clear picture of how copper mining was undertaken in Oman during the Umm an-Nar period. It is apparent that small furnaces were used for smelting locally mined copper bearing ores. The ovens themselves had an internal capacity of only 10 to 15 litres so it is clear that operations were quite modest.

The end products of these activities, in the form of copper pins, chisels, knives, fish-hooks and needles were undoubtedly used by the local population. At Maysar for example a smelting oven together with copper beads, chisels, rings, needles and axes have been found in excavations at the Umm an-Nar settlement there. Thirteen

A selection of copper finds from the Umm an-Nar period at Maysar.

G. WEISGERBER, GERMAN MINING MUSEUM, BOCHUM

bun-shaped ingots of copper were also recovered from a house at Maysar. It has been estimated that between two and four thousand tons of copper was produced in Oman during the Umm an-Nar period.

Having established the production of copper in Oman during the third millennium, and the manufacture of copper implements in the country at this time, the final question is what evidence do we have that these products found their way to Mesopotamia. This, as we have already indicated, is primarily in the form of texts translated from cuneiform tablets recovered from the ruins of Old Akkadian and Neo-Sumerian houses. Up to the time of Sargon, Magan was not mentioned on these tablets, whilst Dilmun was noted as an important trading source of a variety of goods.

In the 'Standard Inscription' of Manistusu we hear how Manistusu sailed south after assembling an army whose fighters were drawn from 32 cities. The inscription states that they rounded up enemy forces from as far away as the metal mines and that they mined a black stone which they brought back to Agade in order to have a statue of himself carved in it. The statue was then dedicated to the god Enlil. The association of black stone, valued by the Sumerians and Akkadians, with Magan

is also commented on in the account of Naram-Sin's attack on Magan. Many authors have stated that the stone referred to was diorite but analysis of two statues from Manistusu's reign, preserved in the Louvre in Paris, have revealed that these were made from olivine gabbro, a stone that is exceedingly common in Oman.

From the same period, two tablets record that copper was brought to the palace from Magan; and that Magan copper was removed from a house. It is also clear that copper was not only imported as unworked ingots for a cuneiform tablet from Adab states that a *za-hum* made from bronze had originated in Magan. One of these texts also tells us that Magan sailors travelled as far as Mesopotamia, both from reference to their ships tying up at the quay of Agade, and from one that records a gift of beer to a courier from Magan during the Old Akkadian period.

Below left: Some of the numerous copper swords, daggers and lance heads found in the al Wasit tomb.

Below: A warrior's grave from the end of the Wadi Suq period was discovered in 1985. It contained a rich assortment of weapons.

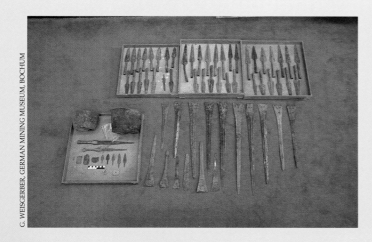

G. WEISGERBER, GERMAN MINING MUSEUM, BOCHUM

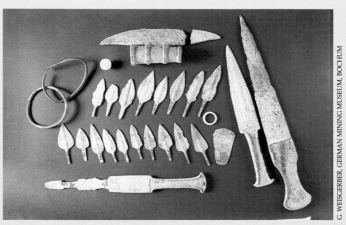

G. WEISGERBER, GERMAN MINING MUSEUM, BOCHUM

P. YULE, GERMAN ARCHAEOLOGICAL MISSION TO OMAN

G. WEISGERBER, GERMAN MINING MUSEUM, BOCHUM

Above: A new generation of archaeologists being trained in Samad al Shan.

THE WADI SUQ PERIOD
2000 BC to 1300 BC

Umm an-Nar culture disappears

The archaeological record for this period is not quite so sparse as has been suggested in many previous accounts of Oman's ancient history. It had been thought that there was a major disruption to the archaeological sequence soon after the beginning of the second millennium, indicating an unexplained disappearance of the Umm an-Nar culture. More recent archaeological studies have shown that, whilst change did occur, it was more gradual than previously believed. Some of the finds at Wadi Suq can in fact be attributed to the mid-second millennium BC and even later, thus bridging the gap between the period 1800 BC and the commencement of the Iron Age in Oman. Potts comments: "It is thus clear that there is no gap in the occupational history of the Oman peninsula during the second millennium, and what was once perceived as a Dark Age in the region was nothing but an artefact of our ignorance" (Potts, Vol I, 1990). Scientists now refer to the period from 2000 BC to 1300 BC as comprising the Wadi Suq period which is split into early (2000 to 1600 BC) and late (1600 to 1300 BC) phases.

Trade with Dilmun

The dawn of the second millennium coincided with the rise of Dilmun as the hub of Gulf trading. Dilmun's gain was Magan's loss and, as the ancient civilization on Bahrain flourished, Umm an-Nar and the settlements that had grown up during the last thousand years among the mountains of Oman waned. The copper traders and merchants of Oman had built their own wealth primarily through direct trading with Sumerian cities. Now that the trade was being diverted through Bahrain they were less able to control the benefits. A re-alignment took place so that Oman's main trading partner became Bahrain and cultural exchanges centred between these two countries, much more than between Oman

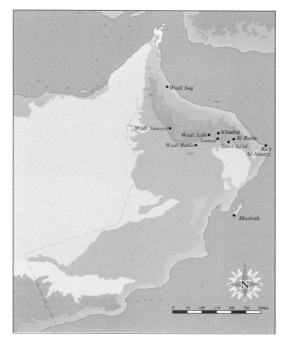

Principal sites of the Wadi Suq period (After Potts, 1990).

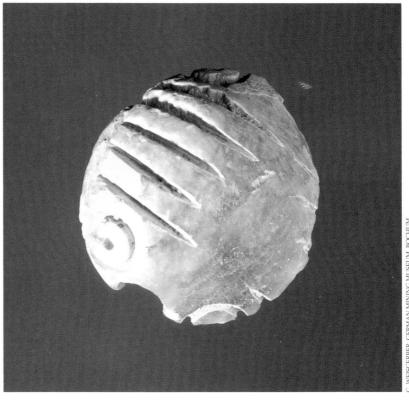

The back of a stamp seal in glazed soft-stone from Samad al Shan grave.

G. WEISGERBER, GERMAN MINING MUSEUM, BOCHUM

A selection of some of the stone bowls which were found in the communal grave discovered by children at al Wasit.

Below: Typical of the Wadi Suq period are lance heads such as these which are still in position at the entrance of a tomb.

Below right: A steatite vessel preserved at Oman National Museum

and Sumeria, as had been the case previously. It was a new situation for both Oman and Bahrain, for in the immediate past there had been relatively little direct communication between them since each had been competing for trade with the rich cities of the north. Oman's prowess in seamanship and boat-building was never in question; neither was the richness of its natural resources, but it could not match the advantage that Bahrain offered in terms of its geographical location and the sheer convenience of its ports for vessels sailing up and down the Gulf.

Funerary ware

In addition to written evidence for the changes taking place, it is confirmed from the finds recovered from graves built at this time, in for example Wadi Suq and Wadi Sunaysil, that Oman's main links were with

Bahrain rather than Mesopotamia. Wadi Suq is a tributary of Wadi Jizzi that runs from the oasis of Buraymi to the coast near Sohar, whilst the graves in Wadi Sunaysil are approximately four kilometres northeast of Ibri. Graves at Wadi Sunaysil comprised stone-lined burial pits below ground level which were covered by mounds of earth and contained by surrounding ring walls. Pottery and steatite found in these graves were similar to a type that had been recovered from graves in Bahrain. Unlike the black-painted red or orange wares of the late third millennium, pottery from these graves, symbols of the Wadi Suq period, were less well fired than those from the Umm an-Nar period, and generally of a lesser quality. Typically they were buff, tan, brown or somewhat orange in colour. One improvement in pottery technique did occur during this period however; that of slicing through the base of pots with a taut string, a method not previously adopted by potters of the Umm an-Nar period. In addition some new shapes appeared, including an open, rounded, somewhat squat jar with a spouted lip.

Steatite vessels attributable to the Early Wadi Suq period show less distinct differences from those of the third millennium than do the Wadi Suq ceramics. The dot in circle pattern is still favoured and vessels

usually had a simple pattern of these around their rim. A slightly later form was the "round bodied suspension vessel with four vertically pierced lugs evenly spaced around the middle of the body, and lid" (Potts, Vol 1, 1990). Later modifications of this took the form of a conical lidded jar with four vertical nose-lugs, and a shallow spouted bowl, both of which are typical Wadi Suq vessels, found in quite large numbers at Wadi Suq period burial sites.

Apart from pottery and soft-stone vessels, a few examples of bronze artefacts have been recovered from excavations of the Wadi Suq period. Favoured weapons were the bow and arrow, in which arrows were tipped by copper or bronze arrowheads; a bronze bladed dagger, and a spear with socketed bronze head.

The written evidence

The early second millennium is well documented on tablets recovered from Mesopotamia. From 1932 to 1866 BC, i.e. the period of the first three Larsa kings, Gungunum, Abisare and Sumu-ilum, there is ample evidence of goods originating in Magan being transported from Dilmun to Ur, and of the Ur traders regularly visiting Bahrain. As we have mentioned above, the merchants from Ur no longer journeyed all the way to Umm an-Nar or the mountains of Oman in order to do business, but contented themselves with frequent journeys to the trans-shipment ports of Dilmun. Texts written during the reign of Rim-Sin (1822 to 1763 BC) further document the sizeable quantities of copper that were still being imported, much of it through a trader by the name of Ea-Nasir who acted on behalf of local authorities and private investors. But the copper boom was coming to an end. Towards the end of Rim-Sin's rule in Ur, in the year 2003, Ur fell to the Elamites from the highlands of Persia and the whole

G. WEISGERBER, GERMAN MINING MUSEUM, BOCHUM

cultural heritage of Sumeria suffered a rapid decline with even the language being lost.

Invasions from the north

Weakened by this upheaval, the doors were opened for a major destabilization throughout the Gulf region. The principle factor involved was a prolonged invasion from the north and east comprising large numbers of Indo-Europeans, many on horseback and armed with battle-axes. They were undisciplined, marauding armies that ransacked towns, burned houses and took whatever booty they could lay their hands on. The settlements of the Gulf, that had lived in relative peace and prosperity for so long, were simply not prepared for such an invasion. Eventually the attackers reached Oman where their aggression had a knock-on effect, contributing to the decline of Dilmun and eventually also of the southern cities at the head of the Gulf such as Ur, all of which had prospered through their involvement in Oman's mining of copper and the trade associated with it.

Silver bowl with constricted rim from the grave of a rich woman in Samad al Shan.

A sandstorm in November provides a reminder of how harsh conditions became towards the end of the Wadi Suq period.

A. SPALTON

Late Wadi Suq period

Before long the name Magan is dropped completely from Mesopotamian records. Apart from the social and economic problems that were heaped on Oman, natural factors also played their part in bringing about a general malaise. Prolonged droughts caused crops to fail, wildlife to die and people to suffer. Massive sand-storms played havoc with all aspects of daily life, clogging houses with unwanted sand and throwing up big sand-dunes. The people of Magan continued to depend to a great extent upon their skills of fishing and sailing. Although trade links were greatly reduced they continued to maintain contact with their neighbours across the Gulf and Indian Ocean but were mainly concerned with trading the essentials for survival such as agricultural goods. It has been suggested that many of Oman's seamen emigrated northwards, up the Red Sea, to the Levant where their descendants were later known as the Phoenicians.

Settlements

A settlement from the Wadi Suq period has been excavated at Ra's al-Junayz just south of Ra's al-Hadd; a site that is known to many of today's visitors to Oman for its important green turtle nesting beaches. The excavated ruins, only a few metres back from the top of the beach, include a mud-brick building over 30 metres long that was used as a storage place for slabs of bitumen. The find of a pottery sherd with Harappan script suggests that this may have been one of the main landing sites for Harappan traders arriving in Oman during the early second millennium. A complex of mud brick buildings at the inland site of Tawi Sa'id near Ibra also dates from this period.

Serious trade did not pick up again in the Indian Ocean and Oman until the second half of the first millennium BC when the Persian Achaemenid kings created new conditions for economic growth and Greek and Roman empires provided new super-rich trading partners.

Turtles have nested on Oman's beaches for thousands of years. When conditions became more difficult inland, people could rely on the sea for an adequate supply of food.

IRON AGE or LIZQ PERIOD 1300 to 300 BC

Bronze: the favoured metal

Although these years are described as the Iron Age, throughout the period in Oman bronze remained the favoured metal and iron is "practically never attested in this region prior to the Seleucid era" (Potts, 1990). The alternative name of Lizq is derived from a fortified site south of the Wadi Samad but there are inherent problems also with the use of this title.

Excavations at Shisr, which some believe to be the ancient site of Ubar.

Ubar: Atlantis of the sands

Following a long period of relative isolation and recession, Oman now experienced quite rapid growth. Biblical sources record how, as early as 2000 BC, camel caravans carried goods from one side of Arabia to the other, from the southern sources of frankincense, myrrh and other goods found in Oman to the burgeoning civilization of ancient Egypt. The journeys involved major organization for man and beasts and depended upon adequate supplies of freshwater. The camel trains advanced in stages, from one major watering or supply station to the next. Among the most famous of these was the fortified city of Ubar, named in the Holy Koran as Irem: "the many towered city of Irem...whose like has not been built in the entire land". A search for this elusive 'Atlantis of the Sands' is recounted by Sir Ranulph Fiennes in his book of the same name, published in 1992. In it he equates Ubar with present day Shisr which lies at the edge of the Empty Quarter and

where excavations have revealed substantial remains of a walled and fortified settlement together with many surrounding settlements. Their studies also showed how the collapse of an underground cavern brought about the end of the city, sending much of it plunging into an enormous gaping hole. Archaeological studies on the site are still at a relatively early stage and are continuing under the direction of the National Committee headed by H.E.the Minister of Information aided by Dr Juris Zarins and other archaeologists. From its position it is clear that this would have been a major staging post on the camel trail with north-bound parties stopping here to replenish their freshwater supplies before heading across the sands to Liwa or to intersect with other routes through Yemen and northwards, via Marib and Mecca, and along the Red Sea Tihama.

The presence of Greek and Roman pottery at Shisr, the believed site of Ubar, attests to its great importance as a link on the great inland trading routes. Given its strategic position and the necessity to protect its fresh-water wells, it is not surprising that major fortifications were constructed. These took the form of a pentagonal walled enclosure, roughly 54 metres by 57 metres, with round and square towers for guards to survey the surrounding land. It was used for many centuries and radio carbon dating confirms that one of the store-rooms was still in operation in 350 AD, suggesting that

Frankincense provided much of the raison d'être for Omani commercial centres such as that of Khor Rori.

Principal Iron Age sites (after Potts, 1990).

Above right: Excavation at Shisr.

Above far right: Ras al Junayz.

Right: View of staircase leading to the Lizq Period hill fortress at Lizq.

the site would have been reported to Ptolemy and included on his map of the time. Interestingly, in the same region as present day Shisr, Ptolemy's map records the presence of Oubaritae, presumably the people of Ubar.

Occupation

Iron Age sites in Oman are numerous and the archaeological record is quite substantial. Many sites have been discovered during recent building activities. In 1979, for example, 550 vessels made from bronze, steatite and pottery were uncovered by a bulldozer working at the village of Selme near 'Ibri. This was the hoard of a grave-robber and most of the material was from the Iron Age. We have already mentioned the site of Bat in our account of the Umm an-Nar period. Finds in upper layers at this site yielded bronze arrowheads, steatite vessels and pottery sherds from the Iron Age. A 100 metre diameter tell on the edge of Wadi Bahla, two kilometres north-west of Bisyah, has eight to ten metres of accumulated debris from its long Iron Age occupation. There are also sites in the Wadi Sumail area. Remains of a small village on the west slope of Wadi Samad, a short distance north of the modern village of Maysar, has been labelled by archaeologists as *Maysar 42*. It was apparently built at roughly the same time as the nearby *falaj* system which has remained in use since its construction. A nearby Iron Age grave site with at least 70 burials had been robbed long ago but still had sufficient artefacts to enable them to be dated to the period.

The site at Lizq deserves special mention. A steep hill, 65 metres in height, stands a short way to the east of the modern settlement. On top of this is a strongly fortified structure made from massive stone blocks. Access is by a stone stairway consisting of 79 steps, held together with mud mortar, and supported on each side by low walls of about half a metre in height. At the top of the stair-well were two towers from which guards could defend the settlement within its impressive walls.

On the Batinah coast there are a number of important Iron Age sites. Beneath the Islamic fortress at Sohar there are considerable remains from earlier times, stretching back into the Iron Age. Other sites nearby are also attributable to the first millennium and a grave complex with at least 200 interlocking graves at Wadi Bosher, inland from Muscat, has recently yielded large numbers of typical Iron Age vessels made from steatite and pottery.

MAGAN-QADE

Oman known as Qade

By 1000 BC the name Magan no longer refers to Oman. In a confusing transposition of names that is perhaps explained by movements of people and exchange of roles, both Meluhha and Magan now refer to Egypt. Is it possible that Magan's emigrants provided a key to unlocking pharaonic Egypt's natural wealth? Certainly, it is inconceivable that Omanis who travelled to Egypt with frankincense did not also share their expertise in the metal trade. But Oman, now known as Qade, was starting to see better times. By 700 BC the uncouth Aryans who had conquered Meluhha were transformed into a much more disciplined and civilized people who had interests in rebuilding the trading links and civilizations they had been responsible for smashing. Trade with Oman was thus re-established. The king of Qade, we are told, travelled from his seat of government at Izki to visit the court of Assurbanipal in Nineveh in approximately 640 BC.

Pade, king of the land of Kade, who dwelt in the city of Iske [Izki] [of which of old(?)] no king had trodden the boundary of Assyria: by the command of Assur of [and] Nin-lil their envoy for good[will and peace], with their rich tribute, travelled a journey of six months, coming to [my] presence. (Istar Slab incription from Nineveh, c. 640 BC)

New irrigation system

This first millennium saw other major improvements to Oman, accompanied by a massive increase in population. It is clear that something had occurred that increased the capacity of the country to feed its inhabitants. That 'something' was an invention introduced to Oman around 1000 BC, probably by the Persians. It was the secret of how to bring water to the desert through an elaborate network of underground tunnels

S. KAY

and surface channels known as *falaj* (plural *aflaj*). According to legend it was King Suleiman, the founder of Persepolis, who was responsible for this ancient example of technology transfer. The story tells that he was blown off course while flying across his kingdom. The gusts took him over the Gulf and he landed at Salut. Seeing that the area had no water he commanded the people to build a *falaj*. Despite the colourful rendering, there is likely to be a grain of truth in the tale since Oman's oldest *aflaj* are indeed found in this region and its people are the acknowledged experts in *falaj* construction. It is a beautifully simple yet highly efficient system of water distribution (see box) and there is little doubt that its introduction transformed Oman.

An ancient falaj.

FALAJ

The basis of Omani agriculture and wealth is water. In very few places in Oman is cultivation possible without irrigation. In some areas, principally on the Batinah, there is widespread irrigation from wells dug into shallow water-bearing levels; however, in most of Oman and, in particular, the interior, the system known as *falaj* is the main source of irrigation water today and has been for at least 2000 years. The construction of these channels, both on the surface and underground, provide the finest examples of Omani engineering skill.

Many *aflaj* were built 2000 or 2500 years ago. The large system around Sohar which is now disused was constructed almost 1000 years ago and others were built or repaired by the great Yarubi rulers. All are of a considerable age. The Arabic word *falaj* derives from a Semitic word of great age concerned with division and distribution. The *falaj* is the livelihood of the village and its water is carefully distributed among the members of the community by means of sluices to open and close subsidiary channels; and is further shared by divisions of time based on

Ancient Falaj.

P. YULE, GERMAN ARCHAEOLOGICAL MISSION TO OMAN

The falaj system may well have reached Oman by the beginning of the 1st millennium BC.
The earliest datable falaj in the Sultanate is located at Maysar and was built in the latter part of the Lizq/Rumaylah period.

the movements of the sun or the stars. A share of the annual water supply is set aside for the maintenance of the *falaj*, known as the *Q'ada*. This portion of the *falaj* water is either sold by auction, or used to grow crops for sale. Income from the sale permits the employmnet of the *bidar* to maintain the communal system by cleaning underground channels, maintaining and repairing masonry, rooks, linings and shafts, as well as the mouth of the *falaj* and the open channels to the garden. There are two types of *falaj* in Oman: the *Falaj Ghayl* or surface channel, and the *Falaj Qanat* or underground channel. The *Falaj Ghayl* taps water from the upper gravels of a wadi bed and carries it in a gentle inclined channel to cultivable land often several kilometres away. Surface channels are also used along the lower courses of *Falaj Qanat*. The water is easily tapped but transporting it often involves constructing a special stone and mortar channel built up alongside, or carved into, the rocky walls of the wadi. Obstacles like rocky ridges have to be crossed by tunnelling. Gently flowing side wadis are crossed with arched aquaducts and stronger flowing wadis by inverted siphons. Inverted siphons are built when the flow of water in the wadi bed is so strong that aquaducts would be swept away. The water is channelled down a vertical tube and underneath the wadi in a well lined stone and mortar tunnel. Provided that there are no leaks at the bottom of the system, the water fills the tube and runs on the other side of the wadi to the same level as the open channel on the

upper side and can be led on towards the fields. The underground channel known as the *Falaj Qanat* taps water from below ground: either underground springs or areas where the water table in the gravels close to the mountains is above the ground level on the plains. First a suitable underground water supply is located by examining vegetation, seepage and anything else

Opening a falaj channel.

S. KAY

43

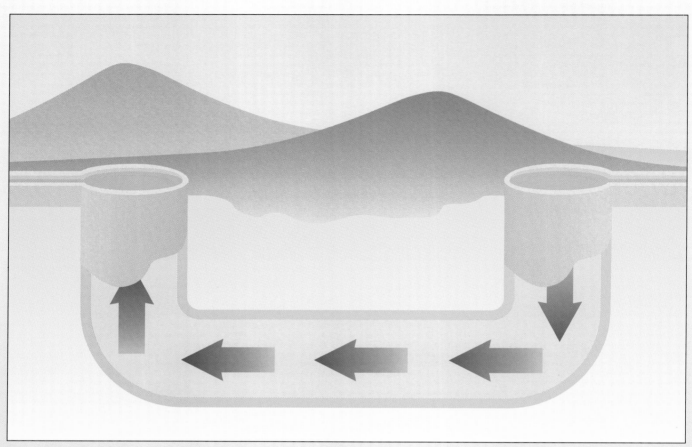

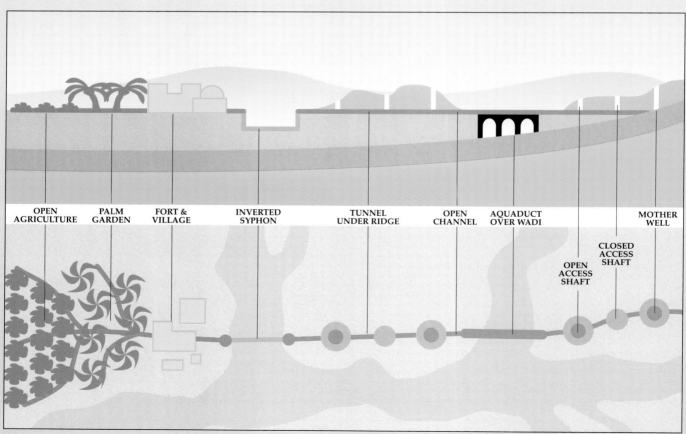

OPEN
AGRICULTURE

PALM
GARDEN

FORT &
VILLAGE

INVERTED
SYPHON

TUNNEL
UNDER RIDGE

OPEN
CHANNEL

AQUADUCT
OVER WADI

MOTHER
WELL

CLOSED
ACCESS
SHAFT

OPEN
ACCESS
SHAFT

A modern falaj channel used for irrigation in Oman.

Opposite: Schematic drawings of how the falaj system carries water from its source to the user. The upper picture shows an inverted siphon used to carry water across a river bed. The lower picture provides a general cross section of an entire system.

that might suggest a spring or abundant water deep underground. The extent of the underground water is tested by digging a well or series of trial wells and measuring the flow by bailing. If the tests are satisfactory work is begun from the mouth of the *falaj*, often several kilometres from the water-bearing mother well, and a gently inclined channel excavated with vertical shafts at regular intervals to provide fresh air for the tunneller and allow removal of debris. Where the tunnel passes through soft soil or sand it is lined with stone or pottery. The most difficult moment of all comes as the tunneller approaches the water-bearing area around the mother well. If the water-bearing strata is penetrated too suddenly a great rush of water may drown the tunneller and destroy his work. The amount of work involved in construction can be prodigious; even with a tunnel half a metre in diameter it is necessary to remove three to four thousand tons of rock for each kilometre dug. The largest tunnels can be nine kilometres long and the mother-well is on average 20 metres deep. The tunnels must be regularly repaired and cleared of silt. Even this can be a major task.

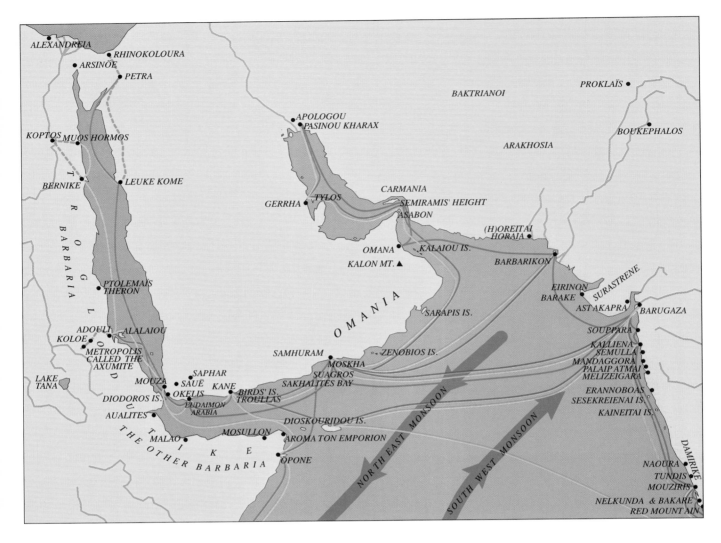

Map of Arabian region as known to the Greeks and Romans.

Greek interest in Oman

After the Persian Achaemenid ruler Cambyses (550-521) conquered Egypt the links between southern Arabia and the Classical Mediterranean strengthened. Cambyses' successor, Darius I (521-484 BC), was very keen to re-establish the old maritime trading of southern Arabia and other Indian Ocean areas with the northern states. In pursuance of this mission he commissioned a Greek navigator, Scylax of Caryinda, to test the feasibilty of sea-routes between India and Egypt. His successful journey from the Indus Valley, via Persia, Oman, the Hadrami coast and up the Red Sea, confirmed that the sea-route offered a viable alternative to long overland journeys, but did little to revive the old Gulf route. However, approximately 200 years later, in 326 BC, Alexander the Great's fleet of 1500 vessels returned from India under the command of his admiral Nearchus. The Greek admiral's journal recorded passing the 'Cape of Arabia', presumably Musandam, from where "cinnamon and other products were exported to the Assyrians". He also mentions the port of Teredon, situated at the head of the Gulf, describing it as the "emporium for the sea-trade in frankincense and all other fragrant products of Arabia". A few years later, shortly before he was killed, Alexander sent a new expedition through the Gulf. Whilst his admiral Archias reached Bahrain, the ship commanded by Hieron of Soli explored the coast of Musandam .

FRANKINCENSE

The information on Frankincense compiled in this section has been prepared from reference to *Plants of Dhofar* by Anthony Miller and Miranda Morris

Gold, frankincense and myrrh are recorded in the Bible as the gifts brought to the infant Jesus in Bethlehem. It is likely that the last two products were exports of Dhofar in Oman. Of the three celebratory gift offerings, frankincense is perhaps the most remarkable, for its uses were incredibly diverse and   Omani frankincense was regarded as the best in the world.

The Omani frankincense tree, *Boswellia sacra*, grows to a height of around five metres. Both it and the trees from which myrrh is derived, *Commiphora* spp., belong to the family Burseraceae whose members have resin ducts in their bark. Apart from the species of frankincense tree growing in Oman, other species also occur in north-east Africa and India. In Oman the trees are found in a relatively restricted habitat, just out of range of monsoon rains but where cool winds depress air temperatures in hot summer months. In addition they are found closer to the coast, within range of seasonal rainfall, but it is believed that many of these have been planted.

Frankincense gum was in Greek times said to have been collected by poorly fed slaves, many of whom died through malnutrition or disease. Once gathered the gum was carried to the main frankincense port of Samhuram where it was loaded on ships under the express permission of the king. It was a highly-prized commodity valued just as much as gold in markets of the Roman Empire.

S. KAY

Frankincense tree, showing the oozing of the frankincense resin.

As well as being burned as an offering to the gods, frankincense was also of importance medicinally and was used as a fumigant to combat disease and evil odours. In the Book of the Dead of the ancient Egyptians (who believed frankincense to be the sweat of the gods, fallen to earth) the authors recommended the use of incense in many of the mortuary rituals and in ceremonial purification. Kindled in clay troughs and the flame doused with cows' milk, frankincense was used for warding off evil and enemies of malevolence. Medicinally, the gum had a place in the treatment, by Greek and Roman physicians, of almost every imaginable disease and remedies employing frankincense also appear in the Syriac Book of Medicine, in the texts of Muslim practitioners of the Middle Ages, and in Indian and Chinese medical writings. (Miller and Morris, 1988).

Frankincense trees are quite abundant in certain areas of Dhofar.

Oozing resin from cut bark of frankincense tree.

The Greek author Theophrastus claimed that clear droplets of frankincense were of better quality than gum scraped off the bark or picked off the ground. Gum harvested during autumn was reported to be better than that collected in spring. The two cutting seasons are also commented on by Pliny. Interestingly, the names he applied to the two seasons, i.e. 'carfiathum' for autumn and 'dathiathum' for spring, are very similar in sound to the words denoting

the two cutting seasons in the present Dhofari language. Frankincense was invariably associated with celebrations in the Greek and Roman worlds. At the height of the Roman Empire, when extravagance was the rule rather than the exception, Plutarch mentions that a statue of a bull was moulded from frankincense, myrrh and other rare products as a meal for the guests of a vegetarian host who was celebrating a win at the horse races! At the funeral of Sulla a full size statue of the dead tyrant was made from a mixture of frankincense, cinnamon and various other spices. Earlier, during the period of Greek ascendancy, when Alexander the Great was still a young boy, he was rebuked by his tutor for wasting frankincense. The story goes that Alexander's teacher suggested that he should save such extravagant behaviour for the time when he was himself master of the frankincense lands. A decade later, upon his successful conquest of Gaza and the start of his southern campaigns, he remembered his old tutor's admonishment, sending him a large consignment comprising 500 talents of frankincense and 100 talents of myrrh.

There were many strange beliefs about frankincense including its classification into 'male' and 'female' types with the 'male' type being superior. The ease with which the aromatic gum can be kneaded and worked encouraged traders to mould it into forms that were attractive to buyers. Pliny records that fragments of frankincense that were the remains of larger pieces after they had been moulded were called 'manna'.

Frankincense was collected by the same methods 2000 years ago as it is by the Dhofaris of today. The writer Theophrastus mentions that trees observed by Greek visitors bore axe marks from which the gum exuded before being removed by an iron scraper, or dripped on to palm-leaf mats spread on the ground. He was amazed to find that such a precious commodity was not guarded day and night but just left on the ground in heaps. According to Pliny some observers recorded that the exclusive right to collect frankincense gum was vested in approximately 3000 families, whereas others stated that the trees were held as common property and the harvesting rights were distributed on an annual basis by the local ruler. One of the customs associated with cutting was that if a cutter had recently been in contact with a woman who had lately attended a funeral then he was temporarily banned from cutting.

Many legends were associated with frankincense. The ancient Egyptians believed that the 'land of Punt', a loosely defined area of southern Arabia, had an exotic sweet smelling bird that carried frankincense in its talons. The Phoenix bird was another legendary species that built its death-bed (nest) from twigs of frankincense and other valuable products. The Phoenix was believed to inhabit Oman and other parts of southern Arabia where it consumed the 'tears' and blossoms of the frankincense tree and the dew from heaven. It was reported to make a long distance flight to Heliopolis every 500 years in order to bury its dead father in a myrrh saturated shroud! It has been suggested that these strange beliefs about frankincense in Egypt are the result of Omani traders spinning yarns to their Egyptian customers, doing their best to keep the true nature of frankincense as secret as possible. There is also little doubt that the Dhofaris themselves had their own legends and beliefs about frankincense. Interestingly, the Hebrew word for the Phoenix (*hol*) is similar to the name of a southern Arabian ancient 'god' (*hwl*). This linkage might explain why the ancient Egyptians believed frankincense was a gift of the gods.

A Roman myth records how a father, enraged by his daughter's love affair with the sun god, set out to burn her to death but that she was rescued by her lover, the sun god, and turned into a frankincense twig that grew into a tree.

But frankincense was much more than the subject of stories and legends. It had a great number of practical uses and each part of the plant was utilized, including the gum, bark, wood, leaves and flowers. Frankincense ground to a fine powder served as a fragrant talcum powder or an additive to render wine sweet-smelling. Apparently this formed a fairly lethal potion, driving imbibers to madness and sometimes death. The aggressive outbursts of frankincensed-wine drinkers inspired the feeding of frankincense and wine to war elephants before taking them into battle! It was also used as an opiate to calm convicts who were due to be executed. A frequent ingredient in folk medicine for a wide range of ailments, it was even used by the Emperor Nero to cover-up the effects of too many late nights!

Khor Rori from the ruins of Samhuram which was once a major port from where frankincense was exported.

Samhuram - Moscha

The Greek's interest in the frankincense trade was hardly surprising for they valued it almost as highly as gold (see box). Trade in Omani frankincense was centred around the port of Samhuram (also known as Samhar, Samaram and Sumhuram), the remains of which can be seen today at Khor Rori, a short distance north of Salalah. A magnificent setting on a raised promontory peninsula that protrudes into the natural harbour, it is not difficult to imagine why the city was sited here, nor why it eventually declined. From the ruins of the extensive stone buildings there is a clear view of the silted harbour, where the ships must have docked, and a line of breakers across the entrance of the bay suggests that the sand-bar eventually closed the harbour. In the fourth century AD Persian conquerors destroyed Samhuram, ransacking the houses which were abandoned. We know from seven inscriptions clearly preserved on large cut stones at the city's entrance and within its narrow streets that it was "founded" in the first century BC by Iliazzyalit I, "King of the Frankincense Country".

Part of the city's impressive ruins were excavated by an American team under Wendell Phillips between 1952 and 1962. Several massive walls stand over four feet high and among the many areas there is the remains of a temple. Finds made include a bronze figurine from India, pottery from Rome, bas reliefs of men and bulls and Greek amphorae. It is clear that a substantial settlement existed at the site long before King Iliazzyalit instructed his builders to construct a city there.

Asaddam Tal Am, son of Kalmum, servant of Iliad, King of Hadramaut of the inhabitants of the town of Sabwa ... undertook according to the plan, the town of Samhuram, its siting and the levelling of the ground and its flow of water from the virgin soil to its putting in order ... the creation and realisation on the initiative and by the order of his master Abiat Salhim, son of Dalma Ali who is commander of the army of the Hadramaut in the country of sacchalan. (Text of an inscription on ruins of Samhuram at Khor Rori).

We know from some of the inscriptions that this was a defended loading site for Oman's frankincense, at least by the latter part of the first century BC. It was known to the Greeks as Moscha. The Romans certainly harboured aspirations to control the frankincese trade and in 24 BC an army under the Roman general Aelius Gallus made an attempt to reach southern Arabia by land, marching down the east coast of the Red Sea. Despite their military prowess they were defeated by disease.

Dhofari frankincense accumulated in Samhuram and was shipped from the city's port to Eudaemon Arabia (around Aden) before eventually being carried up the Red Sea to Egypt and beyond. According to Pliny this frankincense trade made the people of southern Arabia the richest people in the whole world.

Immediately beyond Syagrus, the bay of Omana cuts deep into the coastline and beyond this there are mountains...high...and rock steep....and beyond this is a port established for receiving the sacolitic frankincense. The harbour is a port called Moscha....and ships from Cana call there regularly. And ships returning to Damabaigaza [southern India] if the season is late winter there....and trade with the king's officers, exchanging their cloth and wheat and sesame oil for frankincense which lies in heaps all over the saccolitic country...open and unguarded as if the place were under the protection of the gods for neither open nor by stealth can it be loaded on board ship without the king's permission. If a single grain were loaded without this the ship would not clear the harbour. (Translation from Periplus of the Erythraean Sea).

The above text is alternatively translated as follows:

There is a roadstead designated for the loading of Sachalitic incense - the place goes by the name of Moscha - where ships from Cana are customarily sent; ships coming from Dimyrike [southern India] and Barygaza [at mouth of the Indus], which cruise nearby, spend the winter there due to the lateness of the season, and obtain from royal officials, in exchange for flax, grain and oil, a cargo of this incense which, all along the bay of Sachalites, lies in unguarded heaps; for a divine power watches over the place. It is impossible, either by stealth or openly, to embark on a ship without royal authorisation, and if anyone takes a single tiny lump of it, the ship cannot weigh anchor. (Translation from Periplus of the Erythraean Sea).

Investigating the ruins of Samhuram.

Gateway to Samhuram.

Important ports

Until recently scholars have presumed that Syagrus in the ancient text (probably written between AD 40 and AD 70) corresponded with Ras Fartak. It has been suggested however that it is actually Ras Sajir that lies on the westerly extreme of Salalah Bay. The cliff-girt fortress where frankincense was stored is probably the coastal fort with store-rooms and a partially collapsed encircling wall situated at Raysut. This site possessed a commanding view over the sheltered harbour presently known as Mina Raysut.

In addition to Moscha or Samhuram at Khor Rori and Raysut, there were other ports of importance along the coast of Oman. One of these was to become one of the largest ports in the developing world. Situated at Sohar, it was known then as Omana and was renowned for its boat-builders, who were adept at making sewn boats, and for the dates harvested from palms that grew inland from the port. There was, in addition, a port on the Musandam peninsula known as Acila and the Roman author Pliny (23-79 AD) also mentions *Samhuram and* Batrasave (probably Ras al Khaimah) and *Khor Rori.* Dabenegoris Regio (probably Dibba) as

cities on the Omani peninsula. Pliny's account is of great interest since, among other things, he describes how boats were built by sewing planks together (a technique that has lived through to recent times and is quite widespread in the Indo Pacific, stretching from southern Arabia to the islands of the Pacific) and also comments on how the sailors used the north-east monsoon to sail to India. The voyage along the Arabian coast was quite a hazardous one necessitating the presence of archers on board the cargo ships in order to ward off 'pirates' who plagued the coastal waters.

From the viewpoint of the local people these attacks were probably justified by the fact that foreign forces had taken control of the lucrative trade that had for so long been their main source of wealth. In such circumstances one man's piracy is another man's legitimate protest. Nevertheless, if one compares the situation at the beginning of the

millennium with that which pertained at its close, it is clear that the trade in frankincense, myrrh and other local produce had brought great wealth to Oman, allowing it to grow in tandem with its trading partners in the Classical World of the Mediterranean and in the Seleucid Empire of Persia.

William Facey in *Oman: A Seafaring Nation* comments on events towards the end of the millennium as follows:

Around 100 BC two important developments combined to make south-west Arabia a less indispensable entrepot. First the Hellenistic king of Egypt (Ptolemy VII) began to encourage direct sailings by his merchants between Egypt and India. Second, either on these expeditions or soon after, a Greek called Hippalus discovered a new way of sailing to India, which evidently had not been used before: he learned how to sail directly across the Indian Ocean using the south-west monsoon.

These developments took much of the trade from India to Egypt away from the ports of Oman and led to a local decline, perhaps contributing to the 'piracy' commented on by Pliny. By 50 AD the direct sailing routes with India were so well developed that the prices for aromatic products in cities of the Roman Empire had tumbled to a fraction of their former levels due to over-supply.

Evening sky over Samhuram.

C. VIOUJARD, THE MINISTRY OF INFORMATION

A Samad type grave at Samad al Shan. The male individual is lying on his right side with the head facing south-east. At the feet are large storage jars.

P. YULE, GERMAN ARCHAEOLOGICAL MISSION TO OMAN

SAMAD PERIOD
200 BC to 900 AD

The Late Iron Age

Archaeological studies in Oman show that the Samad Period bridged the Iron Age and Early Islamic Period, extending from 200 BC to c.900 AD. In addition to major structural remains and inscriptions, we have the evidence of many artefacts collected from graves of this time. Men were buried with their weapons and a variety of other goods. Male burials tend to be richer in goods than female burials of this time and it is clear that women occupied a lower social status than the men. Women did, however, wear jewellery in the form of bead necklaces and silver bracelets. It is also clear from these finds that death was an occasion for fairly ostentatious mourning and grandiose grave structures that marked the deceased's status in society. Islamic burial rites are in stark contrast since the Holy Koran urges Muslims to avoid excessive public mourning or over-elaborate tombs.

Immigration of the Azd

Oman had for many thousands of years provided an attractive place to live. Domestication of the camel, around 5,000 years ago, resulted in an opening up of Arabia's interior and a greater communication between tribes. It also led to the blossoming of the unifying language and culture that we know today as Arabic. Arabs were already living in Oman when the people known as Al Azd marched into the country, under the command of Malik ibn Fahm some time during the second century AD (or according to some sources much earlier, during the reign of Darius III (336-331 BC)). Whilst some of the Al Azd settled at Shihr on the Hadrami coast, Malik and his loyal followers made Qalhat their first base in Oman. Aware of the presence of Persian forces at Sohar to the north, Malik began by trying to negotiate a peaceful arrangement with them. Omani history of this period, recorded in the *Kashf al-ghummah*, states

that what appeared at first to be goodwill and diplomacy was rapidly undermined by mutual mistrust that led to a military confrontation. The Persians set out from their garrison at Sohar with an impressive fighting force of 30,000 to 40,000 men together with war-elephants. They met with Malik's forces on the Salut plain near Nizwa where, despite the size of their force, they were defeated. A second attempt, boosted by reinforcements from Sohar, also ended in defeat for the Persians. The victorious Al Azd thus ousted the Persian colonists from Sohar and their other bases along the coast of Oman and opened the way for other members of the Al Azd to enter Oman. By the time of the next Persian invasion of Oman, by the Sasanids, the Al Azd were the dominant force in the country.

Several of the graves at Samad al Shan contained lovely glass beads such as this crumb glass bead, perhaps imported from southern India.

The excavation of the cemetery Samad 21 took place over three seasons and contained over 100 graves dating to the Wadi Suq to Samad periods.

Control of sea routes

The Romans were particularly active in the Red Sea and Indian Ocean, sending their own merchants as far as Ceylon, the Ganges, the Malay Penisula and even to the borders of China. Meanwhile Omani sailors tended to keep to their traditional routes, sailing to Barygaza and other Indian ports. They also traded with Africa, collecting cinnamon that had been ferried to that coast by traders from as far away as South China and Java, and carrying it back to the ancient port at Aden, near the entrance of the Red Sea.

As direct trade between Egypt and India flourished, cutting out southern Arabia, the seamen of the coast continued to skirmish with the foreign vessels off their shores. Frustrated by the losses incurred to merchant ships, Trajan despatched an expedition in 116 AD to put an end to the piracy problem. His soldiers never reached Oman.

Two hundred years later, with the sailors of southern Arabia still intent on taking a share of the lucrative trade, Shapur II (310-330 AD) successfully mounted a punitive raid on the Arabian shore. *The Periplus of the Erythraean Sea*, most likely written between AD 40 and 70, has a more accurate rendering of southern Arabia.

Beyond the harbour of Moscha for about 1,500 stadia as far as Asich, a mountain range runs along the shore; at the end of which, in a row, lie seven islands, called Zenobian. Beyond these there is a barbarous region which is no longer of the same kingdom, but now belongs to Persia. Sailing along this coast well out to sea for 2,000 stadia from the Zenobian islands, there meets you an island called Sarapis, about 120 stadia from the mainland. It is about 200 stadia wide and 600 stadia long, inhabited by three settlements of Fish-eaters, who use the Arabian language and wear girdles of palm leaves. The island produces considerable tortoise-shell of fine quality, and small boats and cargo-ships are sent there regularly from Cana.

Sailing along the coast, which trends north-wards towards the entrance of the Persian Sea, there are many islands, known as the Calaei, after about 2000 stadia, extending along the shore. At the upper end of these Calaei islands is a range of mountains called Calon, and there follows not far beyond the mouth of the Persian Gulf, where there is much diving for the pearl-oyster. To the left of the straits are great mountains called Asabon, and to the right there rises in full view another round and high mountain called Semiramis; between them the passage across the strait is around 600 stadia; beyond which that very great and broad sea, the Persian Gulf reaches far into the interior. At the upper end of this Gulf there is a market town designated by law, called Apologus,

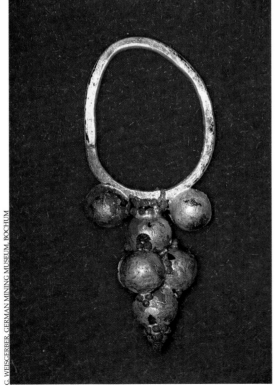

A silversmith's master-piece comprising a single ear-ring worn by an elderly woman is attributed to the Samad period (100 BCE - 629 AD).

G. WEISGERBER. GERMAN MINING MUSEUM, BOCHUM

A chain of 36 cornelian beads as large as cherries from a woman's grave. Perhaps this was an early type of prayer bead chain, but such chains usually have 39, not 36 beads.

situated near Charax Spasini and the River Euphrates.

Sailing through the mouth of the Gulf, after a six day course, there is another market town of Persia called Ommana. To both of these market towns large vessels are regularly sent from Barygaza, loaded with copper and sandalwood and timbers of teak-wood and logs of blackwood and ebony. To Ommana frankincense is also brought from Cana, and from Ommana to Arabia boats sewed together after the fashion of the place; these are known as madaratta. From each of these market towns there are exported to Barygaza, and also to Arabia, many pearls, but inferior to those of India; purple [dye from molluscs], clothing after the fashion of the place, wine, a great quantity of dates, gold, and slaves.

It is much easier to make sense of this record than it is with Pliny's account. The extract from the *Periplus* begins with vessels sailing from the ancient port of Moscha, previously known as Samhuram, situated at Khor Rori north of modern day Salalah in

Dhofar. Soon after leaving this frankincense harbour they would have rounded Ra's Marbat and headed north-eastwards, across the Bay of Halaaniyaat, passing by the Halaaniyaat islands that are here named the Zenobian islands and were previously referred to as the Kuria Muria islands. The *Periplus* then mentions that coastal ports lying to the north of these islands were controlled by Persian forces. The term Persian, in this context, equates to Parthian. Next the text mentions the island of Sarapis which is identifiable with Masira, and where 30,000 loggerhead turtles still nest each year, along with lesser numbers of hawksbill and green turtles. The fine quality "tortoise-shell" to which the *Periplus* refers almost certainly came from the hawksbills. North from here the text mentions that the next major point of interest is the many islands extending along the shore. Known then as the Calaei islands, they are almost certainly the islands we know today as the Daymaniyat archipelago, together with Jazirat Jun and the Suwaidi group of

Below left: A restored copper plate from the hoard found at 'Ibri/Selme. This is the largest such hoard known from the entire Ancient Near East and consisted of nearly 600 objects.

Below: A lion hunt bowl from a rich grave at Sama'il is dated, on the basis of its style and composition, to 200-400 AD.

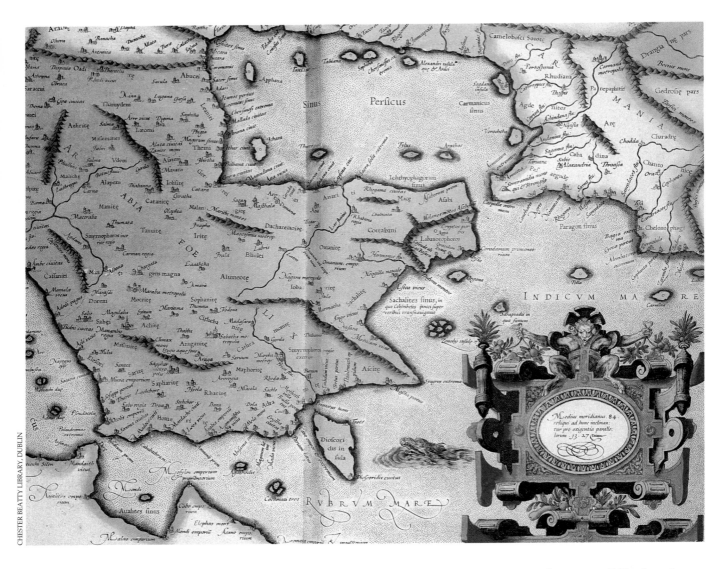

Ptolemy's map showing Arabia, published 1584, indicates placenames known to the Greeks.

islets. Moving further north, the text takes us to Asabon which is surely on the Musandam peninsula and where the main town is still called Khasab.

The next classical source to which we can turn for knowledge of Oman is Claudius Ptolemy whose *Geographia* was written between 147 and 180 AD. The maps which bear his name were compiled much later, based upon his notes, and there is therefore room for different interpretations with regard to the locations of various cities or other features. Moving this time in a southerly direction, after rounding Asabon (Ra's Musandam) Ptolemy mentions a hidden harbour (*Kryptos limen*) that can be identified with Muscat. Next comes *Korodamon* that has been suggested to be both Ra's al-Hadd and nearby Khor Jeramah. Moving further down the coast he mentions *Oragana/Serapdis* which is clearly Masirah island. Inland, Ptolemy's notes on

Oman are somewhat more difficult to interpret. *Ravana/ Rabana/ Rouana basileion* is probably Nizwa or Rostaq but there is not much else that is clear.

References to Oman are also made during the Characene dynasty. Isidorus of Charax, who would have been a contemporary of Christ, wrote of a king named Goaesus who was 'king of the Omani in the Incense Land'. Northward migration of the Azd, who colonized much of Arabia, moving out of southern Arabia, is attested by Pliny who wrote 'the country as far as Charax was inhabited by the Omani'. A little used anonymous reference dating to the early eighth century AD, *Cosmographia*, is based on Roman sources including the work of Castorius. This mentions '*Samematride Castrillum Amarium*' which has been interpreted as '*masani 'Oman*', or fortifications of the Omanis, which has been suggested to refer to the twin ports of Matrah and Muscat.

The Sasanians

The Sasanian Empire, a rival of Byzantium established in present day Iraq and Iran and extending its influence far beyond these borders, was based on a dynastic culture that had its beginnings in southern Persia. Sasanians espoused the Zoroastrian faith that placed emphasis on the dualism of good and evil. Albert Hourani, in his *History of the Arab Peoples* describes Zoroaster's philosophy thus: "the universe was a battle-ground, beneath the supreme God, between good and evil spirits; the good would win, but men and women of virtue and ritual purity could hasten the victory". The Sasanian version of this faith is known as Mazdaism or Zoroastrianism.

The first Sasanian king Ardashir, who campaigned in eastern Arabia around 225 AD, also fought in Oman. An Arabic reference dated to around 1000 AD states that: "Ardashir marched with his troops and soldiers .... and they fought a violent fight and there were killed on both sides a great number. And Sanatruk the king of al-Bahrain, and 'Amr ibn Waqid al-Himyari, the king of 'Uman, were killed". Meanwhile the geographer Yaqut claims that "Ardasir, son of Babik, established the Azd as sailors at Shihr, in Oman, 600 years before Islam". Potts, in his excellent two volume history entitled *The Arabian Gulf in Antiquity*, states that Ardasir's campaign "probably marked the 'return to Oman' which accompanied Persia's fall 'into the hands of the Benu Sasan', as ... the *Khashf al-Gumma* puts it". It would appear however that by the end of the third century AD the Persian influence in Oman had once more been removed.

Khusraw Anosirwan became king of the Sasanian Empire in 531 AD. Soon after his accession he recognized Mundhir as king over a large area of southern Arabia including Oman. In 575 he despatched an army of 800 men to Yemen aboard eight ships, six of which landed on the Hadhramaut coastline.

The *Khashf al-Gumma* records that: "The Persian monarchs used to send persons who had incurred their displeasure or whom they feared to their army in Oman. So it continued until God caused el-Islam to be manifested". Another source reports on a treaty signed by Khusraw Anosirwan and the Azd of Oman. The treaty acknowledged a sphere of Persian influence along the Batinah coastline, and a Persian (Sasanian) garrison at al-Rostaq commemorated in the Arabic name for Rostaq's fort (Qal'at al-Kisra meaning Khusraw's fort). A military control structure was set up which included local rulers (*maraziba*) based at forts in the major settlements; a military command structure, (*asiwara*) that had control over different regions; and finally a local administration within the villages under the *hanaqira,* who have been described as a 'capitalist land-colonizing class'. There was thus a three-layered class system in place, supporting the Sasanian power-base. The Azd inhabitants of Oman were led by a titular head or *Julanda* who was also chief of the Ma'wil clan. He controlled those areas of Oman that did not fall under direct Sasanian control, such as Dibba and the oasis settlement of Tuwam (at Buraimi), collecting taxes from the inhabitants and reporting back to the Sasanian *marzban* based at al-Rostaq.

The *Khashf al-Gumma*, commenting on relations between the Persian occupying force and the Omanis states: "There was peace between them and el-Julanda in Oman, and the Persians kept a force of 4000 warriors in Oman and a deputy with the kings of the el-Azd. The Persians abode on the sea coast, and the el-Azd ruled in the interior plains and hills and districts of Oman, the direction of affairs being entirely with them". We know from several sources that the Julanda's power did not go entirely unchallenged however. Immediately before the coming of Islam, for example, Laqit ibn

These horse sculptures were found in graves in Sama'il and Samad al Shan where the Azd tribesmen are believed to have settled.

Malik Dhu at-Tag was reported to be as strong as the Julanda, commanding a considerable popular following. It seems clear that whilst the local Julanda had for many years cooperated with the Persians in Oman, this power-base was increasingly questioned and challenged by ordinary Omani people.

Early Christians in Oman

Christianity appears to have arrived in Oman during the fourth century AD and it has been suggested that an early Nestorian church was sited at Sohar, although this has not been confirmed and is disputed by some writers. A bishop from Oman, Yohannon, attended a synod in 423/4 AD at which the Nestorian Church proclaimed its independence from Antioch. A bishop of Mazun attended a Nestorian synod in 544 AD, the first such visit recorded since that of 424 AD mentioned above. A later visit took place by Bishop Samuel who attended the synod of Mar Ezechiel in February 576 AD. We also hear of Qais ibn Zuhair who returned to Oman to become a monk following a battle in central Arabia. This suggests that a monastery was in existence in Oman by this time.

Final years before Islam

Under the rule of the Byzantine emperors Justin (517-552) and Justinian (527-556), great efforts were made to dislodge Sasanian forces from their control of the Ethiopian kingdom of Axum, but a major defeat for the Ethiopian army in Yemen only served to consolidate the Sasanian hold over the southern Arabian littoral dur-

ing the second half of the sixth century AD. Pottery remains from this period found in Musandam tend to suggest that Sasanian control spread right along the shores of Oman at this time.

Written accounts of Oman during this final phase of its pre-Islamic existence are quite limited and we must depend in part upon evidence from later writings that refer to this period. One such is Ibn Habib's *al-Muhabbar* that describes the scene at some of Oman's markets around AD 620, i.e. at the very end of the Sasanian period, immediately before the rise of Islam. The following is a translated extract:

Another fair was that of Sohar and Uman. It was usually held on the first day of Ragab and lasted for five nights. Al-Julanda ibn al-Mustakbir used to levy the tithe from the merchants there. Another fair was that of Dibba. Dibba is one of the two ports of the Arabs; merchants from Sind, India, China, people of the East and West came to it. This fair was held on the last day of Ragab. Merchants traded there by bargaining. Al-Julanda ibn al-Mustakbir levied the tithe in this fair, as in Sohar. He used to behave in it like other kings elsewhere. Another fair was that of al-Shihr - Shihr of Mahrah. It took place at the foot of the mountains on which the grave of the prophet Hud is located. At this fair no tithes were levied because Mahrah was not a realm of a kingdom.

It is already apparent that Sasanian influence had waned considerably and the Julanda was in commercial, if not military, control of the Batinah ports.

*Some of the vessels of the
Samad period found in
graves.*

Inside Al-Hazm Fort.
The cannon bears
Portuguese markings.

The ISLAMIC ERA

ISLAMIC OMAN PROSPERS

The Conversion of Oman

According to a manuscript titled *Tarikh al-rusul wa-al-muluk* written by Tabari between 838 and 923 AD (i.e. roughly two to three hundred years after the event) a gentleman by the name Wakidi stated that the conversion of Oman stemmed from the dispatch by the Prophet Muhammad of an envoy, 'Amr ibn al-'As, to Oman where he met with two sons of the recently deceased Julanda. The sons, Gaifar and Abd, were reported to have pledged their allegiance to Muhammad and agreed to the collection of *zakat* (alms-tax) from richer Omanis so that wealth could be more evenly distributed and the poor cared for.

A slightly different version of the same event is preserved in *al-Tabaqat al-kubra* written by Muhammad Ibn Sa'ad some time before his death in 845 AD. According to Sa'ad's account, the emissary arrived with a sealed letter that was addressed directly to two sons of the Julanda, Gaifar and 'Abd. The letter, exhorting the brothers to embrace Islam was given to 'Abd because he was considered to be the most reasonable of the two despite the fact that Gaifar, as the older brother, held prior rank. In deference to his elder brother's position 'Abd handed Gaifar the letter, who read it himself and then handed it back to 'Abd to read. The message apparently made a deep impression on the younger brother.

Texts of two letters sent by the Prophet Muhammad to the brothers are preserved so we have direct insight into the manner of persuasion employed to spread the message. Providing the brothers accepted Islam they were promised power and support by Muhammad; if they refused, he would strip them of their power, surround them with his cavalry, and they would not be allowed to stand in the way of the spread of Islam in Oman. A letter addressed separately to the 'Asbadhites, servants of God and princes of Oman', guaranteed safety and security for those who 'celebrate the offices, discharge the *zakat*, obey God and his Messenger, give their due to the Prophet, and follow the way of the Muslims'. Asbadhites were informed that their property would be respected except for the 'treasury of the fire temple' which would become the property of God and His Messenger. An alms-tax would be collected, calculated at ten percent on fruits, and five percent on cereals.

Gaifar's reported response to the letter according to Wakidi was as follows: 'I have reflected on what you have demanded, but I should be the greatest weakling of all Arabs if I were to give another man rule over all that I possess'. When Gaifar saw that the emissary was making preparations to return in order to convey this message to Muhammad in Mecca, he is reported to have had second thoughts, called him back and embraced Islam. 'Amr ibn al-'As then set about collecting the alms-tax, established himself with the support of Gaifar and his family as a judge, and set about

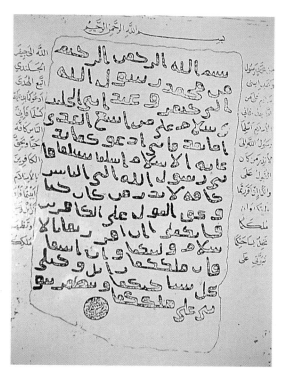

Letter from the Prophet Muhammad to the rulers of Oman written in 630 AD.

A. SPALTON

Camels are driven across the sandy desert of central Oman, providing a reminder of earlier times.

bringing the teachings of Islam to the Omani people. He is reported to have remained in Oman until news reached him of the Prophet Muhammad's death.

A slightly different version of the event is given in *Futuh al-Buldan* written by al-Baladhuri who died in 892 AD. According to this account there were two emissaries, 'Amr ibn al-As whom we have already heard about, and also Abu Zaid. The letter they brought to Oman was addressed to both Gaifar and 'Abd. Upon accepting the terms of the letter the messenger 'Amr was to become their emir or ruler whilst Abu Zaid was to have responsibility for giving religious instruction to the people, assisting in their conversion to Islam. The brothers were in Sohar when the messengers arrived and they accepted the terms of the letter and encouraged others to convert to Islam.

Finally, there is an account of the events in the rich Omani historical source, *Khashf al-Gumma*, which may be translated as follows:

There is a tradition that the first man of Oman to embrace el-Islam was one Mazin-ibn-Ghadhubah, who visited the Prophet and asked him to pray for him and the people of Oman.

Afterwards the Apostle of God wrote to the people of Oman, inviting them to adopt the religion of Islam. He wrote among others to 'Abd and Gaifar, the sons of el-Julanda (who had died a short time before), to the effect that if they would accept Islam, he would confirm them as Governors; otherwise they would be deposed. He sent this letter by 'Amr-ibn el-As, who alighted at a place near Sohar named Damsetjerd, which had been built by the Persians. Thence he sent a message to the sons of Julanda, who were the foremost and most influential chiefs of Oman. The first who met the messenger was 'Abd, who was the most discerning and sensible of the two brothers. He sent on 'Amr to his brother Gaifar with the sealed letter, and Gaifar broke the seal and read it, and then passed it to 'Abd who also read it. The latter then told 'Amr that this was no trifling matter he had come about, and that he would reflect on it, and afterwards give a reply. He then assembled a council of the el-Azd, and sent to Ka'b-ibn Barshah el-'U'di. They all became converts to Islam, and sent to their kinsmen who vowed obedience to the Prophet, and agreed to offer the proper reli-

gious alms. Gaifar sent messengers to Mahra, and Shihr in the south, and to Dibba, and the furthest limits of Oman to the north; and at his invitation all the people accepted Islam, save the Persians who dwelt in Oman. When the Persians rejected Islam, the el-Azd assembled around Gaifar, and all agreed to expel the Persian deputy Maskan and his followers from the country. As the Persians refused either to join Islam or to leave the country quietly, the el-Azd attacked them, killed their leader Maskan and many more, and drove the remainder into their town of Damsetjerd, when they besieged them rigorously, until they sued for terms. The el-Azd granted them quarter on condition they left all their gold and silver and other property behind them and quitted Oman, which they did. 'Amr continued to reside with and direct the el-Azd, until the death of the Prophet. (after translation quoted by D.T. Potts in *The Arabian Gulf in Antiquity*, Vol. 2., p343).

According to some sources, after news of the Prophet's death reached Oman, some of those who had converted to Islam now defected and gathered under the banner of Laqit ibn Malik Dhu at-Tag whom we have mentioned above as holding a strong position in Oman prior to the arrival of Muhammad's emissaries. As Potts comments in his recent book: "One could well imagine that this was aimed more at deposing Gaifar than rejecting Islam". At any event forces from the Moslem army were dispatched under the direct leadership of Hudhaifah ibn Mihsan al-Makhzumi, who joined up with loyal forces under 'Abd and Gaifar. Laqit was killed on the battlefield at Dibba where up to 10,000 rebels are supposed to have died with him while 4000 were taken prisoner. Local people returned to Islam, but a second uprising took place at Shihr which was in turn suppressed by forces under the command of 'Ikrimah ibn Abi Jahl.

Abbasid influence

During the eight to tenth centuries AD Oman enjoyed two centuries of prosperity based upon its agriculture and trading links. This was also the period of Abbasid colonialism and the Baghdad-based power extended its tendrils as far as the inland mountain domains of Nizwa and Bahla; centres of the Ibadi religion. The predominance of Abbasid influence over these two centres meant that their power was effectively spread over a large area of Oman, with the exception of Musandam which remained too remote for a land-based army to effectively subdue. The incentive for the Abbasids was a link-up to the lucrative trade between India, the Far East, Africa and southern Arabia with the Omani ports occupying key positions as major entrepots. This was the heyday of Sohar and an Omani naval force helped to keep sea-lanes clear from piracy.

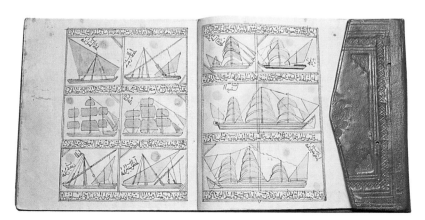

Mercantile developments

The arrival of the militarily strong Seljuks, following their defeat of the Buweyhids in 1062 AD, brought an end to two centuries or more of relatively peaceful trading in the Gulf. The Seljuk dynasty in Oman did not, however, entirely work against trading interests since much of the Indian Ocean trade with the Gulf nations continued to divert through Omani ports. The rise in importance of Hormuz as a regional trading centre during the thirteenth century coincided with growth of the Omani ports of Sohar, Muscat and Qalhat. Now ships from as far away as China were regular visitors to these shores. Tome Pires wrote thus of Hormuz as it was before 1514, when it was taken by the Portuguese:

Ormuz trades with Aden and Cambay and with the kingdom of the Deccan and Goa and with the ports of the kingdom of Narsinga and in Malabar. The chief things the Ormuz merchants take are Arabian and Persian horses, seed pearls, saltpetre, sulphur, silk, tutty, alum - which is called alexandrina in our part of the world - copperas, vitriol, quantities of salt, white silk, many tangas-which are silver coins worth about sixty-five reis, and musk, sometimes amber, and a great deal of died fruit, wheat, barley and foodstuffs of that kind. They bring back pepper, cloves, cinnamon, ginger and all sorts of spices and drugs, which are greatly in demand in the land of Persia and Arabia, and some of which go to Aden when there is a great deal; but as they are already costly at Ormuz I do not think much goes from there to Cairo for dispatch to Italy. They also bring back as much rice as they can, also <u>beatilha</u>, white cloth, and iron, although their great idea is to bring back pepper, rice and gold with them. Horses are worth a high price in the kingdoms of Goa, of the Deccan and of Narsinga, so the Ormuz merchants go to these kingdoms with them every year. A horse may be worth as much as seven hundred xerafins - coins worth 320 reis each - when it is good. The best are the

Part of the ruins of al-Balid.

S. KAY

Arabians, next are the Persians and third are those from Cambay.

With such a hub of trading activity along the coast of Oman and at the entrance to the Gulf, it was not surprising that the Portuguese focussed their atten- tion on this region soon after their navy arrived in the Indian Ocean. In 1514 Hormuz fell to the Portuguese and thereafter Portuguese influence was a major factor for Oman and her neighbours.

Before we leave the maritime trading situ- ation in the early sixteenth century, it is worth quoting another passage by Tome Pires who explained how goods from southern Arabia's ports reached Cairo from where, as we have seen above, they were trans-shipped to Europe.

The merchants there keep the spices by them, and send them to Cairo in this way: they go from Aden to Kamaran, from Kamaran to Dhalak, from Dhalak to the islands of Suakin, whence they go all along the straits of this Suakin, to a port called El Qoseir on the Arabia Felix side, and from there it is three days journey to the Nile and ten days to Cairo; only they do not go this way because of thieves, but after they have reached the island of Suakin they go to Jidda, sailing by day, and many are lost because the straits are stormy on account of the land winds; and those who are going to Jidda unload, when they reach Jidda. At the time of the Jubilee [haj] great caravans come to Mecca, and the merchants join them, since they satisfy the leaders. It is a seventy days' journey to Cairo, and some- times they go from Jidda to Tor by sea; but not

often because it is a main road to Cairo and they are always robbed.

A column from ruins of al-Balid, Dhofar.

Ruins at al-Balid.

Ibn Batuta

On September 29th 1329 the renowned Moslem geographer Ibn Batuta landed on the island of Halaniyyah off the Dhofari coast of Oman. (As we have seen above this island group, until recently called the Kuria Muria islands, was known to the Romans as the Zenobians.) He was on part of his long journey, at that stage between Dhofar and the old port of Qalhat. After landing on the island he climbed its hill to visit a spiritual hermit.

...on top of it is a hermitage built of stone, with a roofing of fishbones, and with a pool of collected rainwater outside it. When we cast anchor under this hill, we climbed up to this hermitage, and found there an old man lying asleep. We saluted him, and he woke up and returned our greetings by signs; then we spoke to him, but he did not speak to us and kept shaking his head. The ship's company offered him food, but he refused to accept it. We then begged of him a prayer (on our behalf), and he kept moving his lips, though we did not know what he was saying. He was wearing a patched robe and a felt bonnet, but had no skin bag nor jug nor staff nor sandals. We spent that night on the beach on the hill and prayed the afternoon and sunset prayers with him. We offered him food, but he refused it and continued to pray until the hour of the last night prayer, when he pronounced the call to prayer and we prayed along with him. He had a beautiful voice in his reciting of the Qur'an and in his modulation of it. When he ended the last night-prayer, he signed for us to withdraw, so bidding him farewell, we did so, with astonishment at what we had seen...

(Quoted by Brian Doe in *Socotra: Island of Tranquillity* 1992.)

PORTUGUESE DOMINATION

Albuquerque attacks

The King of Portugal dispatched three fleets of ships to foreign parts in 1506. One of these, comprising 16 vessels, departed from the Portuguese harbour at Tagus on March 6th and set sail, around the Cape of Good Hope bound for southern Arabia. Under the maritime command of Tristan da Cunha, the fleet carried the Conquistador Alfonso de Albuquerque. The vessels arrived at Socotra in April 1507 and, after a battle against the garrison there (80 dead Arabs, one dead Portuguese plus about 50 wounded), they took possession of the military base. The fact that there were Christians on Socotra made it an attractive base, because they could supply Albuquerque's new base with food and freshwater. He appointed his nephew, Alfonso de Noronha, to command a garrison of 100 men. The fleet then moved to the Arabian mainland where Alfonso de Albuquerque rapidly earned a reputation for savage cruelty against the Moslem inhabitants of southern Arabia. His attempt to take Aden was mentioned by Tome Pires, writing a few years after the event:

Inside the city there is a beautiful fortress, with a captain in it always prepared as he should be, because for the last ten years they have always been afraid of our armadas, and all the Moors help this city so that they shall not be taken. They fear that if it were taken the end would come soon, because it is all they have left. And this city has already had a great battle, and would have been stormed if the ladders had not disastrously broken with the weight of people scaling the walls. And the battle was a famous thing because [to capture] such towns the camp has first to be taken, and this town was all but lost by the Moors. This was a famous exploit, although the city was not taken; and it was not very happy afterwards, and its Kashites [religious priests] feel that its destruction will soon come.

MINISTRY OF INFORMATION

The Omanis had a strong reputation among the Portuguese as skilled and brave fighters. Tome Pires, commenting on the whole length of southern Arabia, wrote:

After Aden comes Fartak, the islands of Kuria Muria and Masirah. The people here are all nomads, merchants and good warriors. Many go from Fartak to Sokotra, Zeila and Berbera as garrison captains. These people also live by trade, but it is not much. From Cape Ras el Hadd inland the land is under the dominion of Ormuz. The people of Fartak have beautiful swords and all other kinds of arms. They are daring men.

Following his initial attack at Khor Jeramah, Albuquerque led his force to Qalhat where a Persian 'ruler' had little choice but to welcome the Portuguese. A few days later, after passing by Tiwi, they landed at Quriyat and committed the first of many atrocities against the Omani people. First they attacked the city's fortifications, then they indiscriminately slaughtered men, women and children as they ran from the scene of carnage. Finally, they

Inside Hazm fort, showing Portuguese cannon.

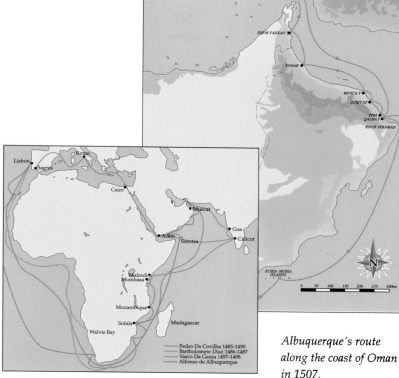

Albuquerque's route
along the coast of Oman
in 1507.

plundered the city, set fire to the houses and burnt ships in the harbour. Word of the barbarous attack ran along the coast like wildfire, reaching Muscat long before the Portuguese navy, which arrived there four days after their vicious massacre at Quriyat.

The citizens of Muscat had barricaded the city, preparing to defend against Albuquerque's impending attack.

At first the Portuguese were somewhat discouraged by Muscat's state of readiness but Albuquerque was seldom one to back down. Those ashore were petrified by the cruel reputation of the Portuguese following the bloody events at Quriyat and, fearing for their lives, two of the town's leaders went out to the fleet moored inside the bay, in order to bid for peace. Soon after the negotiations began however, Albuquerque sensed that these two did not have an absolute mandate from the people ashore to agree his terms. He sent them back with instructions to return the next day. When they did so he set out his demands: an annual tribute to be paid to his navy and the provision of supplies, including food and water, for his planned attack against Hormuz. The Omani negotiators accepted the terms and returned ashore where they found that the people were talking of resisting the Portuguese. That night reinforcements and supplies arrived in Muscat by land and one of the local shaikhs encouraged the town to resist.

As soon as this became apparent, Albuquerque launched an attack on

Upper left: Alfonso de Albuquerque as portrayed in P. Barreto de Resende's Livro do Estado da India.

Left: Myrrh and incense were sources of wealth to Oman for over 2000 years.

Opposite: At doorway of Nizwa Suq.

In August 1544, the Portuguese naval fleet, under command of Fernando de Menezes, moored off Muscat, prior to sailing for Musandam where they were to confront a fleet of Turkish galleys that had rowed and sailed their way around Arabia from their base at Suez. The plate shown here is from Anonimo - Livro de Lizuarte de Abreu, c. 1564.

Muscat, bombarding the shore and town with his heavy cannons. The ships were too far away for this to have any real effect however, so Albuquerque called a halt and held a strategy meeting among his captains. Fearing Albuquerque's anger if they demurred, the officers simply said that they would follow his command. Albuquerque then ordered a two-pronged, flanking attack on the town in which he took charge of the left flank whilst Captains da Tavora and da Costa led the right-hand flank that was to charge the stockade. They landed immediately beneath the fortifications and, despite a brave and determined defence, they broke through on both fronts. Storming into the town, the attacking groups met inside and then drove the residents out, killing or maiming them whenever they had the chance. The attack was a repeat of the Quriyat massacre.

After those who could escape had done so, and women, children and old men were rounded up, Albuquerque personally ordered that they too be killed. Two captains, Antao da Campo and Joao da Nova, played a particularly gruesome role in killing women and they later mutinied against Albuquerque. After the carnage came the pillage and everything of any value that could be carried was taken back to the Portuguese ships. This war booty included 30 guns, bows and arrows, lances and other weapons. The fleet spent eight days at anchor, during which they provisioned their ships with fresh fruits, water and other supplies and Albuquerque was then ready to set fire to what remained of the town. Just before he gave the order a messenger was sent to him to beg that the town be spared. 'Was it not enough that he had killed so many innocent women and children?', the emissary pleaded. Albuquerque, calling up his great reserve of self-justification, replied that the town's people should not have broken faith with him when they reached their initial settlement. Rather than burn it straight away however, he said that he would agree to cancel the plan if he received a ransom of 10,000 *ashrafies* in gold by noon of the next day. Since the Portuguese had already taken all the booty they could lay their hands on, the inhabitants were not in a position to meet the demand. Their houses and dhows (at least 35) were duly set alight and irreparable damage was done to many important structures. In particular, a mosque made from carved wood was completely destroyed.

After Muscat the Conquistador Albuquerque took his tyrannical fleet to Sohar. Further slaughter was temporarily averted there when a delegation from the town travelled out to Albuquerque's flag ship in order to pledge their allegiance to the King of Portugal and to pay whatever huge sum the Portuguese despot demanded. Prior to the fleet's arrival the citizens of Sohar had requested military assistance from Hormuz and it was in the absence of any positive response to this request that they were forced to submit to the Portuguese. After agreeing with the ruler the taxes that were to be collected and paid to him on his next visit, Albuquerque continued his passage northwards towards Hormuz. The next major settlement along the coast was at Khor Fakkan where the same act was played out as had been indulged in at the Omani ports. This time the inhabitants attempted to resist but the sheer strength of the Portuguese force was too much for them and they too surrendered and had the town reduced to ashes. From there the Portuguese sailed to Hormuz, where they were confronted by a much stronger defence, and then back to Socotra where they had left their garrison eight months previously. They found the small Portuguese force in a sorry state, with their men starving to death since the local Christians had failed to look after them, fearing retribution from their Moslem counterparts. On their way back to Hormuz in 1508, Albuquerque and his men again attacked Qalhat, plundering what remained of the town and burning the mosque.

The *Suma Oriental* of Tome Pires, comprising an account of his travels through the East, from the Red Sea to Japan, and written while he was in India between 1512 and 1515, mentions the Oman coastline as part of a province which was called *Arabia Petrea*:

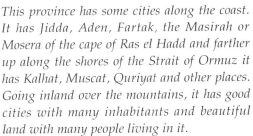

This province has some cities along the coast. It has Jidda, Aden, Fartak, the Masirah or Mosera of the cape of Ras el Hadd and farther up along the shores of the Strait of Ormuz it has Kalhat, Muscat, Quriyat and other places. Going inland over the mountains, it has good cities with many inhabitants and beautiful land with many people living in it.

The people of this Arabia are warlike. They fight on horseback in the same way as we do, with spurs, and holding the reins in one hand and a lance in the other, and they have a great number of men. The horses in this Arabia are better than all the others in any of these parts. They have a large number of camels and oxen which they use, and other animals. They are hunters, very hard working men, haughty and presumptuous.

From 1507, until their expulsion by the Imam Saif ibn Sultan al Ya'aruba in 1650, the Portuguese controlled Muscat and a number of other coastal settlements. Their

The most prominent ancient building remaining at Qalhat, a coastal town pillaged by the Portuguese, is the ruins of the mausoleum of Bibi Mariam.

Two forts constructed by Omanis during the period when Portugal held maritime power in the region - Al Mirani (1588) and Al Jalali (1587) still stand today -a tribute to the craftsmanship of their builders.

greatest legacies are three of Oman's great forts: Mirani and Jalali in Muscat and the fort of Muttrah. These three are the only Portuguese forts still standing in Oman. Other treasures from the Portuguese period are bronze cannon. The finest group comprising five cannon is at the Ya'aruba fort of Al Hazm. Finally, Portuguese boat building techniques influenced those of southern

Arabia. In particular they introduced the method of iron nailing which gradually replaced the sewn-plank method that had been in use for several thousand years.

The Portuguese directed their attention to controlling the major ports of the Indian Ocean and to thus profit from the lucrative trade in spices and silks that passed through these ports. They established 23

fortified enclaves around the Indian Ocean, from Malacca in the east to the Kenyan coastline in the west. The European demand for pepper (from Sumatra), cinnamon (from Ceylon), camphor (from Borneo), nutmeg (from Banda islands) and cloves (from the Moluccas) was reminiscent of the earlier craving for frankincense and myrrh by the Greek and Roman classical civilizations. Once again, foreign forces were drawn to Oman and other coastal states to grab their own share of the high stakes involved in the trade. Coincidentally, the Portuguese taxed other regional trading arrangements such Oman's export of fine Arabian horses to India and India's export of cottons to Africa.

Turkey versus the Portuguese

In 1546 a Turkish fleet lying offshore bombarded Muscat but did not follow through with a landing against the strongly defended, Portuguese occupied city. In 1550 however, the Turkish commander Biri Pasha brought a stronger force to Muscat in order to punish the Portuguese for their support of Arab revolutionaries against the Turks at Basra. In preparation for such an attack the Portuguese commander of the Muscat garrison had commenced construction of a massive fort. At the time of the Turkish attack the new building was still not completed, but it nevertheless provided a good vantage point for the Portuguese defenders. For 18 days the Portuguese remained holed up in the fort whilst the Turks besieged them. Finally, they had no choice but to plea for a safe passage. A shaky treaty was soon broken, however, when the Turkish commander reneged on his promise and killed some of the surrendering Portuguese, handcuffing others, including the Portuguese local commander. The Turks ransacked the fort and took whatever booty they could back to their ships.

Encouraged by this initial success against the Portuguese, Sultan Suleiman ordered further attacks against the Europeans, first in the Red Sea, and later off southern Arabia. The Turkish fleet left Basra in August 1553 but were defeated off Musandam. The remnants of this fleet set sail again the following year in July 1554 and on this occasion they encountered the Portuguese off Khor Fakan. The Portuguese retreated to their safe haven of Muscat but were eventually forced out again and had to face the Turkish ships. Portuguese sailors on board their ships were by now less than certain of victory since the Turks had a credible force and were well matched technically in the skills of naval warfare. Two events of that August day were recorded by Portuguese observers as harbingers of bad luck. First of all, a large whale swam around the Portuguese ships: not an unusual sight off Muscat even today, but its inquisitiveness and seeming lack of fear intimidated the sailors. Secondly, a small meteorite chose that day to fall into the sea off Muscat: one can imagine the consternation this caused among men who were about to fight for their lives.

A sea battle eventually took place a short way from Fahal island which the Portuguese subsequently named 'the island of victory' for it was they, not the Turks, who were to win the day. The battle left the Portuguese with 46 more cannon and a considerable quantity of weapons. But as time passed more efforts were made to oust the Portuguese from Oman. One such attack on Muscat, made by a Turkish commander Meer Ali Beg in 1581, left the Portuguese 'shaken but not stirred' and Meer Ali itching to repeat his qualified success elsewhere. Eventually he was captured and taken to Lisbon where he died, reportedly from the effects of torture. It was raids such as these that led to the construction of the two large Portuguese forts at Muscat, with Al-Jalali built in 1587 and Al-Mirani in 1588.

Joint-action to oust the Portuguese

By the beginning of the seventeenth century Portuguese supremacy in the Indian Ocean was being increasingly challenged by local forces. Hormuz fell to the Persians in 1622 while Julfar was taken by Omani forces. The Portuguese fell back on their strongly fortified base of Muscat from where they continued to operate their system of issuing trading vessels with 'safe-passage' passes in return for heavy payments. There now ensued a period of great tension between the Portuguese and local inhabitants. (It was at this time that the main city wall of Muscat was constructed.) The Persians, buoyed by their success at Hormuz, tried to press home the advantage, wresting control of Sohar but failing to dislodge the European force from Muscat. Admiral Ruy Freire de Andrade, who commanded his forces in defence of Muscat, led them back to Sohar to re-take the port. Unable to mount a frontal attack on Hormuz, Andrade settled for reinforcing a base at

Bahla Fort.

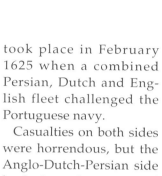

Rostaq Fort.

took place in February 1625 when a combined Persian, Dutch and English fleet challenged the Portuguese navy.

Casualties on both sides were horrendous, but the Anglo-Dutch-Persian side had the advantage of being able to repair and replenish their ships at nearby Gombroon (Bandar Abbas), whereas the Portuguese only had the more distant port of Muscat to fall back on. Rather than evacuate the area, the Portuguese fleet, commanded by Nuno Alvarez Botelho, stayed around the entrance of the Gulf, waiting for the combined fleet to re-emerge. On February 23rd part of the allied fleet re-engaged with the Portuguese, trying desperately to sink the admiral's flag-ship. Both sides ran short of ammunition however, so the result was inconclusive.

Khasab in Musandam, from where he mounted a blockade on Hormuz, pending the arrival of reinforcements from Goa.

By 1624 the Persian position had weakened to such an extent that they appealed to rival European navies of Holland and England to assist them in removing the Portuguese. A major two-day sea-battle

The fort at Marbat overlooks the sea.

Imam Nasir ibn Murshid
(Imam from 1624 to 1649)

The Portguese navy divided after the battle, with many ships returning to their secure Indian Ocean base at Goa, whilst the admiral and a smaller number of vessels remained behind in order to defend their Arabian interests. They were by now being attacked from both land and sea since the Omani leader Imam Nasir ibn Murshid (elected as Imam of Oman in 1624) had been successful in mounting a number of ground attacks against Portuguese strongholds. In 1633 he took the fort at Julfar (in Ras al Khaimah) which had only been built three years previously under the direction of Admiral Ruy Freire de Andrade. The following year his forces took control of Sohar whilst ten years later, in 1644, he ousted the Portuguese from the Musandam fort at Khasab. An attempt to force the Portuguese from Muscat in 1648 almost met with success. The whole town was laid to seige from August 16th to September 11th and the Portuguese were forced to agree to the Imam's peace terms. They consented to the destruction of their fortifications at Sur and Quriyat, the cancellation of taxes levied against Omanis, demolition of Muscat's outer fortifications and a compensation payment of 200,000 *pardaos*.

It certainly looked as if the end was in sight but, having initially agreed the terms, the Portuguese had second thoughts: the siege was re-established and they were not forced back to the negotiating tent until October 31st 1648. New terms entailed evacuation of Portuguese forces from their fort at Muttrah, abolition of taxes, a free-trade agreement, and a promise that no new fortifications would be built by the Portuguese outside of Muscat. Imam Nasir's victory was short-lived however, for as soon as a Portuguese fleet arrived from Goa in November 1648 the Portuguese reneged on the treaty, determined to hold on to Muscat, and strengthened their base at Khasab in

Musandam. Imam Nasser died in 1649, shortly before his cousin and successor, Sultan ibn Saif al-Ya'aruba, finally met with success, ousting the Portuguese from Muscat and consolidating the Ya'aruba dynasty in Oman.

Imam Sultan ibn Saif al-Ya'aruba
(r. 1649-1668)

The famous Omani victory over the Portuguese is described by Humaid ibn Muhammad ibn Razik, in *'Al-Fath al-Mubeen'* as follows:

I, Humaid ibn Muhammad ibn Razik, received this information from several aged trustworthy men, who were brought up in the time of Imam Sultan ibn Saif ibn Malik el Ya'aruby and who all agreed in substance although their words differed, that when the Imam Nasir ibn Murshid died, his cousin remained only a few days in Oman after the Imamate had been conferred upon him and then set out to attack the Christians, who held possession of the towns of Maskat and el-Matrah. These Christians were called Portuguese, who had large territories in India, and at that time they were the most powerful of all the Christian nations, all of whom were their confederates and allies. Every epoch has its heroes.

When the Imam Sultan ibn Saif decided to fight the Portuguese he pitched his camp at Tawy-er-Rula, near el-Mattrah. He had a large army under his command with which he assailed the enemy every morning and afternoon. The Portuguese were well prepared for these attacks, and showed no sign of defeat. They filled the two forts of Maskat with picked men and waited patiently for the coming assault.

The Imam Sultan ibn Seif's troops advanced against them as far as the Bir-el-Rawiyah of Maskat; but the Portuguese had erected towers on the mountains of Maskat and garrisoned them with musketeers, so that whenever any of the Imam's soldiers approached

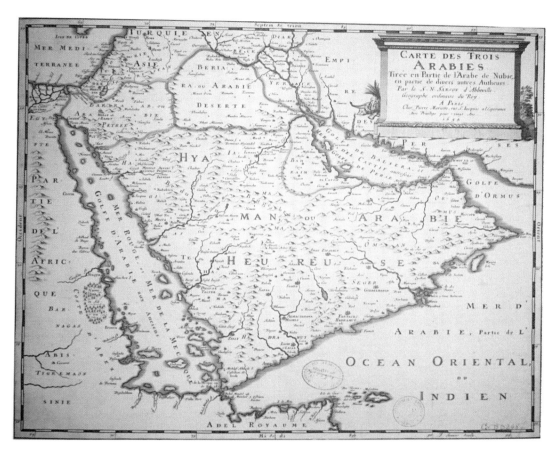

they fired upon them. They had also suspended an iron chain in the air from the tower, now called after my uncle the Tower of Muhammad ibn Razik, to the tower now known as el-Murabba (the Square Tower), whereto were attached iron cradles, in which men were concealed who discharged shot on any of the Imam's followers who ventured near them.

They also occupied the whole of Jebel-es-Saaly as well as Jebel-el-Makulla, and the reverberations caused by the shots fired by those concealed in these mountains and in the other posts, especially towards nightfall, were continuous, whilst their guards and spies went to and fro with news night and day. They showed the greatest determination and were everywhere on their guard. The two batteries they filled with their experienced gunners and musketeers, so that they cut off all means of access to them from without.

The war in the meantime between them and the Imam's troops was of varying fortune: the

Portuguese were unable to expel their assailants from their position at el-Matrah, neither could the latter force an entry into Maskat. The Imam's soldiers, however, used to creep up to them by stealth, and kill any they saw near er-Rawiyah or any that showed themselves near the place called Hallat-el-Ajam-wa-l-Jariyah, and elsewhere, and they used to shout out to the Portuguese on the walls: "Come forth and let us settle matters! Brave men do not hide themselves within forts and behind walls."

They assailed them, moreover, with all kinds of reproaches, but none ventured out, through dread of coming in contact with the swords and spears of the besiegers. On the other hand, the latter were deterred from an assault by the guns and muskets of the besieged.

The struggle went on in this way for a long time, and the Imam and his party began to despair of effecting an entrance into the place, when a dispute arose between the Portuguese and one of the Worshippers of the Cow, to wit,

81

S. KAY

The entrance to Nizwa fort.

the polytheist named Narutem, a Banian, on the subject of betrothal and marriage.

This Narutem had a beautiful daughter whom the Portuguese commandant, whose name was Pereira, had asked in marriage, through the medium of one of the clergy attached to their church in the Western Fort, who acted as Pereira's agent in the matter. Narutem, however, declined the match on behalf of his daughter.

Pereira then offered him a large sum of money, but he still refused, and sent the commandant the following answer: "The thing which the commandant requires neither becomes him nor me, he being a Christian, whereas I am of a different religion. He and his co-religionists hold it lawful to drink wine, and to eat ox-flesh and the flesh of other animals. Neither in ancient nor modern times have Christians intermarried with us."

Pereira's messenger replied: "You must not thwart the commandant, for he has been most generous towards you: he has given you the keys of the shops in the two forts and elsewhere, has made you agent for the treasury and country, and has invested you with plenary authority, and he declares that if you do not give your consent to the marriage I am to marry your daughter to him forcibly, and he will punish you and yours with fines, penalties, and other punishments, such as have not been inflicted on any before you. Hence I advise you to yield, for he who disobeys great sovereigns is sure to bring on himself destruction." Pereira's messenger added many more speeches to the same effect.

When Narutem perceived that there was no chance of escaping from the difficulty except by stratagem, he assumed a soft manner towards the messenger and feigned obedience, saying to him: "Go and tell the commandant to be of good cheer, and you be of good cheer also, for I shall take this matter in hand and shall rely on him."

The two then set out together and found Pereira holding a grand review of his soldiers on the island, and after they saluted him with the salute which Christian subjects give to their commanders, he took his visitors by the hand and, after dismissing his troops, led them up to his quarters and said to them: "What have you decided about the betrothal?"

To this Narutem replied: "Know, O Amir, that the affair submitted to me by your messenger is a very difficult one, owing to the difference of our religions, and because it is unprecedented; but, if it must be so, grant me a year's delay that I may prepare the dress and ornaments which virgins among our women usually wear on marriage. Their fine jewellery can only be made by the goldsmiths of the town of Najinah, but a year will suffice to prepare it; and you know that what is future is not far off.

In the meantime, as one acquainted with the vicissitudes of war, I venture to give you a little advice. The ruler of Oman, Sultan ibn Saif, has not yet withdrawn his sword from you; he lies in wait for you with forces as numerous as the drops of rain, and his soldiers are exulting over you because you are afraid to accept their challenge; hence you are humbled and he is triumphant. I fear, moreover, that his forces will assault you by climbing over the walls like lions. He is even now - so my mind tells me - waiting for an opportunity to attack the town and to force an entry through the gates, and I have no doubt that, with the aid of a few ladders, they might effect that objective and thereby leave you nothing but the two forts, the Eastern and the Western, wherein they would besiege you closely.

In that case you would be cut off from all supplies, more especially water, which he would prevent you from obtaining, and you and your followers would be driven to great distress through thirst, for the besieged cannot stand out against a lack of water.

Now, the water which is in the tanks of the two forts is foul and swarms with insects, and causes disorders of the bowels, and if obliged to drink it the besieged will be sure to suffer from its effects. Again, the gunpowder and provisions which are stored in the two forts and the two batteries are worthless.

My advice therefore is that you let off the water now in the tanks, have them well cleaned, and fill them with fresh water before the siege begins. Let the powder also be brought out and be restored by being pounded anew. The old wheat too, should be discarded, and new grain substituted in its place; for if we put new wheat with the old the weevils in the latter will enter into the new and spoil it, and fatal sickness will be the result."

Narutem added much more to the same effect, on hearing which Pereira commissioned him to carry out these suggestions, for he knew nothing of the artifice intended thereby, and judged that the counsel was sincere. Moreover, he agreed to defer the marriage for one year, as he had been requested.

When Narutem had taken out all the water,

provisions, and ammunition from the two forts, he wrote a letter to the Imam Sultan ibn Saif and sent it by one of his own people.

The substance of the letter was as follows: "You, O Imam of Oman, have been at el-Mattrah besieging the Portuguese in Maskat for a long time, and hitherto you have effected nothing. If you wish to succeed you must proceed in this way. On Sunday next march quickly into Maskat, for I have done certain things to them because of the way they acted towards me about the betrothal.

Consequently, the two forts and the two batteries are now quite stripped of weapons, provisions and ammunition, and the community do not carry their arms on Sunday, that being their feast day, and are engaged in drinking wine and playing musical instruments; therefore if you can make your way into Maskat you will gain your objective. Then hasten on with your force to the entrances of the two forts and set fire to the closed gates, for I have removed all the old gunpowder from them, and replaced it with powder sprinkled with vinegar, which can do no harm . Do not delay beyond the day which I have named for if you reject my advice, and follow the contrary counsel of others, you will not succeed although you prosecute the siege for years."

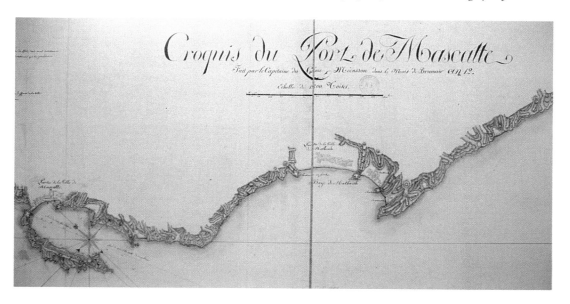

Bahla Fort.

When the Imam read the letter and Narutem's advice as contained therein, and the trick which he had played on the Portuguese in consequence of the dispute connected with the proposed marriage, the truth of which the writer affirmed with a solemn oath, he sent an affirmative reply by the messenger, but kept the matter secret from the nobles and commons.

The messenger returned in high glee to Narutem, who on hearing that the Imam had acquiesced in his proposal was so overcome with joy that he could have flown to the Imam without wings.

Cannon at Marbat.

On the appointed Sunday the Imam offered up the Prayer of Dawn with his people, and then the Prayer of War; after which he prayed that God would give the Muslims victory over the polytheists. He then marshalled his troops and set forth with them at quick time. On reaching the summit of the mountains forming the Great Wadi of Maskat, he selected those who should attack the wall, and those who should rush onward to the entrances of

the two forts and the other posts held by the Portuguese from Maskat to el-Matrah. The selection was made singly and collectively; that done, he set out at their head, they calling out "God is most great! O God, make the orthodox Muslims victorious over the beardless Portuguese!"

On reaching the suspended chain they fired their muskets and hurled stones at those who were in the cradles, but their fire was not returned for God restrained the occupants as they retreated. When the assailants reached the walls they placed ladders against them and

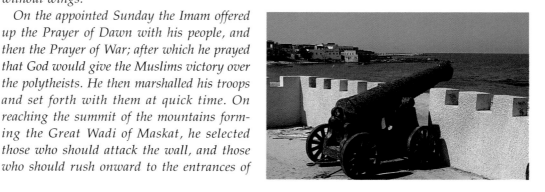

seized all the gates, none of the Portuguese opposing them but such as were reeling drunk, incapable of firing or using their muskets beyond striking with them at random. These the Mussulmans dispatched with sword and spear, and left them prostrate like the trunks of uprooted trees.

They then formed into two divisions, one which rushed towards the Eastern and the other to the Western fort, against which they planted ladders; and when the garrison attempted to fire upon them the guns would not go off, because the powder had been tampered with.

Then there was a hand-to-hand struggle, and swords, spears, and daggers were broken on heads and breasts, the Imam and his soldiers eventually taking possession of the wall, the two forts, the two batteries, and all the other posts of the enemy, with the exception of the tower called Kasim, which was still held by a famous Portuguese warrior, named Cabreta, who sallied against the Imam and his army whenever an opportunity offered. He had a large garrison with him, but one day when he came forth and attacked the Mussulmans who occupied the Island he was obliged to retreat before them. They pursued him as far as the cotton-market where there was a great fight, but they assailed him with spears and rotten-eggs, and slew him and all his followers. So God rid the Mussulmans of him and his polytheist companions.

Then the Imam directed a party of his followers to march against the garrison of the fort at el-Mattrah. He had hardly given the order when the Commandant came in person to the Imam to ask for quarter, and offered to surrender the fort. The proposal was accepted by the Imam, and he accordingly desisted from all hostilities against him or his comrades.

The Portuguese had now but two large ships to oppose the Imam; one of these, which was anchored a good way from the fort of el-Matrah, opened fire upon the town, which was answered by the guns on the fort, but the

Nizwa Fort and, inset, its roof.

shot did no harm, owing to the intervening distance. The other ship began to fire upon the inner port of Maskat, and the shot went beyond Sidab, doing much damage; on seeing which the Imam ordered the Mussulmans to attack it, but they excused themselves, saying that such large ships could only be successfully attacked by vessels of equal size.

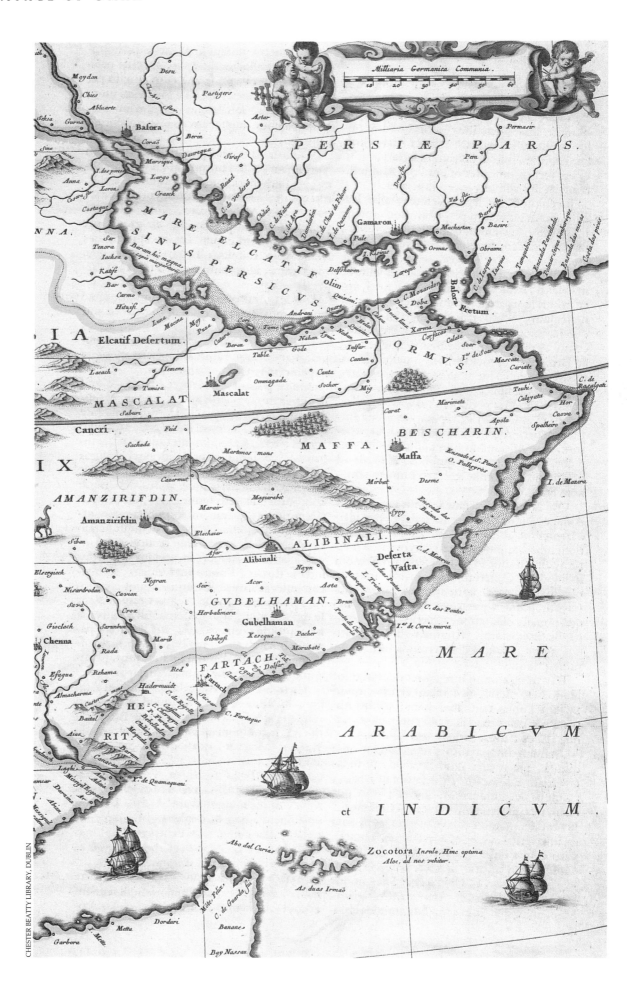

Thereupon the Chief of Auxillaries said to him: "O Imam, lives are valuable, and are only sold for a large price: if you provide the requisite money I will find the men." To this the Imam consented, whereupon the Chief of the Auxillaries went to Oman and chose one hundred men, to whom death was sweeter than wine on the lips of the wine-imbiber. On their arrival he gave them a large sum of money, and they then proceeded to attack the two ships in small boats. And God gave them the victory over the infidels, for they destroyed the two ships and killed all the polytheist crews.

The Imam then appointed Ibn-Bel'arab el-Ya'aruby to be Wali of Maskat, and left many soldiers with him. He enjoined him to be firm, to decree what was lawful and to forbid what was unlawful, and to administer justice impartially. He also exempted Narutem and his family from taxation, as a recompense for the services which he had rendered to him and the Mussulmans

After successfully ousting the Portuguese from Oman, Imam Sultan ibn Saif pursued them elsewhere in the Indian Ocean declaring a Holy War against them. He strengthened key fortifications and was responsible for building the round-towered fort at Nizwa, a project that took 12 years to complete.

With the lesson of Portuguese maritime strength fresh in their minds, the Ya'aruba rulers of Oman were quick to realize the importance of maintaining a modern sea-going fleet of naval vessels capable of protecting their interests in the Indian Ocean and Gulf. They were helped in this by their capture of Portuguese vessels and armaments at Muscat and by the fact that the Portuguese no longer had a safe haven along the coast of Oman. Whilst the land battle was finally won, that at sea was far from over. The Portuguese still had important bases in the Indian Ocean and were still able to harry Arab vessels as they attempted to trade between India, Africa, Arabia, Egypt and Gulf countries.

Increasingly however, the Portuguese came under attack from Omani vessels. Garrisons at Bombay were attacked in 1661/2, Diu in 1668 and 1676, Bassein in 1674 and Kung (on the Persian coast) in 1670. Off Africa, the Portuguese stronghold at Mozambique was assaulted in 1670 and after almost 28 years of pressure from the Arab navy, Fort Jesus at Mombasa was taken in 1698. Despite these successes, the Omani vessels suffered greatly at the hands of the Portuguese during this long period of maritime unrest and the situation has been described as a "stand-off, costly and detrimental to both sides" (Boxer, 1969).

Although the battle against the Portuguese was not quite over, the victory at Muscat, and the ousting of Portuguese forces from the coastal ports of Oman, left these harbours firmly in the hands of agents working for the Ya'arubi Imams who remained based at the inland cities such as Nizwa and Bahlah. Thus customs duties could now be levied by local authorities who gained greater control over development and progress within their regions. Humaid ibn Muhammad ibn Razik, the Omani historian, writes as follows of this period:

Oman revived during his (Imam Sultan ibn Saif's) *government and prospered; the people rested from their troubles, prices were low, the roads were safe, the merchants made large profits and crops were abundant. The Imam himself was humble towards the one Almighty God and compassionate towards his subjects, condoning their offences when such condonation was lawful and never keeping himself aloof from them. He went about without an escort and would sit and talk familiarly with the people, saluting great and small, freeman and slave.*

Map showing Oman, Arabia and the Portuguese dominated Indian Ocean from an Atlas by Blau, 1662.

MID-SEVENTEENTH TO TWENTIETH CENTURIES

Imam Bil'arub ibn Sultan
(r. 1668-1692)

On Sultan's death his son Bil'arub was elected to the Imamate and for a time everything ran smoothly with Bil'arub building on the framework of social improvements and economic growth that had been the hall-mark of his father. He established and financed a college at Nizwa and provided free education for those who attended. In the latter half of his reign a rift with his brother Saif ibn Sultan was the cause of great upheaval. In the end Saif gained the upper hand and was actually declared as Imam whilst Bil'arub still held the title. Saif eventually besieged Bil'arub at Jabrin where the latter was killed.

Saif ibn Sultan
(r. 1692-1711)

A measure of just how successful Oman had become in its international trade is given by the fact that Imam Saif ibn Sultan whose reign bridged the seventeenth and eighteenth centuries (1692 - 1711) possessed 28 vessels, including one 80 gun war-ship, the *el-Falak*, 700 slaves and approximately a third of all Oman's date plantations. His workforce planted around 30,000 date palms in Oman at that time, together with around 6000 coconut palms.

A report by an English visitor to Muscat in 1705 speaks of 14 Omani men-of-war in Muscat harbour and another 15 or 16 reported to be at sea. According to Alexander Hamilton's account of the East Indies, published in 1727, the Omani navy, during the reign of the fifth ruler of the dynasty, Imam Sultan ibn Saif II, comprised vessels of European design including one 72 gun ship, two 60 gunners, one 50 gunner, eighteen 12 to 31 gunners and some smaller vessels wih just four to eight guns each. What constituted legitimate maritime activity in the eyes of Oman's rulers was often perceived as piracy by those whom they sought to control. Little allowance was given for the terror and deprivation imposed upon Oman by the Portuguese, nor of the understandable effort to gain retribution.

Whilst the Europeans persisted in their biased opinions of the Arabs, they apparently saw no wrong in attacking their vessels and terrorising their people. A more objective view of the situation might have been that the Omanis were in fact quite restrained in their responses and were genuinely concerned to build good international relations based on fair dealing. They were rightly determined to defend the territory of Oman, its people, their culture and religion from outside interference. Strangely enough it is their success in doing so that has made the country such a fascinating place for Europeans to visit today.

Imam Sultan ibn Saif II
(r. 1711-1718)

Imam Saif died in 1711 at Rostaq and was duly succeeded by his son Sultan ibn Saif II who moved his military base from Rostaq to Hazm. The fort there is really a monument to him for he is reputed to have spent his entire wealth on its construction. His reign was marked by a continuation of the peace and prosperity that Oman had enjoyed for most of the past century. He was well respected as a strong and just ruler. He died at the fort where he was buried.

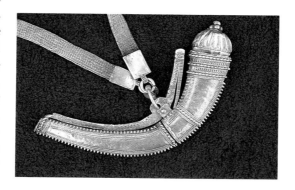

Turmoil in the Imamate

Imam Saif ibn Sultan
(r.1718-1719 ; 1720; 1723—1724 ; 1728 - 1743)
Imam Muhanna ibn Sultan
(r.1719-1720)
Imam Ya'rub ibn Bil'arub
(r.1720-1721)
Imam Sultan ibn Murshid
(r.1741- 1743)

Following the death of Imam Sultan ibn Saif II in 1718, Oman was thrown into a period of internal turmoil as a result of power struggles between rival factions of the Ya'aruba. Saif ibn Sultan, still a boy, was considered by some to be too young to take the reins of power and there were strong moves to place Muhanna ibn Sultan as the Imam. Resistance to this led to Muhanna being killed and the situation was thrown into further confusion with the emergence of several new contenders. Several years of tribal warfare in Oman led eventually to victory in 1724 for Muhammad ibn Nasir al Ghafiri whose tribe had been in fierce conflict against the Hinaween, led by Khalaf ibn Mubarak. The victory was short-lasting however, for Khalaf ibn Mubarak again persuaded his people to resist the al-Ghafiryeen. A major battle at Sohar left Khalaf ibn Mubarak dead and his protaganist, Muhammad ibn Nasser, mortally wounded. Following ibn Nasser's death in March 1728, Saif ibn Sultan was re-elected as Imam with the support of both rival factions. All was not settled however, for now one of Saif's uncles, Bil'arub ibn Hamyar, based at Nizwa, led a rising against him. This was partially successful, wresting control of Nizwa, Sumail, Izki, Nakhal, el-Sharqiyah and the el-Dhahirah. While Bil'arub was declared Imam in the interior, Saif held the coastal provinces, and control of Oman was thus divided.

Internal fighting led to a weakening of Oman's defensive position; a fact that was not lost on the Persians who had never completely given up their interest in Oman. Under the rule of Nadir Shah they were once more becoming a regional force, taking Basra in 1735 and Bahrain in 1736. Imam Saif ibn Sultan asked Nadir to assist him to re-establish control over the whole of Oman, inviting him to bring his army to the country. A Persian victory at Khor Fakkan in April 1737 was immediately soured by the behaviour of the Persian commander, Latif Khan, and Nadir's force withdrew. Protest at the fact that Imam Saif ibn Sultan had invited the Persians to attack Omanis resulted in a new protest against his rule which in turn precipitated a renewed call for assistance from Imam Saif to Nadir Shah.

This time the Persian ruler sent a 6000 strong army to Oman, led by Taqi Khan and Latif Khan. They were well-armed and well-organized, proving a difficult match for the faction-riven Omani forces. By the time the Persian army had seized Nizwa, Bahla and the town of Muscat (but not its two well defended forts), Imam Saif had come to regret what he had started. Many civilians had been killed during the Persian advances and there was widespread distaste for what had occurred. Imam Saif escaped with his ships to the relative safety of Barkaa and set about building a cohesive alliance capable of ousting the Persians. In this he had to turn to his previous enemy Bil'arub ibn Himyar with whom he managed to reach agreement to join forces in opposition to their common enemy. While enemies were uniting, comrades were on the brink of separation. The argument between the two Persian commanders reached such a height of tension that Taqi Khan poisoned his erstwhile companion, the arrogant Latif.

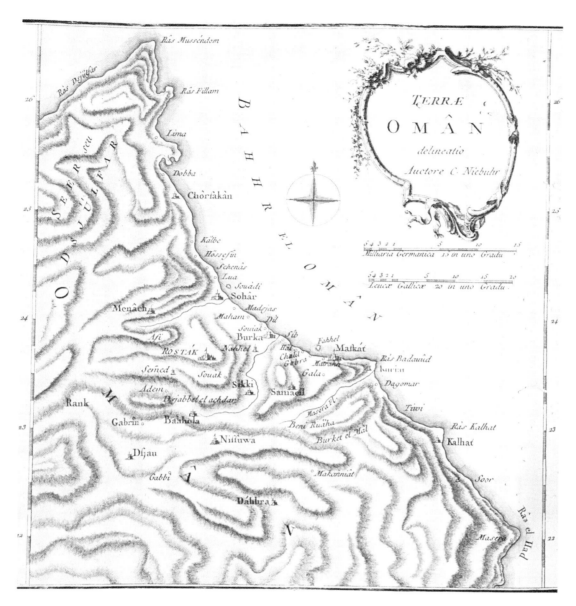

Carsten Niebuhr's map of Oman.

Once more militarily united, Oman was now in a much better position to oppose the Persian invasion. Sumail was retaken and an end was brought to the siege of Sohar, driving the foreign army back to Julfar in Musandam. Meanwhile Nadir Shah was facing difficulties on his home front, led by a revolt of the Gombroon people. He therefore recalled his forces. In 1742 Imam Saif ibn Sultan was finally judged to be too weak as a ruler, and a council of judges and sheikhs asked Sultan ibn Murshid al-Ya'aruba to take over. The inland cities of Sumail, Izki, Nizwa and Bahla supported the new decision and ibn Murshid's army marched on Imam Saif's headquarters in the fort at Rostaq, making him retreat to Muscat.

Meanwhile, the Persian army had reached Musandam and Imam Saif, after sending yet another request for help to Nadir Shah, met them there. Back in Muscat the Oman navy decided that they would side with the newly appointed, and considerably more popular, Sultan ibn Murshid. The planners in Musandam agreed that the Persian fleet would make a two pronged attack with ships under Kelb Ali Khan's command besieging Sohar whilst Merza Taqi Khan, together with Imam Saif, returned to Muscat.

This was the third Persian siege of Sohar; the second having taken place in 1738 when Ahmad ibn Said (founder of the Al bu Said Dynasty) led a determined resistance. On this occasion the Persians besieged Sohar by cutting off its land routes and blockading its port for seven months. The battle at Muscat was a very bloody affair. Initially troops loyal to Saif ibn Himyar confronted

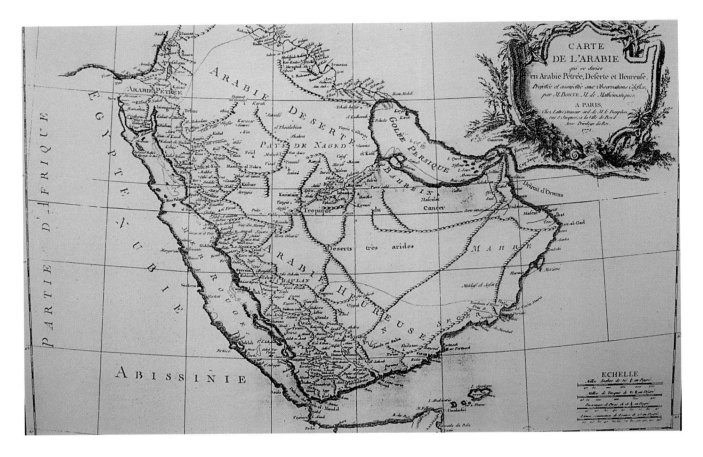

the Persians after they landed, near Saih el-Harmel, and drove them towards Ruwi. On the next day the Persians returned, attacking Muttrah, where they were met by Omani defenders. After fierce hand to hand combat the Persians got the upper hand, killing Saif ibn Himyar and many of his supporters. After this battle many of the Persians rode on horseback to the undefended coastal town of Quriyat where they took women and children prisoners. A second group attacked Maslamat village.

After two abortive efforts to take the al-Jalali and al-Mirani forts, the Persians succeeded on their third attempt. Imam Sultan ibn Murshid gathered forces from the inland cities and rode to Sohar to lend assistance to Wali Ahmad ibn Said who was once more leading the town's resistance against Persian forces. A battle outside the town resulted in the death of the Persian commander, Kelb Ali Khan, and the mortal wounding of Imam Sultan ibn Murshid.

Imam Ahmad ibn Said Al Busaidi
Founder of the Al bu Said Dynasty
(r. 1744 - 1783)

The weakened Imam Saif ibn Sultan had lost the support of his people and it was plain to him that even if the Persians were victorious, there was no way they would hand everything back to him. The forts at Muttrah and Muscat had been won with Persian blood and if Nadir Shah had his way they would remain in Persian hands. Saif ibn Sultan was as much at risk from his own people as he was from the Persians. In deep depression and despair he left Sohar and rode to the fort at Hazm where he is reputed to have told an old comrade: "This is my castle and my grave for the peacefulness of death is far preferable to any happiness that my rule has brought me. I am an eyesore to everyone". He did indeed die soon after arriving back at Fort Hazm and was duly buried there.

It was natural now for the leadership of

Oman's resistance to the foreign invaders to pass to Ahmad ibn Said who had already demonstrated considerable courage. The test that he now faced however was a cruel one. Omani soldiers were simply unable to break the Persian siege of Sohar, despite several gallant attempts to get reinforcements and supplies into the city. Three thousand Omanis were killed in the fighting but Sohar refused to succumb to the Persian pressure.

The Persian commander of the siege, recognizing the tremendous resolve of Wali Ahmad ibn Said and his followers, sought Nadir Shah's approval for a compromise peace settlement by which the siege would end: the Persian troops would leave Oman whilst retaining Muscat; and Ahmad ibn Said should keep Sohar and Barkaa while also paying the Persian ruler a tribute. Nadir Shah approved the deal and an agreement was struck with Ahmad ibn Said. Once the Persians had left however, the Omani ruler saw no point in honouring the aggressor's terms and promptly ceased paying tribute, at the same time arranging that all maritime trade would be channelled through Barkaa instead of occupied Muscat. The traders in Muscat, realizing what was happening, abandoned the city which took on the atmosphere of a ghost town where Persian forces lived in isolation within the Omani forts.

A fortunate chain of events now ensued by which Ahmad ibn Said was able to take back possession of the Muscat forts without spilling a drop of blood. A strong storm blew off course a vessel carrying Majid ibn Sultan, a close relative of the recently deceased Imam Saif ibn Sultan, forcing it to seek shelter at Sohar. Majid was returning from Shiraz, where he had delivered a letter to Nadir Shah, ruler of Persia, from the commandant of the forts in Muscat, asking that he be given permission to hand over the forts to Majid as a direct successor of the recently deceased Saif ibn Sultan. Nadir Shah had agreed to the request and written to the commander instructing him to hand over the forts. When the storm bound ship sought refuge at Sohar, Majid was brought to the Wali Ahmad ibn Said who, after questioning Majid about his mission, took Nadir Shah's letter and read it. Sensing that this was the opportunity for which he had been waiting, he assembled a force of 400 men, led by the Wali of Barkaa Khamis ibn Salim al-Busaidi, who carried the Nadir's letter and instructed them to present themselves at the gates of the Muttrah and Muscat forts. Convinced that they represented the legitimate representatives of Majid ibn Sultan, the Persian commander handed over the forts to them.

With these major defensive structures in Omani hands, they at last had the upper hand over the Persian forces, but Nadir's army was still present and still needed to be repelled. Continuing his strategy of deception, Ahmad ibn Said now requested that his commander at the forts, Khamis ibn Salim, should invite the Persians to his fort at Barkaa. On their arrival they were entertained to several days of feasting and made to feel relaxed, as honoured guests of the Wali. On the third day Ahmad ibn Said invited the commanders of the Persian force to a special reception inside his fort. Around 50 of them attended and once they were within the battlements Ahmad invited his followers to take their revenge upon the Persians, both inside the fort and in the surrounding area. Taken off-guard, the Persians were out-numbered and out-manoeuvred and the pent-up anger of the Omanis was finally given full expression. At the end of the day only about 200 Persians were left alive. A further measure of the deep resentment against the Persians was provided by an incident during the repatriation of the surviving prisoners.

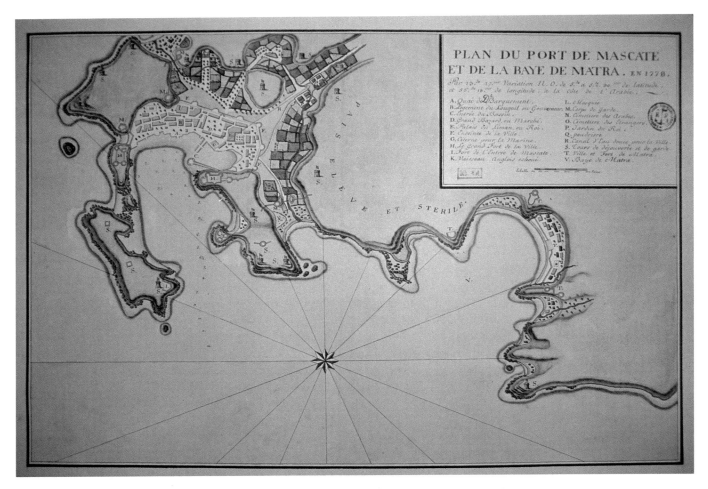

During their transportation by ship from Sohar to Bandar Abbas, Omani sailors set fire to the vessel, leaving the prisoners to die at sea.

In the aftermath of this bloody episode, Ahmad ibn Said set about building a calm atmosphere in the country. Khamis ibn Salim returned to Muscat, together with many of its former residents, people who had lost their homes when the Persian troops had taken over the town. Great confusion was caused by the impact of the occupation since fences and walls had been destroyed, houses turned into stables, and some completely burnt down. Boundaries between different properties were no longer decipherable and heated arguments over who owned what led to clashes and to an outbreak of new internecine violence. Eventually, following mediation by Khamis ibn Salim, the disputes were settled.

Ahmad ibn Said still had to face opposition from different tribal groups in the interior of Oman, particularly forces loyal to Bil'arub ibn Himyar who had been elected as Imam of Rostaq and who commanded the support of the Ghafri people. Determined to unite the country under a single ruler, Ahmad ibn Said confronted Bil'arub and others who opposed his rule. Numerous skirmishes and battles took place which eventually led to Bil'arub ibn Himyar being killed and the Wali of Samad agreeing to follow Ahmad ibn Said.

At last the country was united and Ahmad ibn Said was declared Imam of Oman. The prolonged fighting and unrest had taken a heavy toll however: Oman's position in East Africa had been weakened considerably. The violent death of Nadir Shah in 1747 only brought a brief respite for Imam Ahmad ibn Said, since a new Persian ruler, Kareem Khan Zend, who took power in 1756, represented a renewed threat. Meanwhile, the al-Qawasim were moving into areas of northern Oman. Overall however, Imam Ahmad ibn Said achieved a great deal and was a popular leader among his people. Having spent the best years of his life struggling against oppressors, and having demonstrated great personal courage on many occasions, he earned his fellow countrymen's respect and loyalty. Peace brought with it the chance to repair damage done by the conflicts and to build a more secure future.

Humaid ibn Muhammad ibn Raziq, in his historical account entitled 'Al-Fatth al-Mubeen', comments on a visit by Imam Ahmad ibn Said to Muscat, from his fort at Rostaq. Emphasizing the ruler's popularity, he wrote:

...Then he proceeded to Muscat in a traditional boat with flags flying. Upon his arrival guns were fired in salute to him from the al-Jalali and al-Mirani forts, and from all the naval ships at anchor in the harbour. Crowds of people gathered around him and he held court, asking what requests they had, and wherever possible granting these.

The Omani Navy

The concept of an organised Omani navy was by no means a new one since Ghassan ibn Abdullah al-Fajhi al-Yahmadi had begun the process in around 814 AD when he ordered the construction of special vessels to be used as a naval protection force. Throughout the seventeenth and eighteenth centuries Oman maintained a dominant role in the Gulf and strengthened its influence far beyond Arabian shores to the coast of East Africa. By the end of the seventeenth century Oman's navy was in fact the strongest in the whole Indian Ocean, with large vessels being built for it in India and armed with as many guns as European vessels.

The threat to Oman's security now shifted to a more local confrontation. Increasingly Omani vessels were coming under attack from Qawasim boats based in Ra's al-Khaimah. The Qawasim also mounted what they regarded as legitimate raids against vessels of the East India Company that were using the Gulf port of Bandar Abbas. If the Qawasim were a thorn in Oman's side, the threat of further invasions by the Persians was more like a lance. The new leader Karim Khan, flushed by his success within Persia, demanded that Oman, through the office of Ahmad ibn Said, should pay an annual tribute. This was flatly refused and provided the excuse for a renewed assault against Omani ships.

But by now Oman's navy was not one to trifle lightly with. In 1775, the Omani navy had gone to the aid of the Ottoman Empire, helping to defend Basra from a Persian attack. Ahmad ibn Said's fleet, for this operation alone, comprised ten large war ships, 70 smaller vessels and 50 dhows carrying fighting men. They were successful, much to the anger of Karim Khan, in breaking a Persian siege of Basra, and re-supplying the city. One outcome of this action was that the Ottoman Sultan, Mustafa III, instructed his treasury at Basra to pay Oman an annual contribution. (The practice continued right up to the mid-nineteenth century, and the rule of Said ibn Sultan.)

The following year, after the seizure by the Persians of some Omani vessels, Ahmad ibn Said sent the main body of his fleet of fighting ships to Boshashar to seek recompense. United against their common enemy, the Qawasim joined in the operation, sinking several Persian vessels. When rice supplies to Oman appeared to be drying up, the Omani vessel Rahmany was sent to the Malabar coast to investigate and to put an end to the priacy that was the root cause of the break in trade. It is a measure of how the Omani navy was by now respected that

the governor of Mysore promptly sent an emisarry to al-Rostaq to reassure Ahmad ibn Said that his country wished to live in friendship with Oman. The move was followed by appointment of a permanent representative of the Mysore governor in Muscat.

The Seven Year War between Britain and France (1756-63) was a difficult period for Imam Ahmad ibn Said's navy since Oman had forged ties of friendship with both countries. Several incidents involved French vessels in hot pursuit of British ones, with both entering Oman's territorial waters. This was against local law and the governor of Muscat instructed his vessels to drive the French ships out of the area by firing across their bows. Twenty or so years later in 1781, when another confrontation involving a British vessel (the *Beglerberg*, this time at anchor in Muscat harbour) took place during the rebellion of Imam Ahmad's two sons, the French responded by capturing an Omani 50 gun frigate, the *'al-Salih'*, which they attacked off Sohar while it was *en route* from India to Zubara, Qatif and Basra with a valuable cargo. Most of the Omani crew were killed in the fighting to take the ship and the French commandant, Deschiens, sent the *al-Salih* to Ile de France (Mauritius). On their way there the ship put in at a Maratha port where the local ruler claimed they were at war with Oman and confiscated the ship. A letter, written on September 17th 1781, emphasized the damage that had been done to Gulf merchants as a result of the French piracy:

The Merchants of Zubara and Qatif have nearly all been ruined by the Capture of the Muscat Ship, the cargo of which is valued at 8 Lakhs of Rupees; those of Bussora have also lost considerably and the Pasha, by the stoppage of the trade, has suffered in loss of customs receipts.

Deeply affronted and offended by the French action, the aged Imam Ahmad demanded that the French apologize and compensate Oman for their actions. Slow to respond, the French soon discovered that they were playing with fire. Ahmad's two sons, at that time engaged in a fierce battle over the Muscat twin forts with their father (see below), confiscated a French ship recently arrived from the Red Sea and turned its guns against Imam Ahmad's men. A half-hearted apology was eventually forthcoming (too late to appease Imam Ahmad who had died by the time it arrived) together with the 'gift' of a French vessel the *Escuril*, offered as compensation although it was clearly worth much less than the *al-Salih* and its valuable cargo.

We should not lose sight of the fact that, while various power struggles dogged most of Imam Ahmad's rule, commercial sea trade flourished. In particular Omani vessels were deeply involved in the lucrative transport of coffee to Basra, trading with Cochin, and generally taking a leading position in Gulf trading.

Sadly, the latter years of Imam Ahmad's reign were tainted with more violence and bloodshed, this time instigated by members of his own family. Two of his sons, Saif and Sultan, probably incited by Wali Muhammad ibn Suleiman al-Ya'aruba of Nakhal, rebelled against their elderly father and seized the fort at Barkaa. It was really more of an internal family feud than a rebellion since Saif and Sultan were motivated by a desire to gain their share of the power and wealth that their father was in the process of distributing to his sons. They resented the fact that their half-brother Said, was destined to succeed as the overall ruler and had already received command of Rostaq, Nizwa, Izki and Samail. Imam Ahmad ordered that the fort at Barkaa be re-taken and the sons surrendered. Although Imam Ahmad forgave his sons he

harboured a lasting grudge against the Ya'aruba, whom he blamed for the incident.

A short while later, in 1781, Ahmad's sons again rebelled, this time tricking their way inside the al-Mirani and al-Jalali forts. This brought their father from Rostaq down to Muscat where he personally instructed them to surrender. When they refused he ordered an intense bombardment which was eventually halted by an agreement, reached in June, that Imam Ahmad's forces, led by his loyal son Said, could hold al-Mirani fort while the two rebellious sons, Saif and Sultan, would hold al-Jalali and the fort at Barkaa. It was a short-lasting truce however, for during December Saif and Sultan tricked their half-brother Said and imprisoned him in al-Jalali fort. Aided by one of the slaves, Said managed to escape, and early in 1782 Saif and Sultan took refuge on the Makran coast where they were greeted by the Baluchi, Nasir Khan, who gave them a section of coastal territory to utilize as their base.

Imam Said ibn Ahmad
(r. 1784- 1793)
The death of Imam Ahmad ibn Said, on December 14th 1783, was widely mourned throughout Oman for he had provided strong leadership through very difficult times. Ahmad's eldest son Said was duly elected to the Imamate at Rostaq in January 1784, but there was no reconciliation with his two half-brothers and the legitimacy of the election was disputed. Saif, now loose in the Indian Ocean, turned his attention to seeking support to unseat Said's forces from the Muscat forts. It was off the East African coast, at Kilwa, that he found his potential ally. Joining forces with the Sultan of Kilwa, he made an appeal for French help, promising the Europeans free access to Omani ports and even a French counting house in Muscat, which would be able to fly the French flag. It was not to be however

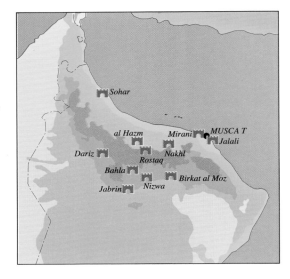

Principal Forts.

since, after a brief and abortive attempt to unseat the sultan of Zanzibar (foiled by a relief force jointly commanded by Saif's brother and erstwhile comrade in arms Sultan, together with one of Imam Said's sons), he retired to the Lamu coast where he died.

In 1786 an English visitor, Julius Griffith, commented as follows: "The French , from the Isle de France, in time of war particularly, make frequent voyages to Muscat, from whence they obtain cargoes of wheat, and what is almost equally valuable to their possessions in Mauritius, numbers of asses". It was also at this time that Tipu Sultan deposed the Raja of Mysore and set about cultivating trade with Oman. The latter imported rice, cardamom, timber, cloth, sandalwood and pepper, whilst ships returning to Mysore carried dates, mules, and horses from Oman together with pearls, silkworms and sulphur which originated from Gulf ports.

Al Sayyid Sultan ibn Ahmad
(r. 1793-1804)

The period of Said's rule immediately after his father's death was one of great uncertainty and unrest in the country that was finally ended by the accession of Imam Ahmad's rebellious son, Sultan ibn Ahmad, who took power in 1793. During the interim period commercial trade continued and in particular the French slave trade, based at Zanzibar, flourished. Sultan, who held

Muscat, attached great importance to the close ties that had been established with Zanzibar and other centres of trade along the East African coast. He was renowned for his love of Zanzibar, taking great care not to lose control of the place. In the year of his death, 1804, an observer remarked: "...The choice of commanders becomes daily more difficult, and nowadays, he [Sultan] only appoints eunuchs, and even divides [the civil and military] powers between them. The armed forces are under a Banyan or an Arab whose rich estates in Muscat guarantee his fidelity to the Prince. He has farmed out the mainland to a third person who has similar sureties to give him". By the end of the eighteenth century it was clear that a major rift had taken place between the seaward looking military base of Muscat and the inland parts of Oman that had traditionally provided the seat of power and the spiritual centre of the Ibadi faith.

Sultan ibn Ahmad's reign (1793-1804), spanning the end of the eighteenth and beginning of the nineteenth centuries, was also marked by enmity between the French and British in the Indian Ocean, underpinned by the Napoleonic Wars (1792-1815). Oman had maintained reasonably good relations with both countries in the past, but now the British were keen to see that the French did not gain the advantage in Muscat. A series of incidents with visiting ships and talk of a French factory to be established at Muscat left the British feeling vulnerable. The nearest permanent British representative at this time, under the aegis of the East India Company, was based at Basra and had the task of reporting from afar on events in Oman, among other parts of Arabia. Samuel Manesty, who held this post in 1791, wrote to the Secret Committee of the Company, based in London, as follows: "We are still ignorant of the success of the negotiations of the

French for the establishment of a factory at Muscat, but we have reason to think that the Imaum, from motives of interest, as well as friendship, would show an active inclination to comply with the wishes of the British government on all occasions". But the subject of a French establishment did not go away and the British Governor-General at Calcutta adopted more of a scare-tactic approach, writing directly to Sultan ibn Ahmad that he should not be beguiled by French charm for, "after putting their King to death, and abolishing religion, [they] are attempting to create disturbances all over the World, and to introduce the same anarchy and disorder in other kingdoms..."

Sultan reassured the British that he had no intention of siding with the French, or of giving them a permanent base in Muscat. Meanwhile, the East India Company representative in Basra was told to put his eye back on the commercial ball. An official document criticized him in these terms: "...the vaunted interests of the Establishment [at Basra] are confined [by Manesty] to watching the motions of a few suspected French emissaries whose access to India is open by a variety of channels beyond the reach of Mr Manesty's knowledge or control, and to its convenience as a Post for conducting our business with Europe".

Napoleon's invasion of Egypt in July of 1798 brought renewed fears by the British of an expansionist French policy in the Indian Ocean and with it concern over maintaining special relations with Oman.

Imam Ahmad ibn Said Al Busaidi
c. 1744-c. 1783

Hilal	Qais	Said c. 1783-c. 1784 claimed imamate until death in 1811		Saif			Sultan 1793-1804		Talib	Muhammad
	Azzan	Hamad c. 1784-1792		Badr 1804-1807 regent	Salim 1804-c. 1821 co-ruler	Hamad	Said 1804-1856			
Hamud	Qais		Khalid	Hillal	Thuwaini 1856-1866	Majid	Ali	Turki 1871-1888	Abdul Aziz	Barghash
Faisal	Azzan 1868-1861	Ibrahim	Salim 1866-1868	Hamad	Harib	Muhammad	Faisal 1888-1913	Fahad	Muhammad	Khalifa
			Khalifa				Taimur 1913-1931		Hamud	
			Abdulla				Said 1932-1970		Ali	
			Jamshid deposed 1964: end of dynasty in Zanzibar				Qaboos succeeded 1970			

The Al bu Said Family Tree
Sultans of Oman
Rulers of Zanzibar

Sultan ibn Ahmad received a special visit, under instructions from the British Governor-General in Bombay, from the East India Company's new representative at Basra, Mirza Mahdi Ali Khan. Mahdi's case for a 'French-Out' policy seemed to be well taken by Sultan (who did not tell the British that he had already agreed to a French factory at Muscat) and discussions were opened on the subject of a British factory at Muscat. The visit also served to highlight the extent of Sultan's (and thus Muscat's) sphere of influence and political control. Mahdi reported that strong commercial and diplomatic links existed with the Sawahil of East Africa, Makran, Hormuz and Bandar Abbas. Whilst Sultan was playing both sides, having done good business with the French at Zanzibar, and the British in India, he was aware that the British could make good their threat to close Indian ports to Omani vessels, an act that would be ruinous for Oman's commercial trade.

Tension remained however, and a number of incidents demonstrated that Oman was determined to maintain relations with both European powers. A reciprocal supply agreement, for British ships visiting Muscat and Omani ships visiting Indian ports, had been signed in 1798, but had been severely tested the following year by an incident involving French privateers and their captured British vessel, the Pearl, which was partially off-loaded at Muscat. This led to a renewed treaty between Sultan ibn Ahmad and the British, and to the establishment in 1800 of Britain's first Political Resident in Oman, Archibald Bogle, who also served as Sultan's doctor. Bogle died within months of arriving in Muscat so never had the opportunity to build on the appointment. The few despatches that Bogle managed to write record Sultan's campaigns against the Qawasim (for which he requested British assistance) and against the Wahhabis.

As we have seen, from his base at Muscat

Sultan ibn Ahmad controlled a considerable empire extending beyond the shores of southern Arabia. He was not, however, in full control of a united Oman. On taking power in 1793 his personal rule was limited to Muscat and Barkaa and to those areas where his brothers held sway: Sur, under Talib; Suwayq, under Muhammad; and Sohar and Mattrah which were under the control of Qays. The rest of Oman remained under local shaikhs, heads of the dominant tribes. Thus, Nizwa and Yabrin were held by the Bani Ghafir; Bahla by the Al bu Said; and Nakhl by the Ya'aruba.

Even in Muscat itself Sultan's power-base was challenged by the considerable influence of Khalfan who had been Wali of Muscat since appointment to the position forty years previously by Ahmad ibn Said. Supported by his son, Muhammad ibn Khalfan, these two had kept Muscat running as a centre of commerce throughout a period of political turmoil in Oman. By 1802, Sultan was in control of an army of 24,000 Omanis, 300 slaves and 1700 mercenaries from the Sind and Baluchistan. At sea, he had a sizeable fleet of impressive ships including the Gunjava, a square-rigger of 1000 tons displacement and armed with 32 guns; three smaller 20 gun square-riggers; 15 frigates of 400 to 700 tons; three brigs, and at least 15 large dhows that carried men and supplies.

In 1799 a conflict arose with Bahrain over payment concerning gumruk which was a charge for safe-passage levied by Sultan on ships using the Gulf. This tax was levied at 2.5 percent of the value of all goods carried by ships sailing into the Gulf from Indian Ocean ports. If ships failed to purchase the 'safe-passage passes' they risked attack from forces loyal to Sultan based at Hormuz. Not happy with this the Utub (and in particular the Al-Khalifa of Bahrain) challenged the arrangement and tried to impose their own tax.

When Sultan's navy attacked three vessels returning to Bahrain from India in the spring of 1799, the Bahrainis turned to the ruler of Persia Shaikh Nasir ibn Nasir for assistance. In return for a promise of loyalty and a tribute, Nasir sent a sizeable force to Bahrain causing Sultan's ships to withdraw. Sea-battles and skirmishes between the Omanis and Utub continued right through the summer and at one stage Kharg island was temporarily held by Sultan.

In 1800, the Wahhabi threat to Oman took on more serious dimensions with an incursion by Abd al-Aziz's general, Salim ibn Hilal al-Hariq (a Nubian slave), into Oman with the objective of taking Sohar. Clever tactics by Sultan and his brother Qays, who was Wali of Sohar, prevented this operation but led to considerable loss of life and was only settled by a truce that left the Wahhabi in control of the oasis at Tuam (which became a base for subsequent attacks by the Wahhabi in 1803).

Another Wahabbi raid the following year, against a different inland town in Oman, led to the killing or taking prisoner of around 150 men. Word came of a possible full scale invasion by a 25,000 strong Wahhabi force. An additional twist to the equation was the defection of the Suwaidi to the Wahhabi camp after Sultan was forced to evict them from Hormuz (following an ill-advised attack against British vessels that were supposed to have been exempt from the *gumruk* or 'safe-passage tax').

The second attack on Bahrain mounted by Sultan in 1801 was more organized than his previous one. A series of events had led the Persians to side with him, creating a force of 2450 troops and a fleet including the impressive 32 gun, 1000 ton, *Gunjava*, plus two brigs and at least ten dhows. The Omani force succeeded in landing on Bahrain and imposing Sultan's son Salim as Wali. In 1802, a combined force of the Al Khalifa and Wahhabis gathered at Zubara in order to mount a counter-offensive. They successfully dislodged the Omanis and re-took Bahrain. In the summer of 1802, Sultan made one more attack against the Utbi fleet in the Gulf, but events in mainland Arabia drew his attention to defending Oman from the Wahhabi. His pilgrimage to Mecca in 1803 left a temporary power vaccuum in Muscat, leading to an attempted coup by his nephew Badr, and also brought down the ire of Abd al-Aziz, leader of the Wahhabi, who was incensed by Sultan's gall in entering the Hijaz with his armed forces. This triggered a major confrontation with the Wahabbi in which the Qawasim and Utub were requested to abandon their pearling season in order to blockade Oman.

The constant pressure led eventually to a truce by which Sultan agreed to pay 12,000 Maria Theresa dollars per year, for three years, to Abd al-Aziz, and to permit a Wahhabi political agent to be based at Muscat. It was a short lasting agreement however, for the Wahhabis soon attacked again, encountering Sultan's forces, commanded by his nephew Muhammad ibn Hamid, a short distance outside Suwaiq on the Batinah coast. Muhammad was killed and the Wahhabi force victorious. News of Abd al-Aziz's murder, combined with word of a strong force established by Sultan to ride against the Wahhabi, led to their rapid withdrawal however, and a temporary halt to this particular threat.

News of an Ottoman resistance to the Wahhabi movement took Sultan to Basra on board his large war ship the *Gunjava* in September 1804. He had hoped to gain Ottoman assistance to resist the Wahhabi in Eastern Arabia, but found that they were not yet ready for such an action. On his way back to Oman he left the *Gunjava* in order to land at Qishm, but the smaller dhow was attacked as it sailed in and Sultan was killed.

101

Said ibn Sultan in a copy of a contemporary portrait by Henry Blosse Lynch.

Sultan Sayyid Said ibn Sultan Al Busaidi (r. 1804-1856)

Sultan's death left Oman in a state of confusion and temporary civil war. A fierce struggle for control took place between various factions of Sultan's extended family. Eventually the reins were taken up by Sultan's son Said ibn Sultan, who reigned from 1804 to 1856. Said faced a new set of problems, not the least of which was increasing competition from Indian ivory and cloth traders who threatened Oman's commercial dominance in the region. Meanwhile, the lucrative slave trade was coming under pressure from the British. In an effort to counter the effects of this, Said ibn Sultan ordered the planting of many clove trees in Zanzibar. It was partly the need for close supervision of these plantations that led Said to make Zanzibar his primary residence from 1841. This encouraged many other Omanis to settle there.

Soon after he took power, in 1807, Sayyid Said ibn Sultan signed a Friendship and Trade Agreement with the French, but the British effectively put an end to this when they defeated the French at Isle de France. From that point on Sayyid Said developed close ties with England. In Oman's long standing feud against the Qawasim, Said was firmly supported by the British who viewed these people as pirates. (This subject has been carefully reviewed by Sultan Al Qasimi in his book: *The Myth of Arab Piracy in the Gulf*, 1986.) The British believed that their support for Oman was, among other things, an important balancing factor against the Qawasim. Following a period of prolonged conflict, peace agreements were signed in 1820, paving the way for a loose confederation of Trucial States which provided a basis in the twentieth century for establishment of the United Arab Emirates.

Sayyid Said's rule was a long and highly successful one. His biographer Salil wrote of him as follows:

Praise be to God through who Said, the happiest of rulers, attained quiet prosperity and perennial glory, decreeing to him sublime eminence in the sphere of happiness and renown, insomuch that by the Divine aid vouchsafed to him he subdued the sovereigns of his time, acquired dignity by the battles which he fought with his enemies, conquered with the sword hitherto unknown countries and made a straight road over the dissevered necks of the rebellious.

He was a man of great personality and charm, as noted by Lieutenant J.R. Wellstead who described him in 1835 in the following terms: "He possesses a tall and commanding figure; a mild, yet striking countenance; and an address and manner courtly, affable and dignified".

Although Said's interests extended across a wide area from the Persian mainland to East Africa, his chief focus was on Zanzibar which became his second capital. He travelled widely by sea and took great pride in his navy, frequently taking personal command of his flag-ship the *Shah Alam*. His close ties with the British were marked by

regular exchanges of gifts, particularly on the occasions of the coronations of William IV and Queen Victoria. In the former case an Arab broodstock mare was given to William IV in 1830 while Queen Victoria received a stallion. Proud of his ships, Said also presented King William IV with one of his naval vessels (later to be named the *HMS Liverpool*), a gesture that was reciprocated by a gift of a British ship (*Prince Regent*) to the Omani ruler. Donald Hawley, in his excellent book *Oman & Its Rennaissance* comments further on the bizarre nature of some of these gifts which included (from Queen Victoria to Said) a state carriage and harness for use on Zanzibar where there were no suitable roads; and (from Said to Queen Victoria) the "Kuria Muria islands ... as a gift in perpetuity on 14th July 1854, a gesture which promoted an embarrassed gift of a snuff box from her Foreign Secretary, Lord Clarendon. They were returned to Oman in 1967" (Hawley, 1977).

Princess Sayyida Salma, daughter of Sultan Sayyid Said ibn Sultan Al Busaidi, who reigned 1804-1856, married a German from Hamburg, Herr Ruete, and took the name Emily.

Far left: Ahmed bin Na'aman, special envoy to New York depicted in 1840.

Sultan Sayyid Thuwani ibn Said
(r. 1856-1866)

Sayyid Said ibn Sultan ruled both Oman and Zanzibar with great insight and firmness, but the sense of unity that had existed between the African island and Arabian Oman died with Said in 1856. At the time of his death the bulk of the Omani navy was tied up at Zanzibar. The ships were not returned to Oman but came under the control of Said's son, Majid ibn Said, who was present in Zanzibar at the time of his father's death. Whilst Majid claimed power in Zanzibar, his brother Thuwani did the reversal of Oman's pre-eminent position as one of the strongest naval powers in the Indian Ocean. On top of the fact that Thuwani lost the best part of Oman's fleet to his brother in Zanzibar, the Omani merchant fleet faced a new challenge from steam-packet ships of the British India Steam Navigation Company. These modern vessels, no longer dependent upon seasonal winds for their sailing schedules, were fierce competition for the traditional Omani wooden dhows that had for so long provided the mainstay of the Indian Ocean fleet.

In consequence of these and other factors, Oman experienced a serious economic slump that provided fuel for internal strife. Thuwani was blamed for Oman's ills and his rule was challenged on several fronts, including an uprising in Sohar led by his brother Turki; a rebellion of several tribes inspired by Qais ibn Azzan of Rostaq; and an invasion by the Wahhabi supported by Janaba and Bani bu Ali tribes. He finally met his death while enjoying a siesta at the fort in Sohar: his son Salim shot him with a double-barrel pistol.

same in Oman. Following a series of arguments between the two, together with the threat of military action by Thuwani in order to force his brother to pay his annual "rent" for his occupation of Zanzibar, a settlement was reached with British assistance, whereby Majid was recognised as ruler of Zanzibar and Thuwani retained his position as Sultan of Oman. In recognition of Oman's prior claims to Zanzibar, Majid also had to pay an annual fee of 40,000 crowns.

A rapid change of events in the mid-nineteenth century brought about a sudden

Sultan Sayyid Salim ibn Thuwani
(1866-1868)

Salim's aspiration to rule Oman was finally achieved, but it was a very short-lived victory. The manner of his accession was widely abhorred and opposition to his rule grew rapidly. The instability brought a further weakening of Oman's position, with the Zanzibar Sultanate refusing to pay their annual fee to Salim, and the Persians terminating the Omani lease of Bandar Abbas before renewing it at a greatly increased rent. After less than two years of unsatisfactory reign, Salim was forced to leave Oman when Azzan ibn Qais led his followers in a rapid series of successful attacks on the Barkaa, Muttrah and Muscat forts. Some years later in 1873, Salim tried to stage a come-back in Oman during the reign of Sultan Turki ibn Said. By this stage however, the British had formally recognized Turki as the Sultan of Oman and *HMS Daphne* arrested Salim, sending him to Hyderabad where he died the following year.

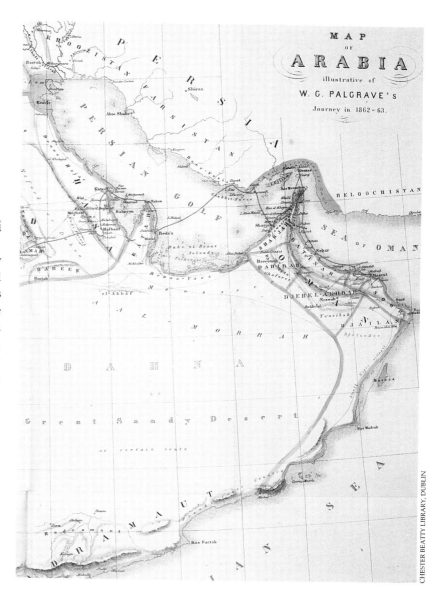

CHESTER BEATTY LIBRARY, DUBLIN

Imam Azzan ibn Qais
(1868-1870)

Imam Azzan's rule was characterized by a strongly fundamentalist religious philosophy. The country was united under his control and this renewed strength enabled him to oust the Wahhabi from the oasis at Buraimi which they had been using as a base-camp since 1800. An arrangement between Imam Azzan and Abu Dhabi's ruling family was established so that Buraimi would be protected from future incursions. But Azzan's rule was also a short one since he met opposition led by Turki ibn Said, brother of Thuwaini, that gained support from the Sultan of Zanzibar and Shaikhs of Dubai, Ajman, and Ras al Khaimah. The two opposing forces met in a battle at Wadi Dhank in which Imam Azzan's side was defeated. Azzan took refuge in Sohar and was killed a short while later in a battle at Mutrah in which Turki was again victorious.

Map of Arabia from W.G. Palgrave's journey in 1862-1863 (Narrative of a Year's Journey through Central and Eastern Arabia (1862-63) *by William Gifford Palgrave).* Please note that this map has no relevance to current international borders.

105

Sultan Sayyid Turki ibn Said
(1871- 1888)

Turki began his rule with a large number of groups opposing him, including his younger brother, Abdul Aziz ibn Said (who, like Turki, was a brother of the murdered ruler Thuwaini), Salih ibn Ali (a member of the Hirth tribe), and Ibrahim ibn Qais (brother of the recently killed Imam Azzan). Following a very difficult few years, Turki succeeded in 1875 in gaining the allegiance of Ibrahim ibn Qais. This marked the beginning of a long association between Ibrahim's family and Oman's

Sultan, with Ibrahim's son Ahmad serving as Minister of the Interior for Sultan Said ibn Taimur right up to 1970. Opposition from Salih ibn Ali did not subside however, and he deeply embarrassed Turki by attacks on Mutrah and Muscat. These eroded Turki's following, and in 1875 he retired to Gwadur, leaving his brother Abdul Aziz to rule Oman. This was not, however, the end of Turki's rule for, after spending a few months out of the limelight convalescing and recharging his spirits, he returned unannounced to Mutrah and Muscat during a period when Abdul Aziz was on a trip to Wadi Samail.

Two years later in 1877, Salih once again launched an attack against Turki's rule, claiming that it did not respect religious values. On this occasion he was repulsed with help from the British vessel *HMS Teazer* that bombarded Salih's encampment. A renewed effort to oust Turki was made in 1883 when Salim joined forces with Turki's brother Abdul Aziz who had briefly tasted power eight years previously. Once again British assistance was given to Turki, this time in the shape of *HMS Philomel* which shelled the attacking forces. He was also assisted by his allies from the Hirth and Masakira who came to his assistance; and by his son Faisal who led a pursuit of the rebel forces, bringing them back into line with his father's rule.

Despite these power struggles, so long a feature of Oman's internal politics, Turki's rule was constructive and positive in its influence on Omani life. He exercised good judgement and strove to reconcile differences between tribes in Oman while conducting a pragmatic foreign policy. Grateful for assistance rendered by the British and concerned over injustices of the slave trade, Sultan Turki signed a treaty with Britain's representative Sir Bartle Frere in 1873, which aimed at bringing the trade to an end.

Sultan Sayyid Faisal ibn Turki
(1888-1913)

Faisal was able to command loyalty from his father's long-standing adversary Salih ibn Ali, whose cousin Aliya Faisal had married in 1881. He took over the Sultanate at the young age of 23 and had to face some older and more experienced antagonists led by his uncle Abdul Aziz who had battled unsuccessfully against Faisal's father Turki. Supporting this renewed coup attempt was Hamad ibn Jahafi. A change in the Sultanate of Zanzibar in 1893, under which Ali ibn Said was replaced by Hamad ibn Thuwaini, brought support for a Zanzibar-led take-over of Oman. Faisal, helped by the British, repelled an attack on Muscat and Mutrah, but not before the rebels had briefly held Muscat. Faisal learnt a lesson from the encounter, counting himself fortunate to have survived. He strengthened defences and took a stronger hand in leadership, maintaining his position as Sultan up until his death in 1913.

At the turn of the century Oman found itself torn between powerful lobbying by French and British interests. France and Russia sought to weaken the British hold on the Indian Ocean and French efforts to strengthen their presence in Oman formed part of this approach. The age of steamships necessitated strategic siting of coaling stations where ships on long voyages could re-bunker. Muscat offered such a site, ideally situated for ships travelling east-west between the Red Sea/Suez route to Europe and the Gulf, India or beyond. Both France and Britain had bid for refuelling bases and Faisal took the diplomatic course of granting both countries equal land areas and permitting identical buildings to be erected on the shores of Muscat Bay. These buildings stood until 1972 when they were finally demolished to make room for the naval base.

Oman was linked to the rest of the world by telephone cable in 1901 and Faisal continued to consolidate his position during a period of relative peace and stability until his death in 1913.

Sultan Sayyid Taimur ibn Faisal
(1913-1932)

A photograph of Sultan Sayyid Taimur ibn Faisal from Alarms and Excursions in Arabia (George Allen & Unwin, 1931).

Faisal was succeeded by his son Taimur (whose mother was Sayyida Aliya) in 1913 and was almost immediately faced with a rebellion led by the elected Imam Salim ibn Rashid al Kharusi, who had the support of both the Hinawis and the Ghafiris. The conflict culminated in an attack on Muscat in 1915 under Salim ibn Rashid's leadership. A force of 700 British India troops, loyal to Sayyid Taimur, met them at Seeb and succeeded in driving them back. Following several false starts, a compromise was achieved that brought peace between the tribes of the interior and the coastal provinces, together with a general recognition of the Sultan's role. This arrangement continued to operate satisfactorily throughout the Immamate of Salim ibn Rashid al Kharusi and his successor Imam Muhammad ibn Abdulla al Khalili, but broke down following Imam Muhammad's death in 1954.

Bertram Thomas served under Sultan Sayyid Taimur and recounts some of his experiences in his book, *Alarms and Excursions in Arabia*, first published in 1932.

The book carries a dedication that reads: "To his Highness the Sultan of Muscat and Oman, Sir Saiyid Taimur Bin Faisal Bin Turki Bin Sa'id, K.C.I.E., C.S.I., with acknowledgements for many favours enjoyed at his hands and in token of five happy years spent in the service of his State". In his book Bertram recounts his experiences in Musandam where Sheikh Hasan of Khasab led the strongly independent Shihuh, who refused to allow a survey party from the British vessel *HMS Ormonde* to step ashore in order to raise a survey flag on one of the hill-tops, and ignored a letter from the Muscat-based government, thereby temporarily frustrating Bertram's survey party. Thomas commented that the challenge was mounted in 1930 towards the end of Sultan Taimur's reign at a time when the Shihuh of Musandam were flexing their muscles. But this was not the end of the affair. The Al Sa'idi, under command of Captain Rashid, returned to Musandam that April and brought Bertram Thomas to negotiate a peaceful settlement of the dispute. Having held initial talks with one of the recalcitrant shaikhs of Musandam, Thomas suspected that they were mustering a defensive force to repel any landing. A British warship appeared on the scene and Thomas describes the incident as follows:

Bertram Thomas on his favourite camel, "Khawara" as depicted on the frontispiece of Alarms and Excursions in Arabia, 1931.

Four Bells had just been struck as Captain Rashid came to report the approach of one of H.M. ships. Arriving from seaward was a man-of-war. Long and low of hull, tall of mast and with two squat funnels, she was a beautiful and dignified model of lead, looking spick under a tropical sun. For me it was an unexpected visit, as Al Sa'idi was not equipped with wireless. But we soon established flag touch, and I went over to make my number. She was H.M.S.Lupin, the Acting Senior Naval Officer's ship, through which I had to report the situation ...

Muscat was taking the situation in Musandam seriously but, as Thomas recalls, eight weeks of patient negotiation to obtain local approval for placing a flag on the jabal met with a staunch refusal conveyed in writing by Shaikh Muhammad ibn Sulaiman who ended his letter with a firm warning: "It is requested from you to fend off this matter and do not interfere in our precincts and property. Your despotism be upon yourselves and your danger be upon yourselves. Do not blame us and salaams". In the end the survey party chose another hill and Shaikh Muhammad enjoyed a temporary victory. Finally, on April 18th, an ultimatum was issued to the people ashore, ordering them to "surrender ... unconditionally to your Government, the Albu Sa'id Government, in the gunboat Al Sa'idi within a period of 48 hours from the receipt of this ultimatum by you. If you do not so submit yourself, Muscat and British forces will bombard property...". But there was no

A British navy 'Persian Gulf Sloop', Cyclamen, photographed in about 1930, lying off the coast of Oman. The picture appears in Bertram Thomas' book, Alarms and Excursions in Arabia, published in 1931. The vessel was sent to support a conflict between the Muscat government and the Shihuh of Musandam.

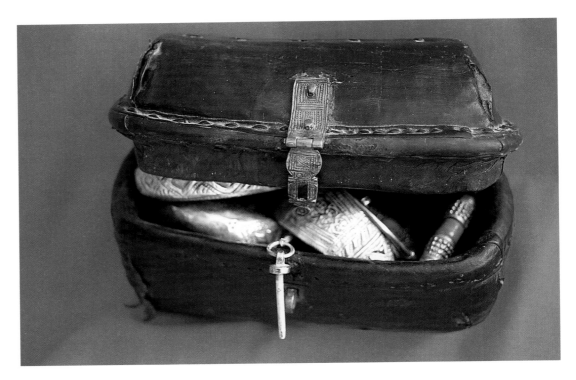

response and the bombardment did take place as Thomas graphically describes, and it brought the sought-for climb down, written in classic language and worthy of repetition here, if only to gain a flavour of the communications of the time and place:

To Saiyid Malak, Son of Saiyid Faisal, Sultan of Muscat and Oman:
May God save him and keep him and glorify him and protect him and make the Paradise his dwelling and the Peeping Nymphs for his reception, and then we are all your people and your slaves from before Qada, we inform your high and noble position. O our lord! we are your people and slaves and the dust of your feet from the time of our fathers and forefathers, and now as it is not concealed from you that Hasan had become a governor over us, and today we do not want him to be either Shaikh or Governor at all, and today we beg your pardon and forgiveness and we are under your orders and command and cannot disobey you. You are our Imam and Sultan, and we want a reply from you soon by hand of the bearer of this letter, and whatever your commands we are obedient to you and we beg of you pardon. Pity us, O lord! Make us a favour, You are the people who grant favour, and whatever is demaded of us that shall be given.
From all the Shihuh of Qada, Shaikh.

Thomas insisted on a climb down from Shaikh Hasan himself. Further bombardments took place and Shaikh Hasan's house was hit. Finally, on May 7th, following the intervention of a peace-maker in the form of Shaikh Sa'id from Dubai, Shaikh Hasan surrendered and was taken back to Muscat as a prisoner. Such were events during Sultan Saiyid Taimur ibn Faisal's reign. Financial problems plagued much of this period and in 1932 he handed over to his son, Sayyid Said ibn Taimur whilst he retired to live in Bombay, where he passed away in 1965.

Sultan Sayyid Said ibn Taimur (1932- 1970)

Sultan Sayyid Said was father of Sultan Qaboos, the present ruler of Oman. He inherited a country with severe financial problems and followed a policy of fiscal rectitude that gradually placed the country's finances on a firmer footing. He faced a number of crises during his reign, primarily focussed on shifts in tribal loyalties and internal politics. When a new Imam Ghalib ibn Ali was elected in 1954, a movement for secession grew in central Oman. A firm military response controlled the initial uprising, but in 1957 a renewed effort, led by Ghalib's brother Talib, and supported by, among others, Shaikh Sulaiman ibn Himyar, was quelled with British assistance.

The advent of the Oil Age also had its impact on Oman during Sultan Sayyid Said's reign. Following the first Arabian oil finds in Bahrain in 1930, and subsequent finds in Saudi Arabia, the whole of south-eastern Arabia captured the interest of international oil companies. An oil survey actually took place in Sayyid Taimur's reign in the 1920's, but it did not lead to any oil discoveries and interest waned. An oil exploration concession was granted to Petroleum Concessions Ltd in 1937, but not much happened until after the Second World War when the renamed company Petroleum Development (Oman) conducted geological surveys of northern Oman in 1954, at Fahud. Although the geological indicators were positive, efforts to locate an oil field there were initially unsuccessful. It was discovered in 1962 that the exploratory well had missed a major oil field by only a few hundred metres. Discoveries in Oman did not come with the relative ease that they had done in Bahrain and Saudi Arabia and £12 million was spent before the first commercial find was made at Yibal in 1962. Once the break-through was made other finds followed: the Natih field in 1963 and Fahud in 1964 which was the first to come on stream, in 1967.

The early exploitation of oil in Oman during Sultan Sayyid Said's reign, together with the income this generated, brought new hopes and aspirations for social development within the country. However, Sayyid Said's inability to cope with the rapid rate of change and a reluctance to move with the times with regard to progress finally led to his enforced abdication in 1970. From 1958 to 1970 he had remained in Dhofar, issuing decrees from there and never visiting northern Oman. Prior to the discovery of oil there had been very little money available to tackle the social needs of the country in terms of roads, schools, hospitals, communication networks and so on. It was not surprising therefore that Oman's ruler had taken a very cautious approach to public expenditure, nor that he found it hard to change his style of government towards the end of his life. His abdication permitted his son, Qaboos ibn Said, to take over the reins of power and to lead Oman along its present course of carefully managed development and advancement. Shortly after Qaboos ibn Said took power, Oman was formally admitted to membership of the United Nations and the Arab League, marking an important milestone in Oman's nationhood. Sultan Sayyid Said died in London in 1972, two years after his son began the task of leading Oman on its present forward path: a story that we develop later in this book.

*The Government of
Oman has provided
modern recreational
facilities for its people,
whilst preserving tra-
ditions and the envi-
ronment. This is a view
of Riyam Park.*

MODERN OMAN

H.M. Sultan Qaboos bin Said.

MODERN OMAN

There is no doubt that the economic aspect of every nation is the artery of its life, the source of its strength and the pillar of its policy and stability...We, therefore, concentrate our attention on finding ways and means, and on initiating projects, to develop the economy of our country and provide opportunities for employment and a good standard of living for every Omani citizen. [H.M.Sultan Qaboos bin Said]

One of the most endearing aspects of Oman is that it seems to have balanced the advantages of the technological age against the need to preserve the strong cultural, traditional and spiritual values that characterize its people. True progress is development without the destruction of all that is good within a community or nation. The government of Oman has clearly focussed its efforts on improving the lives of its people without destroying the country's unique culture, human values, or respect for the environment. When one looks at modern

MINISTRY OF INFORMATION

Oman and the considerable achievements that have taken place during the rule of Sultan Qaboos bin Said, one must also recognize the national priorities that have guided the decisions behind the remarkable growth that has occurred over the past two and a half decades.

Education is a priority of the present government. Whereas in 1971 the country had only three primary schools with 909 boys, in 1993/4 there were 474,888 students in Oman.

Sport is encouraged at all levels and football is very popular.

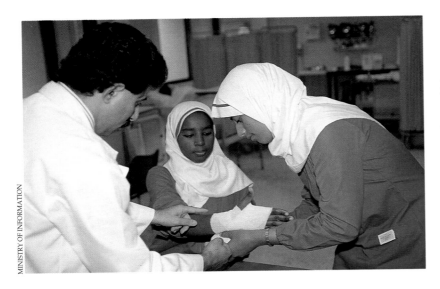

MINISTRY OF INFORMATION

Vocational training is a vital element of Oman's education policy. Trainee nurses receive instruction at the Institute of Health.

Education

Let us start with some simple statistics. In 1971 there were no preparatory or secondary schools in Oman. There was a total of three primary schools in the entire country in which 30 teachers taught 909 boys. Female education was unknown. Just ten years later, in 1981, the picture was already vastly different. The number of pupils had increased by 13,437 percent to 122,143, who were taught in 177 primary schools; 210 preparatory schools; 21 secondary schools, seven Islamic preparatory institutes; one Islamic secondary school; one commercial secondary school; one agricultural secondary school, four teachers training colleges; and one special school. The total number of teachers had climbed, in ten years, from 30 to 6745, a staggering increase of 22,483 percent! It would be hard to find any other country in the world where such an explosion of education occurred over such a short time span. Taking the picture ten years forward, to 1991, we see a consolidation of the surge and further dramatic increase in numbers, with the total number of students almost tripled, from 122,143 to 360,066 and a parallel increase in centres of learning. Furthermore, there has been a slight drop in the pupil/teacher ratio at primary schools from 35:1 in 1971 to 28:1 in 1991. It is perfectly clear from these figures that a high

priority of Sultan Qaboos' government has been to provide free education and equal opportunities to all of Oman's people. It has been a mammoth task which still continues but the progress has been quite remarkable.

Such progress fully justified Sultan Qaboos Bin Said's comments when he stated: "Education, culture and awareness are the foundation stones in our development. Our duty is to build schools, educate the citizens and open the windows of civilization for our country". In addition, he explained that: "Our aim is to provide education in all parts of the Sultanate so that every Omani gets a fair share in accordance with their aptitude. We also plan for the eradication of illiteracy; and shall concentrate particularly on technical and higher education so as to meet the needs of the country in trained Omani manpower". Not only is it true to say that few countries have experienced such a tremendous surge in education over such a brief period, but it is also clear that Oman's most impressive strides commenced from the accession of Sultan Qaboos bin Said on July 23rd 1970.

Summarizing the philosophy that has guided Oman's educational policy, a document prepared by the Ministry of Education comments that "faith, knowledge and work are the main pillars of social progress and development in Oman" and that "the Sultanate of Oman, aware of the social, cultural and economic challenges which face its people, who are awakening after a long period of stagnation, confronts these challenges by utilizing all its efforts and capabilities for the sake of creating a modern society capable of shouldering its responsibilities and carrying out its national obligations". The fruits of Oman's efforts to confront the enormous challenge that it faced in 1970 are clearly evident today in the faces of educated young people who are the product of a progressive and enlightened education policy that considers the whole being and each person's potential role in society. The basic philosophy has been to develop the full range of human faculties including Islamic understanding; mental capacity; physical capabilities; sensitivity towards and appreciation of nature, society, science and the arts; career skills and the work ethic; economic skills and management abilities; a sense of civic and political duty; an ability to appreciate and use leisure-time and finally the idea that education does not end with school or university, but continues throughout one's life. In this sense, the education policy is broad based and forward looking. It is an essential basis for development of modern Oman.

Oman's achievement in this field is even more surprising when one considers that, despite its short period of development, it is considered as a "model of education progress in developing countries in general and Arab countries in particular". Oman's criterion for success in this field is not, how-

ever, whether its policy can be regarded as advanced or archaic, but whether it is regarded as successful in developing the wide range of human faculties.

It would be quite wrong however to give the impression that Oman is resting on its laurels so far as education is concerned. This is not the case and it has in fact been taking a critical look at its achievements and whether there are ways in which the system can be further improved. The focus now is on quality rather than quantity. Detailed analysis of syllabi and curricula objectives has recently been taking place in order to bring the practice of teaching in the classrooms more in line with the philosophical and objective aims of education policy. A recent study in this area has focussed on three skills, i.e. observation, measurement and data handling. Tests and questionnaires were given to pupils at 15 Omani secondary schools and the results were used as a basis for planning improvements to the system.

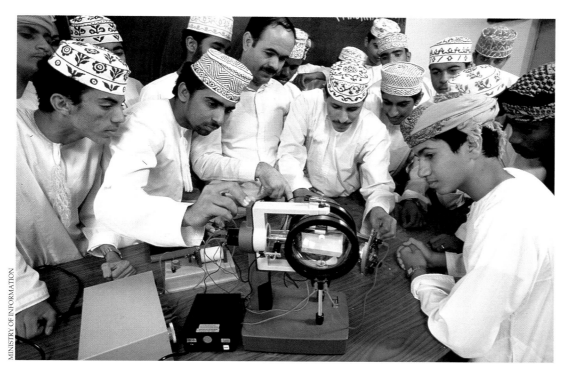

Science education is based upon plenty of practical experiments, preparing Omani students for technical employment in the future.

Health care standards have improved just as much as levels of education. The National Health Programme, launched by Sultan Qaboos, has produced impressive results.

MINISTRY OF INFORMATION

Health care

Health care has experienced the same incredible growth that education has seen. Here one can measure success, not simply by the number of hospitals and clinics that have been built, or by the number of patients that have been treated, but by the great improvements in health of the population. In 1960 Oman stood at 129 out of 131 in the world national league tables for child mortality rates, only exceeded by Sierra Leone and Afghanistan. At that time 378 children out of every thousand died before they reached five years old. Infant mortality rates, i.e. babies dying before they reached one year old, were also horrifically high, at 214 per thousand. The National Health Programme, launched by Sultan Qaboos, has produced results that cannot fail to impress; reducing infant mortality and dramatically lowering the incidence of infectious diseases. The programme is divided into seven separate sections: i.e. Expanded Programme of Immunisation, Control of Diarrhoeal Diseases, Acute Respiratory Infections, Oral Health, Prevention of Blindness, Mother and Child Health and Control of Tuberculosis. Over 90 percent of the country is covered by the programme; the incidence of TB has been

decreased from 861 cases to 482 cases in a five year period while the infant mortality rate was reduced from 45 to 29 per thousand in the same period, and to 23 per thousand in 1993. A system of field health centres ensures excellent communication between the central administrative network and the people the programme aims to help.

These developments have improved both the quality and longevity of life in Oman. In 1960 the average life expectancy was only 38 years old, a figure that was obviously distorted by very high infant and child mortality rates. By 1993 life expectancy was 67 years old and still climbing as improvements in health care, housing, social welfare and education continued to have a positive impact. Such a dramatic impact on a nation's demography is unprecedented and provides the best possible testimony to the success of Oman's development programmes. A UNDP document, entitled 'Human Development Report - 1990', set out to measure various countries' economic development in terms of their success in meeting human needs rather than purely financial goals. It included estimates on how 108 different countries would manage to reduce under five mortality rates to 7 percent or to halve the existing rate in those countries where it was already less than 14 percent. Oman was the only country in the entire list to achieve both the UNDP targets before the report was even written. A summary of the analysis is shown in Table I.

The report also summarized the coverage of immunisation programmes in many different countries. Once again, Oman came out near the top of the table with its 90 percent immunisation of children.

Insofar as statistics provide an indication of Oman's modern development, those on health confirm the country's commitment towards improving living standards for its people. In 1971 there were 216 hospital beds in the entire country. Twenty years later, in 1991, there were 3431 beds and new hospitals were still under construction. Table II summarises the enormous investment that took place in the health area.

TABLE I

Target year to achieve	Country/number of countries
1988	**Oman**
1990-1995	UAE, Kuwait, Cuba, Costa Rica, Chile, Hong Kong
1996-1999	15
2000-2025	40
2026-2075	22
2076-2100	5
Beyond 2100	9

after Miller, Economic Development & Planning in the Sultanate of Oman, United Media Services, 1991

TABLE II
DEVELOPMENT OF HEALTH SERVICES

Year	Hospitals	Beds	Clinics	Doctors	Nurses
1971	5	216	10	46	77
1981	14	1886	17	348	1025
1990	47	3431	91	994	3512
1993	46	3625	81	1565	4728

MINISTRY OF INFORMATION

Oman's industry is based upon its natural resources. Dates are a small, yet traditionally important part of its agricultural base.

MINISTRY OF INFORMATION

MINISTRY OF INFORMATION

MINISTRY OF INFORMATION

TABLE III
QUANTITATIVE DEVELOPMENT OF ESSENTIAL SECTORS 1980-1990

Item	1980	1990
Gross Domestic Product	2063.5	4154.9
Oil sector	1279.5	2054.2
Non-oil sector	784.0	2100.7
Schools/Institutes	388	800
Students	108323	360066
Teachers	5259	15587
Hospitals	14	47
Omani exports (million riyals)	4.6	68.9
Roads/ asphalted (kms)	2192	4960
Telephone lines	15044	107409
Trade Balance (million riyals	616+	1034+
Oil production	103.7	250.1
Electricity production (mn/kw/hr)	787	4503

SOURCE:Statistical Yearbook 1990, July 1991, Directorate of National Statistics.

Top left:
A cloth factory combines traditional skills with the advantages of modern technology.

Left:
A chain-link fencing factory provides modern materials to accomplish the task once filled by natural wooden fences.

Development statistics
Health and Education are only part of the story however, albeit a vital part. If one looks at housing, roads, or any other basic economic and social indicators there is a similar story to be told. It is of course relatively easy to achieve incredibly high growth rates when one is beginning from extremely low levels such as those that pertained in 1970. For ten years, the government was engaged in building a basic infrastructure to the country. From 1980 to 1990 there was a process of further development and consolidation, as we can see in Table III.

MINISTRY OF INFORMATION

Population increase

One inevitable facet of Oman's rapid growth rate has been an increase in population, presently estimated at around 3.5 percent per annum. The overall population, at the time of writing (September 1994) is just over 2 million. As at November 30th 1993 the figures were as follows: 537,060 expatriates, 755,071 male Omanis; 725,460 female Omanis. This placed the expatriate population at around 26 percent of the total, a figure which was regarded by Mohammed bin Moosa al Yousef, Development Council Secretary-General and Chairman of the National Census Committee, as "an acceptable ratio and in harmony with the needs of the current development phase". The country's medium term policy is however to reduce the number of expatriates by a process of Omanization, thus maintaining overall population size whilst the Omani national sector increases. The fact that over 70 percent of Omanis are under 40 years of age suggests that population growth will be one of the major characteristics of Omani society during the coming years. It is already an important factor in government policy-making where it is seen as a positive feature but one that will require careful planning to meet the increased needs of a growing population.

Most of the population is engaged in agriculture, trade, fisheries, traditional indus-

tries and handicrafts. Oman's population is centred in relatively few areas with 1993 figures showing a maximum of 31.1 percent of the whole population located in the Muscat area, closely followed by the Batinah with 26.9 percent. Table IV shows the overall figures for population distribution.

Projections of population growth have been made, based on several different scenarios. Assuming a 4 percent increase per annum in the Omani national population, and a starting point figure of 1.48 million at the end of 1993, this would increase to over 1.9 million in the year 2000. In less than 30 years time, if the 4 percent growth rate is maintained, it will reach, in the year 2025, 5.9 million. Whilst it has been argued that some increase in population could be desirable, the Government is concerned to control population growth and the Sultan has spoken publicly about the need for birth control measures and effective family planning.

TABLE IV Population Distribution 1993		
Muscat	622506	31.1%
Dhofar	174888	8.7%
A'Dakhliya	220403	11.0%
A'Sharqiya	247551	12.4%
Al-Batinah	538763	26.9%
A'Dhahira	169710	8.5%
Musandam	27669	1.4%
Total	2001490	100.0%

SOURCE: General Secretariat of the Development Council. Census carried out 1-10 December 1993

Top left: In celebration of the National Day, these pupils wear an attractive form of traditional dress.

Bottom: Oman's youth provide great promise for the country's future. They have benefited from education, health care and modern social facilities, whilst retaining respect for their traditions and culture.

TABLE V POPULATION MAKE-UP BY AGE GROUPS					
Age Group	65+	45-65	15-44	5-14	0-4
Percentage	2.33	9.46	34.78	33.02	20.42

MINISTRY OF INFORMATION

Food sector

It is also clear from these figures that Oman's workforce is strengthening and the demand for employment opportunities is set to rapidly increase. Government strategy in this regard has been to educate and train people for the wide range of opportunities that exist in such a burgeoning economy. This does not mean that traditional activities have been neglected. If anything there has been a stronger focus on these areas than on new sectors since the traditional occupations have proven their sustainability over a long period of time. Thus, great importance is attached to the food sector, all of which falls within the remit of the Ministry of Agriculture and Fisheries.

Agricultural production in Oman is greatly helped by the fact that certain parts of the

country have quite significant rainfall. Approximately 40,000 hectares are considered suitable for cultivation. Main crops are dates, bananas, coconuts, wheat, maize, alfalfa and certain vegetables. The Public Authority for Marketing Agricultural Produce (PAMAP), a government run institution, was established in 1981 in order to encourage Omani farmers to produce fruit, vegetables and other agricultural produce, and to provide an effective link between farmers and the trade. It runs a series of distribution and collection centres that have helped to reduce the time taken from farm to consumer, thus increasing quality. A fleet of refrigerated transport vehicles, quality control laboratory, training unit, food processing unit and a specialized banana receiving and packing unit complete the range of services provided by the PAMAP. Processed or packaged agricultural products promoted by PAMAP include a growing list of enticing commodities such as honey; frankincense attractively packaged with a burner; leaves from the *sidr* tree (traditionally the ground green leaves of *sidr* were used as a hair shampoo in Oman; they strengthen the hair while preventing dandruff); tomato powder; garlic powder; onion powder; henna powder; dry lime;

MINISTRY OF INFORMATION

sohari (powder of the dry lime regarded as a good appetizer, rich in vitamins, calcium and potassium); pickles; papaya jam; dry dates; hot chilli pepper powder (*al-hamra*); dry dates powder (*busr*), used as a nutritional supplement, served in a drink, or in jellies, biscuits, cakes and pastries, and finally *al-khiran*, a preparation from the natural powder of dry limes, especially prepared and packaged for mixing as a drink.

Improved methods of irrigation have increased production but placed additional strains on the water-table which, in some areas, has fallen. The focus now is on improvements in yields through use of improved seeds, insecticides and fertilizers rather than increasing water pumping. On the animal husbandry side, veterinary services have been provided and advice is given to farmers in order to prevent problems arising or to treat those that do occur. The establishment of Animal Resource Research Stations, a fodder factory and veterinary clinics has provided an important stimulus to production of cows, goats, sheep, camels and poultry and the emphasis on these has been to add value to the raw products.

C. VIOUJARD/MINISTRY OF INFORMATION

The fisheries sector has derived great strength from the productive marine environment along the 1700 kilometres of shoreline that forms part of Oman's renewable natural resources. Valuable stocks include small pelagics such as sardines and anchovy, and large pelagics such as tuna and kingfish. In addition, the shelf areas yield groupers, snappers, many other bottom-feeding fish and several important invertebrates such as crayfish, cuttlefish, and abalones. Artisinal fishing remains the main sector: methods of capture include set gill nets; set wire traps; seasonal beach seines and hook and line fishing. Over 1600 small fishing boats operate along the coast, whilst the larger trawlers work further offshore. As with virtually all of the world's fisheries, there has been a tendency to over-exploit stocks but this has been brought firmly under control and present planning is aimed at ensuring sustainable catch-rates. Landings in 1980 totalled 75,000 tons, while those in 1988 peaked at 166,079 tons, following which there was a drop in landings to 117,536 tons in 1989 and a steadying out at around this level in sub-sequent years.

Modernization of fishing methods has greatly assisted Omani fishermen in carrying out their onerous and often dangerous work. At least 120,000 people directly derive their livelihoods from fishing in Oman. Government subsidies have been directed at providing safer, easier to maintain fishing boats and reliable outboard engines or other gear. Training schemes have also been introduced to show Omanis how to take best advantage of technological developments in the field. Aid is distributed from a special Fishermen's Fund established by the government to assist

fishermen. Further technical back-up is provided by the Marine Study and Research Centre. Success with aquaculture has been an elusive goal so far but there is little doubt that fish-farming will become in important industry in Oman, once the biological problems are tackled. One area where help was needed, and has been provided in considerable measure, is in provision of suitable landing, storage and marketing facilities. A number of Fishery Centres have been built along the coast, each of which is equipped with cold-storage facilities. Commercial fishing has also been developed in partnership with overseas companies, based on medium to large trawlers and industrial size processing plants. High quality fish has been exported to the Gulf States, Asia, Europe and North America. In the final analysis however, the strength of the Omani fishing sector depends upon the skill and perseverance of Omani fishermen. Government can help, encourage, and make certain aspects of the task easier, but the fishermen, with their knowledge of local fish stocks and marine conditions, remain linch pins to the fishery development programme. A measure of the importance attached to this sector of the economy is provided by the fact that, at the time of writing, fishing accounts for over 30 percent of the total non-oil exports of Oman; a level that ensures that it will remain on the government's priority list.

PDO

Oil and gas

While the traditional pursuits of agriculture and fisheries have sustained Oman throughout its history, the discovery and exploitation of oil in Oman introduced a vital new industry to the country, and one that has played a key role in financing the socio-economic growth that has been described above. Oil exploration in Oman began in 1924 but oil was not found until 1962 at Yibal, a discovery followed shortly thereafter by the first commercial find, at Fahud in 1964, which remains the largest single oil discovery in the Sultanate. Oil exports began in August 1967 when 20.9 million barrels were exported. By 1970 this figure had risen to 121.3 million barrels. After the Iraq Petroleum Company (IPC), a consortium of oil companies, withdrew from Oman after several years of unsuccessful oil exploration, Petroleum Development Oman Ltd. (PDO) was granted the concession, in which Shell was the major shareholder with minority shares held by Compagnie Francaise de Petroles (CFP) and Partex. By 1980 annual production had reached 229 million barrels and

PDO became a majority owned Omani company in which the Sultanate took 60 percent of the equity, with Shell retaining 34 percent, CFP 4 percent, and Partex 2 percent. The company is run by a Board of Directors consisting of nine members, five representing the government of the Sultanate and four representing the three commercial companies. Chairman of the Board is H.E. the Undersecretary of the Ministry of Petroleum and Minerals.

Production sharing agreements, signed by the government with other oil companies that have been granted concession areas in the Sultanate, stipulate that Oman shall receive between 80 and 85 percent of the oil profits. If a concessionaire fails to find commercial quantities of oil or gas the company still has to shoulder the entire cost of exploration as well as other developmental expenses. In the event that oil is struck in commercial quantities however, the concessionaire is permitted to recoup costs of exploration, development and production from the oil revenues; providing these do not exceed the 40 percent level. The remainder of the revenues are then divided

between the government and the concessionaire in accordance with provisions of the oil concession agreement.

During the course of preparing material for this book I was pleased to interview H.E. Said bin Ahmed al-Shanfari, Minister of Petroleum and Minerals. I asked him to comment on the current exploration programme. "In general", he replied, "we are quite happy with the results of oil exploration in the last 20 years because our proven oil reserves are increasing continuously and have now reached 4.5 billion barrels. We endeavour to add each year at least the level of crude oil produced during the same year. Our oil production has reached a record level of 750,000 barrels per day. If we compare our proven oil reserves with those in 1971 (which stood at 1.2 billion barrels), and our production at that time, which was 300,000 barrels per day, we find that there is a big jump. These figures demonstrate our success so far.

"You should also remember that in 1970 there was only one oil producing company in Oman (PDO) but now we have four: PDO, Occidental Oman (USA); Japex

(Japanese) and Elf (French). It is also possible that other oil concessionaires may find oil. The exploration of large amounts of gas has encouraged the government to establish a gas liquification plant (LNG) for export. The government owns 51 percent of this project, while Shell, Total, Partex Mitsubishi, Citoh and Mitsui own the rest of the shares. The LNG project is slated to cost around nine billion US dollars and the first LNG shipments are expected in the middle of 1999.

"Currently Oman is carrying out an intensive oil and gas exploration and appraisal campaign. During 1992 several oil and gas discoveries have been made and most are under testing and evaluation. At the present time it can be said that some of these new finds have promising oil or gas potential, such as Mabrouk; Al Bahair; Al Noor and some other medium sized oil fields such as Waha; Hazar; Tauish; Wifaq and Nawal. As for gas exploration our proven reserves have doubled and reached 17 trillion cubic feet. We are very much encouraged by our exploration success and hope to double these reserves in the near future".

Al Fahud main pumping station is operated by Petroleum Development Oman. It boosts oil from northern Oman through the main export line at Mina al-Fahal.

Such statistics can hardly fail to impress, but the Minister was not losing sight of the fact that oil and gas are non-renewable resources. Although proven reserves can be increased each year as a result of exploration work, exploitation of those reserves will eventually lead to their depletion. It is for this reason that the Oman government has adopted a strategy of looking far into the future, not just at how the present young generation will view their stewardship of these valuable natural resources, but how future generations hundreds, or even thousands, of years hence will view their actions. It is a very serious responsibility and one that is not taken lightly. If oil and gas are to be exploited at this phase of Oman's development, then it is essential that best use should be made of the financial benefits that accrue from this exploitation. We have already seen how oil revenues have helped to finance programmes in education, health, road building and other socio-economic schemes. I asked the Minister what policies were being taken in regard to the question of employment since it seems clear that Omani nationals should benefit as much as possible from the economic activity created around the oil and gas industries.

"Following directives of His Majesty the Sultan", the minister continued, "training and Omanization of jobs has become a national goal in the public and private sectors. Training is pursued inside and outside Oman. In the PDO Omanis occupy 63.13 percent of all the jobs at all levels. Senior level employment of Omanis in the PDO has reached 43.89 percent while it is at 72.82 percent at the junior level. According to the training and Omanisation plan the percentage of Omanis at the senior level shall reach 48.72 percent next year while the junior level shall climb to 78.35 percent. In 1993 the overall level of Omanis in the PDO should be 66.18 percent and we hope to achieve a 75 percent level in 1995 with between 90 percent and 93 percent by the year 2000". He went on to explain that similar Omanisation programmes were operating in other companies including the Oman Refinery Company (ORC), Japex, Occidental Oman and Elf Oman.

Before leaving the Minister's office I asked him what he felt were the great challenges and achievements of the oil and gas sector in recent years. "In terms of challenge," he answered, " our goal is to find more oil than we exploit in each year in order to increase our proven oil reserves. The same thing applies to gas, which is used locally and not yet exported. In the field of development there are several projects such as the Lekhwair, Yibal and Birba schemes which have been implemented in order to increase the capacity of our facilities in line with increase in oil production. Of these the Lekhwair project is the largest and most expensive, costing 500 million US dollars".

The project at Lekhwair, on the edge of the Empty Quarter is truly remarkable. The Lekhwair field was discovered in 1968 and brought on stream in 1976. Between 1976 and 1984 the producing wells at the field were increased to 42 and production reached 25,000 barrels per day. Trials carried out with water injection, aimed at sustaining reservoir pressure and maximizing recovery from the field, proved promising and plans were laid for installation of a water injection system. Collapse of the oil price in 1986 led to a delay in the development but finally, in February 1990, PDO's shareholders approved the Lekhwair Waterflood Development which they described as "the most complex oil and gas development in PDO's history". Built in an extremely hostile environment, the project comprises a mini-town isolated among the

PDO

Offshore oil and gas exploration has been a modern feature of Oman's petrochemical industry.

Seismic vehicles operating in the Bahja area form part of Oman's ongoing exploration programme.

dunes of the desert. The 170 people employed there enjoy air-conditioned accommodation and a full range of recreation facilities. Electricity is provided by its own 50 megawatt power station. The project effectively quadruples oil production from the field, bringing it to around 100,000 barrels per day and contributing to approximately 13 percent of the Sultanate's total oil exports. Oil from the field is of a very fine light quality, helping to sustain the premium quality of Oman's light export blend. In addition, a new $15 million gas transfer line carries up to 1.5 million cubic metres per day of treated Lekhwair gas to the Government Gas Plant and from there into the national gas network.

A pioneering effort of engineering in more senses than one, it is the first use by PDO of state-of-the-art computerized Distributed Control System (DCS) technology, enhancing operational efficiency; the first use in Oman of corrosion-free glass reinforced epoxy (GRE) pipelines in crude oil service, extending the life of the system and reducing maintenance costs; the first application in Oman and one of the first ever applications of the environmentally friendly SulFerox gas sweetening process from Shell which results in zero atmospheric pollution while reducing both capital and operating costs; the first application in Oman of variable speed fluid drive couplings on gaslift compressors, improving reliability while reducing capital and operating costs; the largest application in the world of polyethylene sleeving in the 16 inch water injection ringmain, preventing corrosive products from entering the reservoir; the largest high pressure water flood of a tight limestone formation in the world; the first turnkey drilling contract awarded in Oman and one of the largest in the world, won by an Omani contractor, NDSC; and finally the first major oil and gas manifolds fabricated by 100 percent Omani contractors in Oman. When one contrasts these tremendous achievements with the situation just 20 years previously, when Oman was emerging from the shade, lacking any of the skills, know-how or technical expertise to drill an oil well, let alone create one of the most advanced facilities of its kind in the world, the full scale of achievement at Lekhwair swings more clearly into focus.

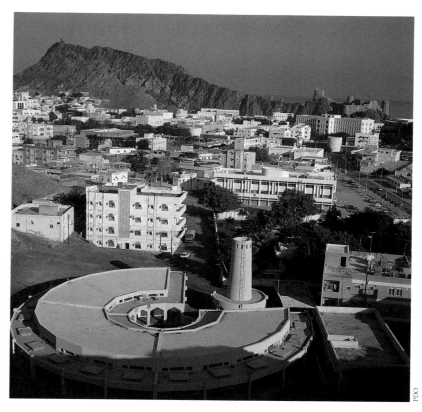

Muscat

Development programmes

Oman's oil and gas industry has made a tremendous contribution to the national economy but it is widely acknowledged that it will not last forever. Every five years a new Development Plan is unveiled which sets forth a programme of investments and projects for the next five year period. The plans are based on a series of clearly defined development objectives; i.e: (i) to develop new sources of national income to augment and eventually to replace oil revenue; (ii) to increase the ratio of national investments directed to income generating projects, particularly in manufacturing, mining, agriculture and fisheries; (iii) to distribute national investments among geographical regions with a view to spreading prosperity and progress to all regions of the Sultanate; (iv) to support the maintenance of existing population centres and communities, in order to safeguard those communities from potential emigration to densely populated urban centres, and protect the environment; (v) to attach high priority to the development of natural water resources; (vi) to attach high priority to the development of human resources, and to improve their capacity to contribute to the national economy; (vii) to meet infrastructural requirements; (viii) to support commercial activities by removing market deficiencies, particularly in the areas of transport, communications and storage, and other obstacles to competitive trading, with a view to enhancing the emergence of a competitive market; (ix) to provide for the creation of a national economy based on private enterprise and free from monopolistic practices; (x) to enhance the efficiency of the government's administrative machinery.

There have been five phased development programmes established to meet these objectives: i.e the preliminary period from 1970, when Sultan Qaboos became ruler, to 1975; followed by four five-year development plans, the latest of which runs from 1991 to 1995. A brief summary of previous development plans is necessary to place the present one in context. The initial period, 1970 to 1975, was spent creating the right atmosphere for peaceful progress and

Al Khawdh road cut reveals part of Oman's geological history.

131

MINISTRY OF INFORMATION

socio-economic development. The first Five Year Plan (1976-1980) provided a strategy for the future development of the country. The period was also one in which a boom in oil revenues occurred. Exploration of natural resources was given a high priority and development programmes were aimed at providing a sound infrastructure while encouraging private enterprise, thus promoting a free national economy. The second Five Year Plan (1981-1985) saw further significant increases in oil income associated with a rise in world prices. Emphasis was again on infrastructural development and, in particular, on water resources and water distribution. The third Five Year Plan (1986-1990) covered a period in which oil prices fell quite sharply and the previous development programmes were thus tested in terms of the country's ability to survive on lower oil revenues than expected. Government trimmed back on its development programmes and demonstrated that the Omani economic system retained a high degree of stability. The fourth   Five Year Plan, like its predecessors, is based on lessons learnt from the past and seeks to consolidate the gains made to date. Its principle features are briefly summarised below.

Firstly, the plan seeks to expand further on the Omani economic base and its diversified activities. Despite the tremendous increase in oil revenues during the period 1975 to 1989, the non-oil contribution to the domestic product over the same period increased from 33 percent in 1975 to 55 percent in 1989. This was achieved during a period in which government contribution to economic activity decreased while the private sector contribution increased. The second main plank of the new policy is to tackle problems and issues related to impact of development, particularly in the areas of reducing dependence upon oil income and expatriate labour. Thirdly, the plan places Oman's progress and future development in the international sphere, acknowledging changes taking place globally with, for example, major economic groupings such as the European Union forming new economic power centres. It notes that economic competition between world powers is increasing, and rapid advances in communications and information technology demand flexible development strategies.

Oman's gross domestic product (GDP) increased dramatically between 1970 (106.8 million Omani Riyals) and 1985, following which it dipped slightly before regaining its upward momentum to reach a 1990 level of 3,521.9 million Omani riyals. The oil and gas sector contributed 45.1 percent of the GDP in 1990. During the period from 1971 to 1976 average oil production was 300,000 barrels per day whilst in the period of the previous Five Year Plan, i.e. from 1986 to 1990, it reached 614,000 barrels per day. Figures for the current period are showing a further increase. The contribution of the non-oil sector has shown a very healthy increase during this period with Agriculture and Fisheries contributing 18.3 million riyals in 1976 and 125 million in 1990; whilst the industrial sector's input over the same period increased from 4.3 million to 151 million.

Other resources

In addition to oil and gas, Oman has a number of other valuable underground resources including copper, chromium, iron, manganese, nickel and magnesium. Copper mining is, as we have seen at the beginning of this book, an activity that can be traced to the very early period of Oman's prehistory. Commercial mining of copper was re-started in 1983 and has proven to be a success. Modern techniques of geophysical surveying and mapping have provided a much clearer picture of the country's mineral deposits. The commercial operation, run by the state owned Oman Mining Company, at Wadi Jizzi, near Sohar, mines the ore which is processed with the aid of a crusher, and refinery, into copper cathodes. In 1990, 12,000 tonnes of these cathodes were produced. Additional rich veins of copper have been identified at Rakah and Hayl al Safil, approximately 200 kilometres from the refinery near Sohar. These are now being mined by the open-cast method with their ore transported to the existing crusher concentrate site near Hayl al Safil, before being taken to the refinery. Exploration of other sources of copper is continuing.

Chromite, accidentally discovered in 1971, is also present in commercial quantities with estimated reserves of around two million tonnes. The Oman Chromite Company, established in 1991, has been established to mine and export the

chromite. Coal is also present in considerable quantities near Sur, where reserves have been estimated at 36 million tonnes. Plans are being considered for a coal burning power station to utilize this fuel source.

A valuable by-product of the copper mining industry is gold with around 2400 kgs projected for production from eight years of operating the Hayl al Safil copper mining and processing site. Oman's gold reserves are now the subject of an evaluation programme which is likely to continue for a number of years before any plans are laid for commercial mining.

Industrial development

Prior to the oil era, Oman's industries were confined to those that served the traditional needs of its people. Boat-building, various handicrafts, textile manufacture and silver-work had all been practised for centuries and Omani products in these fields were sought after both within the country and throughout the region. Advent of the modern age, stimulated by the discovery and exploitation of oil and gas, spawned a new industrial base and one that continues to grow at a satisfying pace. Much of the growth that has taken place is the result of private sector investments, encouraged and supported by government. Increased local wealth stimulated demand for imported products and where these could be locally manufactured, private entrepreneurs were encouraged to do so. A important key sector in this industrial development was, not surprisingly, associated with the construction industry.

The non-oil sector of Oman's economy presently forms over 50 percent of the GDP and exports from all divisions within this sector are continuing to rise. As we have mentioned, this industrial boom has been created in part by the discovery of oil and gas in Oman, but it is also the result of several other important factors, including its strategic location as the gateway to the Arabian Gulf; its abundant natural resources; an enlightened government policy of industrial incentives; and a consistent striving for quality before quantity that has given Omani manufacturing a good reputation, both regionally and internationally.

At the heart of Oman's industrial success is its creation of a number of industrial estates. The pioneer of these, and the largest, is the Rusayl Industrial Estate (RIE) which is approximately 45 kilometres from the centre of Muscat. Established in 1984 with the aim of stimulating non-oil economic growth, over 60 factories have located there, manufacturing a wide range of products from "tea to tyres and biscuits to bedding". The industrial estate complex offers companies a range of advantages including a well established infrastructure of roads, ample supplies of water, electricity and gas; an efficient telecommunications network; waste disposal facilities; and the full range of services one would expect in a modern town. Companies wishing to set-up there are assisted through the necessary procedures by what amounts to a 'one-stop shop' for business documentation, including customs, and documentation required by ministries of Labour, Foreign Affairs, Trade, and Commerce and Industry. Attractive rates for building rents and energy add to the practical value of the incentive package.

The incentive programme is a far reaching one that seeks to encourage industrial growth in Oman. Companies establishing new ventures in the country are exempt from all taxes for the first five years of operation and this tax holiday can, under certain circumstances, be extended. Industrial machinery and equipment are permanently

PDO

GROWTH IN CONTRIBUTION OF MANUFACTURING SECTOR
TO GROSS DOMESTIC PRODUCT OF THE COUNTRY AT CURRENT PRICES
IN MILLION R.O.

YEAR	1975	1976	1977	1978	1979	1980	1981	1982	1983	1984	1985	1986	1987	1988	1989	1990
Manufacturing	2.1	4.3	6.7	8.5	11.5	15.6	27	39.6	49.7	72.1	82.3	103.1	111.5	122.7	137.1	151.1
Oil Refinery	-	-	-	-	-	-	-	-	4.1	13	9.9	8.6	10.1	10.3	13.4	14.4
Others	2.1	4.3	6.7	8.5	11.5	15.6	27	39.6	45.6	59.1	72.4	94.5	110.4	112.4	123.7	136.7

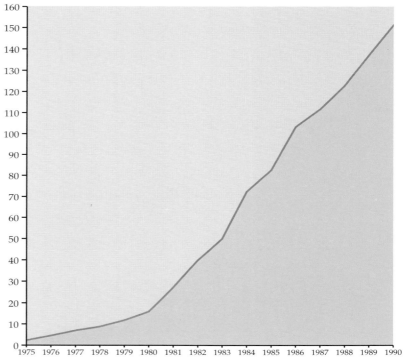

exempt from import duties while raw and semi-processed materials are exempt for the first five years with discretionary renewal periods after that. Where products manufactured in Oman face competition from imported products a policy of tariff protection may sometimes be applied in order to allow the young national company to establish itself in the competitive open-market environment. Interest free loans are available from the Ministry of Commerce and Industry while low-interest loans are provided by the Oman Development Bank. Omani graduates from tertiary level education are offered a special incentive package to establish businesses in Oman, including grants of 40 percent of project costs, together with interest free loans for a further 40 percent. The graduates must find 20 percent of the cost from their own resources. The Ministry of Commerce and Industry also operates a start-up benefit package for other, non-graduate, investors who may receive grants of 30 percent of project cost for Muscat based ventures with up to 50 percent provided for projects outside of Muscat.

MINISTRY OF INFORMATION

Tourism

One area of investment and development that looks set to flourish in Oman is that of tourism. Already the country offers a number of first-class hotels and some stunning wild scenery. When one adds the attractive preservation of culture and the thoughtful conservation of wildlife, together with a climate that promises sunshine throughout the year, it is apparent that the vital ingredients are already present. Developments during the first and second five year plans were focussed on providing a basic infrastructure into which tourism could fit, including construction of hotels, rest-houses and various transit facilities. A programme of renovation of historic forts and other monuments was also carried out, and is continuing. Although this was not done with the purpose of attracting tourists, but as part of a national programme of cultural preservation, it has nevertheless helped to create some fascinating visitor centres. A study of Oman's entire coastline has been prepared and suitable sites for future hotel development have been ear-marked. Seeb International Airport has been expanded to accommodate the increased number of air-

craft and passengers and airport facilities have been upgraded at other centres.

Availability of adequate supplies of fresh water is essential for all the above developments and Oman's achievements in this field are most impressive. In 1970 Muscat produced just 156 million gallons of fresh water, all of which was pumped from deep wells. In 1977 production of freshwater leapt to 1002 million gallons, mostly as a result of the country's first major desalination plant. By 1994, Muscat's freshwater production reached over 13,535 million gallons. Similar exponential growth in water production occurred in Salalah.

Concern that the demands of modern development should be tempered by the need to protect the environment has been a consistent theme of Oman's planning under the guidance of Sultan Qaboos bin Said. On the occasion of the 15th Anniversary of the Sultanate's National Day the Sultan reminded his people of this fact in the following manner:

As a result of our great concern for protection of the natural environment, and our achievements in this respect, Oman has gained a respectable position among nations concerned with environmental protection; yet, we still have to exert yet more effort and consider the special conditions relevant to this issue, when we come to plan and implement development projects. We must proceed to develop contacts with regional and international organisations concerned. It is a duty which must be undertaken by each citizen, to guarantee the protection of our natural resources and public health against any harmful effects, and protect the beautiful and distinguished nature which God Almighty granted to our beloved Oman.

Firm evidence of Oman's commitment to these environmental issues is provided by government policy that requires, for example, the issuance of 'No Environmental

Objection Certificates' for all private and government projects subject to planning legislation. The certificates are designed to prevent any negative effects of development. In summing up the government's policy in this regard, the 1992 report to the United Nations Conference on Environment and Development made the following statement: "There is an environmental cost associated with industry. It can either be paid as a controllable value added to goods, or as the indeterminable cost of ill health, discomfort and loss of resources resulting from pollution and environmental damage associated with uncontrolled industrial development. The Oman Government has chosen the value-added option, a decision which, it is believed, will be of long term benefit to the country". It is an example which many other countries would do well to follow.

International relations

This brief overview of Oman's modern development would be incomplete without a comment upon its international relations and activities. Uniquely among the States of Arabia, Oman has a history of several hundred years of power and influence, not only in the region, but extending to Africa and the Far East. In spite of incursions at various times by the Persians and Portuguese, Oman was never a colony, and the Omani people developed a national pride and sturdy independence of spirit which has stood them in good stead in defending their national integrity in a turbulent and unstable region.

Unhappily, Oman fell into a state of stagnation during the 18th and 19th centuries. This was brought about by a number of factors: internecine strife, the erosion of its overseas trade - notably, through the advent of the steamship - and lack of social and economic progress which compounded this stagnation. This deterioration continued even after oil revenues began to flow, and it was only on the accession of His Majesty Sultan Qaboos bin Said in 1970 that a true renaissance began.

On his accession, His Majesty defined certain principles that were to guide Oman's foreign policy; these principles have been followed to the present day. They are the intention to establish friendly relations with all countries, regardless of their political complexion, on the basis of mutual respect and non-intervention in each others internal affairs.

In 1970, it is true to say that Oman had virtually no diplomatic connections with the outside world, although a tenuous relationship had existed for some time with Great Britain and the United States. It was therefore one of His Majesty the Sultan's primary objectives to establish these relations, a policy which has been energetically and successfully pursued. Today, the

Sultanate is a member of the United Nations, the Arab League and many other international bodies devoted to the cause of peace and the enhancement of standards of living of mankind.

Oman joined the Arab League in 1971, and the United Nations later the same year. In 1972 the Sultanate joined the Islamic Conference Organisation, and in 1973 became a member of the Non-Aligned Group. The election of the Sultanate to the UN Security Council in 1994 was a tribute to the Sultanate's influence and standing in international affairs, and the respect which it has earned from the world community.

The Sultanate, under His Majesty's leadership, was foremost in advocating the formation of what became the Arab Gulf Cooperation Council, a body of six member states - Oman, Bahrain, UAE, Kuwait, Qatar and Saudi Arabia - which was formed in 1981. The aims of the Council are encapsulated in the intention, not only to improve the quality of life of their own people, and to preserve the integrity of their territories, but to exert a joint influence in the region for the good of all.

Over the years, His Majesty has rightfully gained a reputation as a powerful mediating influence, not only in the region, but in connection with the preservation of peace in the rest of the world. This has been notably evinced in recent years by His Majesty's successful efforts to improve relations between Saudi Arabia and Iran, to provide a venue for talks between the leaders of north and south Yemen in the hope of averting war between the two parts of that country, and in his prudently neutral stance at the time of the Iran-Iraq War, which provided a notably effective stabilising factor which prevented the likely expansion of hostilities to other areas of the region. Similarly, His Majesty sought until the last moment to persuade Iraq to withdraw from Kuwait, but, when these latter efforts failed,

Oman contributed to the coalition forces which implemented the directions of the UN.

Earlier still, the Sultan's far-sightedness and accurate analysis of the political situation had resulted in the Sultanate being virtually the only country to support the Camp David Accord which, after many vicissitudes, has led to productive efforts to secure a final, honourable, settlement for the Palestinian people.

His Majesty has also followed a policy of developing relations with Europe. It was on his initiative that a meeting of Foreign Ministers from the AGCC States and the European Community - the first of its kind - was hosted in Muscat in 1990. The Conference had modest success in reaching agreements over international tariffs and, notably, moving towards successful conclusions of the standing petrochemical disagreements between Saudi Arabia and Germany. Latterly, in his National Day speech in 1994, His Majesty stressed the dangers of violence resulting from the activities of those who seek to distort political and religious realities to their own ends. In other speeches, he has called for united action on the part of the world community to eradicate a new form of conflict: that between groups within countries, as is being witnessed in what used to be Yugoslavia.

Oman today is not Oman of the past. Its gloomy face has brightened and it has shaken off the dust of isolation and stagnation and opened its gates and windows for the new light to bring this country into direct contact with the outside world so that it may react positively to development and the course of events.

[H.M.Sultan Qaboos bin Said]

Crowned sandgrouse.

NATURAL HISTORY

PERSONAL OBSERVATIONS

Jiddat al-Harasis

The gazelle saw our vehicle from at least a kilometre away, long before my myopic eyes focussed on their elegant forms but, perhaps, not before the sharp-eyed Harasis ranger Mahmoud silently noted their presence. He did not veer from his chosen route across the stony desert and it was sheer chance that we happened to pass within 50 metres of the herd that, to my great surprise, continued to munch on the thin layer of grasses and herbs carpeting the arid terrain. Mahmoud did not display any surprise or interest in their presence, no word of excitement, wonder or pleasure at seeing so many endangered gazelle alive and well in this remote wilderness of southern Arabia. I could not take my eyes off them, nor could I resist the temptation to gesticulate and superfluously cry: "Gazelle!". Mahmoud, failing to disguise a faintly quizzical smile, kept driving.

A short while later, still bucketing across the seemingly limitless Jiddat al-Harasis, under a bright blue bowl of sky patterned by a few cotton-wool clouds, the unflappable Bedouin pointed at the ground ahead of us. "Inta shuff?" he asked. I stared ahead, straining my eyes to see anything unusual, but all that I could see were stones, sand, and the occasional desert shrub. I shrugged my shoulders, "Ma shufta" I declared. Again he pointed, "Hinak, houbara" he explained and now at least I knew what it was I was supposed to be seeing. I searched again in the direction he pointed, but to no avail. Finally, as we advanced the magnificent bustard stood-up on its long legs and ran away. "Ah, yes! Houbara bustard," I announced - unnecessarily.

A few minutes after we left the houbara behind the radio cackled into life: "Yalooni, etnain. Yalooni, etnain." Mahmoud reached for the microphone and replied to the call: "Etnain, Yalooni. Etnain, Yalooni," and then began a rapid exchange on our own

whereabouts and that of our quarry. The conversation was as much a routine social call as serving any particular function. I never doubted that my guide knew precisely where he was heading despite the total absence of roads, signs or any other modern aids. True, our vehicle had a compass but not once did I see Mahmoud refer to it. We had been going now for about 25 kilometres from the base camp at Yalooni. In addition to the first herd of gazelle I had seen others, and had lost count of how many individuals we had encountered. Sometimes they sprang across the desert, half running, half flying; while at other times they took little notice of us. Normally, I might have requested that we stop and admire the gazelle, perhaps try to photograph them, but they were clearly not on Mahmoud's agenda for this trip.

Suddenly, our course altered by about 15 degrees and we made a bee-line for the shimmering horizon. "Inta shuff?" he asked again. There was no way that I could see anything unusual and I reckoned we had a clear view for about six kilometres or more. At 40 kilometres per hour it takes about seven minutes to reach the 'horizon' and yet I was still unable to see the quarry two minutes later. Eventually, even I realized

The Jiddat al-Harasis wildlife conservation project is staffed by local people whose traditional skills have been put to good use for the protection of oryx, gazelle, ibex and other wildlife.

A wild oryx herd graze a vegetation patch on the Jiddat al-Harasis.

Oryx keep their calves within easy reach in order to protect them from predators.

The Harasis ranger, Louti, is renowned for his skills as a tracker.

that the white spots seemingly suspended above the horizon in the heat-haze could be nothing but Arabian oryx. This time I bit my tongue and resisted telling the driver what he had known for at least the previous two minutes. The oryx group to which he had brought me did not disappoint. Having observed captive oryx in Jordan, Saudi Arabia, Bahrain, Qatar and the UAE, the thrill of seeing them so healthy in the wild was deeply satisfying. No amount of photographs, scientific reports or films would ever substitute for the sheer pleasure of witnessing the real thing. We parked about 50 metres from the 16 oryx and watched them quietly through our binoculars. There were two recently born calves, twelve adult females and two adult males: one young one and the dominant bull of the herd. As we watched, a mother and calf wandered away from the herd and the bull quietly rounded them up, escorting them back to the main party. This type of behaviour does not occur among gazelle or other large mammals and helps the oryx survive in habitats where few other animals can exist.

Mahmoud began pointing out individual animals within the herd. Over by the acacia tree the larger male stood with three females. "Hada, Khalifa wa Kateeba wa Hababa" he explained. Khalifa, the male, had been born in January 1983 in Jordan and, like Hababa, born in April

1982 in the USA, had been transported to Oman as part of the reestablishment programme. Kateeba on the other hand was pure Omani, born in February of 1983 inside the settlement enclosure. A short distance away from them stood two of the newest additions to Oman's oryx population, Sabha and Samira, both less than a month old and both born in the wild. In all there were 131 oryx living in the wild on Jiddat al-Harasis at the time of my visit in December 1992. Sixty-three were males and 65 females, with three calves too young to be certain of their sex when observed through binoculars. The statistics for the project were extremely impressive with 165 oryx born on the Jiddat since 1980, 113 of which were still alive. During the same period 41 animals were brought in to the Jiddat, 29 from USA, five from Shaumari and seven from the Oman Captive Breeding Centre. But statistics cannot convey the real success of the White Oryx Project for it is about much more than the reintroduction of Arabian oryx into the wild. Although it is true that this challenge originally provided the *raison d'etre*, and continues to be the central focus, the project's administrators

A. SPALTON

remain as interested in caring for the Harasis people as they do for the oryx. (In fact the official government title of the project is the 'Jiddat al-Harasis Development Project, Part B'.) The two are more interlinked than one might imagine, for it is the unique skills, desert-lore, and deep sense of commitment to wildlife preservation displayed by the inhabitants of the Jiddat that have ensured the project's success.

Like the oryx, the Harasis face the inevitable impact of modernization which is threatening to undermine the sustainable nature of their long existence on the Jiddat. As with other Bedouin groups in Oman, they are proud of their ancestry and retain many of their tribe's traditional values and customs. Their love of the stony expanse of the Jiddat is linked to the region's great natural beauty and the fact that it is uniquely blessed by a moist fog carried in from the sea, providing moisture even when there is no rain. The Jiddat's plants and animals depend upon this elevated plateau's sea-fogs and the Harasis people have raised their camels and goats through long periods of drought, when little or no rain fell over much, if not all, of the Jiddat's 250,000 or so square kilometres! For many centuries the Harasis depended upon their camels for transport but now many have four-wheel drive vehicles. With this mechanization came the need for petrol and it is around the Shell Garage at Haima, on the main Muscat to Salalah road, that a whole new community is developing. Already providing an administrative headquarters for the Wilyat of Haima, the expanding town also

Wildlife biologist, Andrew Spalton, took this picture whilst making a camel trek with members of the Harasis tribe.

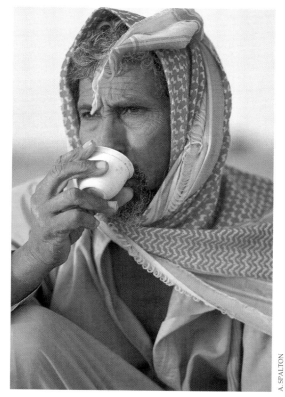

Life in the desert has a soothing rhythm set by sunrise, sunset, prayer-times and by breaks for Arabic coffee and dates.

145

A. SPALTON

Children of the Harasis tribe face conflicting influences of their traditional life-styles and the benefits of modern development, which draw them towards urban communities.

Harasis women with child.

has a new school, new mosque, a nascent supermarket, bank and a host of other small service centres together with an estate of new low-cost houses. Whilst the Harasis welcome the prospect of an "improvement" in their lives, they also worry about the social and economic implications of such a rapid pace towards modernisation. Mahmoud, my guide and ranger on this excursion, was already facing practical difficulties associated with these changes. His son was boarding at the Haima school

whilst his two daughters had recently entered the local girls' school which does not take boarders. This created special problems for him since he could not move his goats from their traditional pasturage areas deep in the heart of Jiddat where he normally lives, but had to provide a home for his daughters to sleep near the school. In an effort to solve the problem he split the family in two, with one part looking after the goats near Yalooni, and the other part in a new tent structure that he pitched in the desert a mile or so from Haima. He was already a troubled man, finding it difficult to provide for two homes and to ensure the safety and security of his extended family. As his son and daughters grow-up enjoying the benefits of modern education, there is little chance that they will wish to return to their traditional desert existence. Mahmoud will either be faced with giving-up his much loved life in the desert, or watching his family become even further divided. But perhaps there is some light at the end of this dark tunnel.

Just as Man was responsible for the decline and eventual rescue of the Arabian oryx, so the oryx may provide answers for the survival and adaptation of the Harasis. As the wild oryx population increases and attracts greater interest, both nationally and internationally, it becomes ever more vital that the Harasis continue to provide their special guardianship of nature. By protect-

A. SPALTON

A. SPALTON

ing the oryx they have also ensured that other wildlife is safe from Man's predations. The enormous nature reserve under their care, covering around 150,000 square kilometres of the Jiddat al-Harasis, now abounds with gazelle, and provides a home to one of the world's healthiest populations of Nubian ibex together with a host of other wildlife, including such forms as the caracal lynx, golden eagle and Rüppell's desert fox. Such a nature conservation project is important and worthwhile in its own right, even if the general public never had the opportunity to view the region's wildlife. However, given the worldwide pressure on wilderness areas and the widespread fascination in Arabian oryx, there seems little chance of withstanding the pressure to open the area to visitors and already an Omani tourism operator is planning to bring nature-seeking tourists to see the oryx and other wildlife. It is likely that this trend will develop and it may even provide a new impetus for the conservation effort in future. It could well be that Mahmoud and his family will have their futures secured by the White Oryx Project that will give back to the Harasis in the same way that they have given to it.

My visit to the Jiddat al-Harasis took place in December 1992, when the area was enjoying the benefits of two rainfall episodes that had occurred earlier in the year. Desert plantlife was unusually green for the season and plentiful grazing had brought all wildlife to peak condition. Predicting this natural abundance, the oryx had mated after the rains and now many of the females had recently given birth or were about to do so. A year previously it had been a very different story with the wild oryx only just managing to survive the effects of a prolonged drought. Grazing had become so scarce that mothers could obtain only sufficient food to keep themselves alive. Their calves, starved of adequate milk, died. It was a story happening throughout the region, affecting not only oryx but other large mammals such as gazelle and ibex. A year later the survivors, enjoying the benefits of recent rainfall, were probably the healthiest Arabian oryx, gazelle or ibex anywhere in the world.

The Harasis people have a reputation as excellent wildlife rangers. Their skills are

Wildlife rangers of the Harasis tribe travel by camel as well as by modern four-wheel drive vehicles.

Gazelle are abundant in Oman, thanks to a country-wide conservation policy.

A. SPALTON

A. SPALTON

The Harasis cross the sabkha of the Huqf depression during May.

tested every day since they must keep track of the movement of wild oryx over an area at least the size of East Anglia in UK. Unlike oryx held in fenced reserves elsewhere in Arabia, these animals are truly free to go anywhere they wish. There are no fences and no restraints on their movements. Eventually it is hoped that they will re-invade the Wahiba Sands to the north. For the present however, they appear to be satisfied with the Jiddat al-Harasis, a well chosen site for their re-introduction into the wild. Each day Harasis rangers set out from the project's base at Yalooni in order to track the oryx and monitor their progress.

Each two-man team spends three days in the desert before returning to their base and reporting their findings. In this way, without the use of radio-collars, satellite tracking or any other monitoring gadgetry, the oryx rangers guard their priceless wards.

One of the Harasis has a different mission. Working alone, in one of the most dramatic desert landscapes of all Arabia, his task is to track the shy and elusive Nubian ibex. Louti has earned himself a unique reputation as a wildlife ranger, able to read the minutest signs left behind by the rare ibex that inhabit the rim of the Huqf escarpment. Having heard of his skills as a tracker, I was keen to see him in action. Accompanied by Roddy Jones, field-manager of the Yalooni White Oryx Project Headquarters, I was taken first to meet Louti at his desert campsite. We found him brewing coffee on an open fire next to a small copse of bushes, about 15 kilometres from Yalooni. After sharing dates and coffee, we set off again towards the Huqf with Louti at the wheel.

Wildlife ranger, Louti, searches for ibex along the edge of the Huqf escarpment.

A. SPALTON

Ibex on the Huqf.

He is a quietly confident man of about 40 years old, modest, soft-spoken and with untold hidden reserves of endurance. Louti had been asked to show me the ibex. Roddy was quite sure he would accomplish this mission despite the great difficulty of producing wildlife on call. I confess that I retained a degree of scepticism.

Our first approach to the edge of the Huqf left me breathless with the unexpected magnificence of the scenery. We had been driving across a gradually rising stony plain criss-crossed by the dried-up beds of flash-flood wadis. Louti parked the vehicle in what appeared to be an unexceptional part of this moonscape and I followed him as he walked away from the Landcruiser, towards the edge of a steep drop-off. Massive broken slabs and boulders of limestone lay tumbled along the face of the escarpment, ripped apart by the occasional torrential floods that had eroded a mile-wide, rift-shaped wadi displayed in front of us. The deeply incised escarpment face prevented a clear view along the drop-off. Promontories to each side of us effectively restricted our field of observation to the area immediately in front and for 50 or so

metres to each side. It was in this stony bowl that Louti now scanned the rocks for any sign of ibex. Meanwhile Roddy used his binoculars to study the vast flood-plain beneath us. After about five minutes, Louti turned and walked back to the vehicle. There were no ibex to be seen. Close to the Landcruiser he stooped down to pick up a minute leaflet, lying on the ground, next to a yellow-flowered *Tribulus* plant. This apparently was evidence that ibex had been feeding there earlier in the morning. Nearby he showed me a single depression in a patch of sand surrounded by stones. It was an ibex footprint. Fearing that this might be all I would see of the creature, I tried to photograph it but it resembled nothing more than a slight depression. There were no clear hoof marks and no obvious way of indicating that it had been made by an animal. I gave up and followed Louti back to our transport. We set off again, driving a few hundred metres back from the escarpment edge, seeking another potential ibex hiding place. This time after parking the car, we crept towards the escarpment edge. Louti, leading the way, crouched down and peeped over the cliff.

*An Arabian Tahr
resting in shade.*

A. SPALTON

Roddy and I followed suit but once again there were no ibex. We were on the right trail however, Louti pointed to a metre-wide concavity in a patch of sand resting between two large boulders. The ibex had slept there last night but they had moved on. As we walked back to the car, Louti's eyes were on the ground. This time the tracks were easier to read. There were three ibex and they had gone to the south. We climbed back into the Toyota and Louti drove without speaking.

About two kilometres further on we again approached the cliff-face and came to a halt. Taking care to prevent the car doors slamming, we set off for the rim. Just before we reached it Louti bent down and picked up a dozen or so tiny rounded black balls that were hidden among the pebbles. He whispered to me that these were from an ibex calf. Almost as soon as we reached the rim a mother and twin calves bounded up and pranced along the top of the cliff-edge away from us. I quickly worked my camera but realized that the pictures would be little more than a record of fleeing ibex. We were after more than this but it was a good start. By now I was totally convinced that Louti could indeed produce ibex like rabbits from a conjurer's top-hat. Over the next half hour he proved me right. He showed how he could track the animals while driving, how

he recognised the difference between a female ibex and a stag simply from their footprints, and how he could second guess where the ibex would be at any time of day. We visited a rain-pool in which the ephemeral desert shrimp, *Triops*, were living and saw six more ibex before heading back to camp.

Much later, back at Yalooni, I reflected on what I had experienced. Over the course of two days I had observed more desert wildlife than in 20 years of travelling in Arabia. How could this be possible, for Yalooni is itself a man-made project? Here a small village has been established in the heart of the desert, with all the support facilities which such a modern human settlement requires, including generators, houses, fuel storage, work-shops, water tanks, office, and laboratory complete with computers. All this effort is directed at putting back into the natural ecosystem what Man had removed from it. Despite the seeming incongruity of ugly modern technology in the heart of a wilderness, the project is singularly successful. Not only has it provided the means to set-back the clock so far as the extinction of Arabian oryx in the wild is concerned, but it has also protected a wide range of associated wildlife and provided a source of sustainable income for the Harasis people.

Seascapes

Fahal Island's sheer cliffs and elevated sandstone plateau are the most prominent feature of Muscat's seascape. It has formed an important navigational beacon for sailors down through the ages: from the Maganites and their ancestors who fished these waters four to eight thousand years ago; for Greeks and Romans who explored this coastline; for the Arabs and their persecutors the Portuguese, who fought historic battles in the shadow of its falcon-inhabited crags; and for the modern oil tankers and cargo vessels that scan it on their radar from 50 miles away. To Omani fishermen it provides valuable shelter from seasonal winds and good fishing grounds, and for an increasing band of SCUBA divers it offers some of the finest underwater scenery and marine life in the Muscat region.

The islands' cliffs are so steep that they cast a strong shadow over the surrounding sea and one's choice of diving location is dictated as much by time of day as by conditions of wind and tide. Although there are no all-weather anchorages, several small bays provide suitable sites for mooring small boats. Depending on where one dives, the rock continues its steep descent underwater or forms a less precipitous slope in which tumbled fragments of the eroded cliffs create countless crannies and small caves inhabited by moray eels, numerous small fish, crayfish and octopus. At night the latter emerge from hiding, the crayfish to feed on algae and the occasional spiny urchin, while octopus feed on the crayfish. During daytime a truce is declared as both take refuge from lemon sharks, rays and large groupers. Flaming purple soft corals decorate the rocks along the eastern side of the island, creating a magnificent tropical marine garden in which birds and brightly coloured insects are replaced by an assemblage of equally attractive and bizarre fish whose common names, butterfly fish,

frog fish, damsel fish, hawk fish and porcupine fish, are reminders of our much greater familiarity with life above-water and our tendency to interpret what we find

Coastal scenery near Mughsayl in Dhofar shows rich intertidal.

A cuttlefish swims over sea-grass beds.

Collared butterflyfish,
Chaetodon collare.

*Manta rays feed
on plankton in
Omani waters*

beneath the waves on this basis. The analo-
gy is not entirely without validity for, just
as with terrestrial habitats, each species living here is adapted to a particular niche.
And here also the base of the food-chain
depends upon the energy of sunlight converted to carbohydrates by a variety of
plant-life, ranging from microscopic single-
celled zooxanthellae, so effectively farmed
by corals, to delicate blue-green algae coat-
ing rock surfaces and finally, further south,

where the ocean's deep cool waters rise to
the surface each summer, to massive kelp
weeds that form the equivalent of a deciduous woodland, complete with leaf-canopy.

Schools of collared butterflyfish hover at a
cleaning station, taking turns for a cleaning
wrasse to pick parasites from their scales.
Persistent damsel-fish protest at our entry
into their algal-coated territories; a small
electric ray lies half covered by sand, over-
head schools of caesios feed, unmolested
for the time being, on plankton. We keep
eyes peeled for whale-sharks that frequently feed along this section of the island, but
this is not their day. In close to the cliff, on
my way back from the dive, I investigate
the over-hanging wave-cut cliff whose surface is permanently in shade and where
hawk-fish cling tenaciously to the steep

face, eyes peeled for unwary fish fry. Also among the shallows I encounter a large octopus masquerading as a coral head. My diving partner swam directly over it, and perhaps that is why it's slight movement caught my eye. Nearby, two large crayfish hid among boulders. Fahal is regularly visited by a host of oceanic marinelife, from the greater hammerhead shark and whale-sharks to large whales and prancing schools of spinner, common and bottle-nose dolphins.

Oman's marine mammals have been described as one of the diving world's best kept secrets but now the cat is out of the bag. At a recent meeting of cetacean experts in Nairobi, marine biologists Robert Baldwin and Dr. Rodney Salm showed their pictures of Omani whales and dolphins to the eminent gathering of marine mammologists. The response was an enthusiastic endorsement of what many who have been diving these waters for years already suspected: Oman is among the world's best localities for whale and dolphin watching. It is only a matter of time before the rest of the world catches on to this fact. The dolphin experts were not only impressed by the abundance of these friendly and fascinating creatures in Oman, but they were also excited about the possibility that the pink-bellied spinners, so familiar to local fishermen and divers, may represent one of the first Indian Ocean records of the dwarf spinner (*Stenella clymene*), or perhaps be a sub-species or even a new species. But what most surprised the experts was the great variety of marine mammals present in Oman. The Oman Natural History Museum has been collecting data on washed up whales and dolphins for many years. From this evidence they have pieced together a list of marine mammals in Omani waters and have created an impressive Whale Hall in which their findings are presented to the general public. Four species of baleen whales occur here: humpback, Bryde's, sei and minke. Toothed cetaceans are more numerous, with ten confirmed species including five (and possibly six) dolphins; i.e. Indopacific humpback, bottle-nose, common, spinner (possibly two species) and Risso's; and five-toothed whales including the false killer whale, killer whale, sperm whale, dwarf sperm whale and Cuvier's beaked whale. Several of these are believed to breed in Omani waters.

Following our dive at Fahal we went in search of dolphin schools; heading south, directly offshore from Muscat, where we were able to observe fishing boats returning towards the shore from their night-missions. For a while I thought that we were going to be disappointed. Despite a mirror-calm sea and perfect viewing conditions, there did not seem to be any big schools breaking the surface. After about half an hour of searching however, we caught sight of some dolphins in the distance. As we approached we could see from their wild leaps that they were spinners. Suddenly the sea was alive with their antics and we were surrounded by at least a hundred dolphins.

Dolphins and fishermen search for fish off Muscat's rocky shoreline.

153

Coastline at Fins, between Muscat and Sur.

Dolphins are common off Muscat where large schools of spinners create a dramatic sight.

In addition to the spinners, common dolphins were also present, swimming to one side of the spinner school while a short distance away, a group of bottle-nose dolphins were playing their own games. Because the different species were so close, it was quite easy to distinguish the various forms. Many of the dolphins swam with young alongside them and it is clear that they breed in Omani waters. I tried out my usual method of getting close to these beautiful creatures underwater, taking a tow-line from the bows and being pulled along with my body against the boat. It worked and I was able to observe the dolphins at close quarters, diving deep under the boat before surfacing in exuberant leaps. It was a great way to end a morning's outing in the waters of Muscat Bay.

Arriving in Dhofar

As the Oman Aviation flight approaches Salalah, one is greeted at first by a crinkled plateau of eroded hills gouged out by thousands of runnels, connecting at their bases to wide, snaking wadi beds pock-marked by clumps of trees - unidentifiable from this height but a bumpy ride in a four-wheel drive vehicle would later confirm these to be frankincense for which the Dhofar region is renowned. Gradually as the aircraft descends towards the sea, a long ribbon of clouds marks the crest of the *jabal* which runs parallel to the coastline of this southerly province. Immediately beneath the plane the land still looks completely arid but we rapidly approach the clouds and the plane responds to the strong thermal currents by issuing an uncomfortable shudder. As the plane continues its descent, turning at right angles to the coast, it rapidly passes over the various zones characterizing the coastal strip. Now we can look down at the clouds and admire hillsides whose thin veneer of greenery seems to have protected their surface from the more obvious consequences of erosion. Here hill-slopes are less jagged and more easily traversed than those further inland; their relatively rounded forms criss-crossed by tracks of various vehicles whose purpose appears, from the air, to have been nothing more than to place illegible signatures on the landscape.

Dhofar's green and pleasant land seems out of context with the widely held but erroneous view that Arabia is devoid of lush vegetation.

Pivot irrigation has revolutionized agricultural production in many parts of Arabia. Here the method is seen at Dhofar Cattle Feed Company's farm in Salalah.

Almost immediately we come across the first sign of habitation in the form of an isolated mountain village. The plane banks sharply above a band of denser cloud and, for a moment, our view of the ground is obliterated. As we emerge a few seconds later we catch our first clear glimpse of the sea, then once again the cloud thickens and we are left with a momentary tantalizing impression of long white beaches washed by rolling breakers. When we emerge for the second time I am surprised to see, immediately beneath the aircraft, a seaward facing precipitous mountainside with lush green vegetation, more reminiscent, from this height at least, of the tropical rain-forested slopes of the granitic Seychelles islands, a thousand miles due south in the Indian Ocean, than of anything one expects to find in Arabia. No amount of reading about the combined effects of the tropical monsoon and the coastal upwelling responsible for Dhofar's unique climate had dampened my initial excitement at encountering such an island of profusion surrounded by Arabia's harsh but equally evocative desert.

It was almost sun-set and the colours below were somewhat subdued but there was no mistaking the solid canopy of trees which formed this mysterious and enticing forest. Looking back, over the top of the mountain, one could still see the arid hill-scape stretching as far as the horizon. But now the plane was on its final approaches and we were able to distinguish many more details on the ground. Walled enclosures, where Man has harnessed fresh-water, sculpting his own islands of greenery, appeared more frequently and then an enormous circular green carpet, the result of pivot irrigation, which I later identified as belonging to the Dhofar Cattle Feed Company. As the landing strip looms up, we pass over houses whose gardens are packed with trees, oases of greenery in an arid brown land.

Before touch-down, more irrigated land, reminding me of the green of Ireland, and in the distance the town of Salalah. Wheels down and we arrive in Dhofar Province, the land of Queen Sheba, of frankincense, and of countless other natural wonders. As we taxi towards the terminal, I look inland again and see the rising peaks of the *jabal* neatly dressed with a topping of cloud which only minutes before had obscured my view of those elusive mountains. Above the clouds, the sky is still a clear blue but it is already past six and in only a few minutes time darkness will draw its own veil over my first view of this fascinating region of Oman.

156

S. KAY

Ancient and modern

Turn right out of the Intercontinental Hotel's seaside entrance and walk a few hundred metres along the beach, towards the cliff top modern houses of Ras al - Hamra, first recognised as a prime residential location by neolithic Man. Before long progress is slowed or arrested by a channel that cuts across the beach and leads into (or out of depending on the state of the tide) an extensive mangrove 'swamp'. Swamp is a misleading term at the best of times and certainly on this occasion, for the ground among the mangrove trees that line the channel is firm under foot and not the least bit threatening. Skirt the edge of the channel, up over the beach and around in a sweeping arc, arriving at the point where clear sand beach gives way, grudgingly at first, but a few metres further on with complete abandonment, to that strange and much maligned maritime bush, the mangrove. Walk in a little way, taking the trodden path where aerial roots of the mangroves have been cleared by the feet of fishermen. Depending on the tide's state, you will either have a dry walk or finish up wading through ankle deep water. Either way it is quite clear where the blackened flats give way to the tide-gouged channel, for this is at the outer edge of the man-groves, demarcated by a tangle of their roots and branches dipping into the channel. Anyone who has ever doubted the conserva-

tionists' cries for preservation of m a n g r o v e s w o u l d d o well to stand here and to quietly take in the scene so vividly revealed as the tide floods in and out.

Glistening green kingfishers flash between the over-hanging branches and the shimmering surface, spearing their prey of small fish. They do not go hungry. Packed among the micro-jungle of roots lining

Mangroves create unique green habitats for birds and important nursery and feeding grounds for marine-life.

River kingfisher, Alcedo atthis, *at Azaiba.*

HANNE & JENS ERIKSEN

the bank are literally millions of fry. They shelter close to the side, taking care not to venture too far into the main channel where they risk being attacked by larger fish. These are the stock from which will grow many of the larger pelagic fish that are commercially caught offshore. Decline of fish stocks is not only caused by over-fishing, but equally by loss of habitats such as key nursery grounds. I wish that I could have shown this scene to those decision-makers throughout the tropics, who have argued that mangroves do not need to be preserved.

Fishermen have been visiting Qurm mangrove for at least 6000 years. One look at the ground at one's feet provides a clear explanation of why the seaside bushes have been such a magnet. Forget for a moment the constant leaps and splashes of young and not so young milkfish and snapper in the channel (although these too must have offered an attractive harvest for they are easily scared into jumping clear out of the water and into the mangrove branches); fishermen did not even need to get their feet wet to harvest nutritious food from these mangroves, since the ground among the radiating aerial roots is scattered with edible oysters and whelks. The oysters are so prolific, and the water is so rich in food, it seems clear that their population is limited by suitable surfaces on which to settle rather than by any other factor. Such sites in many tropical countries have been converted into extensive oyster-farms by packing the shallows with upright wooden stakes on which grow tons of oysters. Here in Oman this particular stretch of mangrove, thanks to the efforts and concerns of a conservation-minded government, has been mercifully preserved in its natural condition, forming an impressive nature reserve surrounded on three sides by modern developments, and on the fourth by the open sea.

But that is not all. Apart from the commercially and socially significant fish, oysters and whelks, and the aesthetically pleasing birdlife, this mangrove habitat is alive with claw-waving fiddler crabs. I have known wildlife cameramen and biologists travel thousands of miles to study or film these curious crabs but here they are in profusion with few people even aware of their existence. It was here also that I gained my first view of that attractive wading visitor to Oman's shore, the pratincole.

Wildlife documentaries, magazines and books have served both to educate and confuse the general public. On the one hand we have gratefully appreciated and admired the stunning scenes of nature brought to us by intrepid and dedicated photographers, while on the other hand we have been led to expect that what we see on television, in the cinema, or among glossy pages of green literature is nature in the raw. Of course it often is unadulterated but we do not all possess 600mm lenses or camouflaged hides through which to observe the wildlife we encounter in our daily lives. This is another reason why sites such as the Qurm mangrove are so important because, not only do such places provide tranquil settings close to major connurbations, but they also offer television-style nature-watching to the general public. They can thus serve to reinforce our own appreciation of nature and our understanding of the vital role played by key wildlife habitats.

Whilst it is relatively easy to visualize the impact of modern development on Oman's wildlife, and in many cases to take action to minimize these effects, we seem to be only vaguely aware of how the status of wildlife has changed down through the years. Habitat destruction began with Stone-Age man and has continued at a variety of paces, right up to the present time. Archaeologists have helped us to piece together evidence of previous epochs, when climatic differences in Oman helped to sustain creatures that no longer live there - some of which are extinct. Apart from the ancient bones and fossils that have provided such evidence, there are also a number of written descriptions of the ancient natural history and sociology of Arabia. Several of these date to around 2000 ago, including that by Pliny; the anonymous *Periplus of the Erythraen Sea*; and a recently translated text by Agatharchides of Cnidus, a Ptolemaic author who is particularly interesting for what he reveals about the marine environment of southern Arabia, including Oman.

The importance of such texts for enhancing our understanding of Oman's historic wildlife can, in my view, hardly be overstated and yet few biologists have turned to these sources. In addition, scholars translating and interpreting the ancient texts do not seem to have taken biological evidence into account. The first time I really became aware of this was on reading the Epic of Gilgamesh, the world's oldest epic poem preserved on tablets recovered from Mesopotamia which were written over 4000 years ago. The story tells how Gilgamesh, having led an exciting youth, reached a mid-life crisis and sailed to the land of Dilmun in search of an elixir. A priest on Dilmun (Bahrain) eventually took pity on him and told him "the secret of eternal youth". He was informed that if he dived into the sea he would find a 'black spiky flower ... sharp so that it pricked like a rose' and that this held the secret of eternal youth. The story relates how Gilgamesh did indeed jump in and how he plucked the 'flower'. Unfortunately he lost it a short while later to a serpent and this creature thus gained the powerful 'secret of eternal youth'.

There is more to the story but it was this section that interested me most because I felt that there was enough here to guess at the source of the legend. Anyone who has jumped into shallow-water around Bahrain, or indeed around much of Oman, will already have met the 'flower of eternal youth' since the description perfectly matches that of the black-spined sea urchin *Echinothrix*, which is very common and could easily have been caught by Gilgamesh. As an interesting side issue, sea urchin gonads are still regarded in many parts of the world as an aphrodisiac. The fact that the urchin was described as a flower should not cloud the issue since, even today, many people would mistake spiny sea urchins for plants rather than animals. But what of the rest of the story? During the Gulf War I worked on a film and book about the war's environmental impact *(Tides of War)* and this took me to Bahrain for some underwater filming. It was my first close encounter with sea snakes. For almost a week we did nothing but film these reptiles and became very familiar with their behaviour. It seemed obvious that these were the serpents of the Epic of Gilgamesh and that it was hardly surprising that the story ended with 'serpents' stealing the 'secret of eternal youth' for we watched the snakes in ankle deep water casting off their old skins and emerging, as if by magic, as fresh, brightly coloured 'born-again' sea snakes. We had a particular interest in this since the newly moulted snakes had much clearer vision than the ones whose skins were older and whose scales over their eyes had become encrusted. The sea snakes were so common in the shallows that it was inconceivable that the ancients were not familiar with them and with their strange behaviour.

With this experience in mind, it is worth taking a second look at the passages in Agatharchides that are relevant to Oman. First with regard to the 'Fish-eaters', who lived along the Arabian shoreline, he writes:

159

Coastal features of Oman's shoreline near Fins.

flows back through the stones and passage-ways towards the depths that attract it, but the fish that remain behind in the hollows are easy prey and food for the Fish Eaters. The other fish, as we have said are easily subdued, but when sharks, comparatively large seals, sea-scorpions, eels and all creatures of this sort fall into the trap, the enterprise becomes dangerous.

All the areas of deep water near shore are hostile to their way of life, as also are those lying along beaches. For such territory provides neither abundant catches of fish nor of similar creatures. The homes of the fish-eaters are located along rocky shores which have deep depressions, irregular ravines, narrow channels and curving inlets. Where these exist...they place rough boulders in the depressions so as to form several narrow passageways. Then when the tide is borne in to the land from the sea....the sea covers the whole rock shore. It also brings with its surge from the strait many fish which remain near shore browsing in the sheltered recesses for food. But when the ebb tide occurs again, the water

Now this was written around 110 BC and is a fine account of the method by which the fish-eaters gained their food. It is clear that inhabitants of the coastline were already aware of how to use tidal rise and fall in trapping fish. One of the interesting points it raises is the presence of "large seals". There are at present no seals known to be living in the Red Sea or northern Indian Ocean and the species referred to is therefore presumably extinct. This is a great pity for it was a very friendly species of seal, unafraid of man, as we hear in the following brief description:

"The houses of fish-eaters are located along rocky shores which have deep depressions, irregular ravines, narrow channels and curving inlets"
(Agatharchides c. 100 BC).

Most amazing of all, seals, which live with these people, themselves fish in a way similar to that of the men. Likewise, also with regard to their lairs and the safety of their young, these species treat each other with the greatest good faith, or

The people who live near the never thirsty Fish Eaters, as though an unbreachable treaty had been concluded between them and the seals, do not harrass the seals nor are they harmed by them. Without plotting against one another, each group strictly respects the other's prey, and, thus, they live in close association with one another in a way that would be difficult to parallel among men who live with other men.

The Ptolemies were perfectly familiar with seals since monk seals inhabited the Mediterranean where a few still survive. They knew what they were describing and we can be assured from the details given that seals were quite common at that time along the shores of the Red Sea and southern Arabia. The account is even more credible when one looks at some of the more recent evidence for seals in the region. French sailors who first arrived in the Seychelles islands in the eighteenth century described seeing seals hauled out on sandbanks. Wellsted saw a skin of a young seal in the early nineteenth century near Ras Banas in the Red Sea and was told by local fishermen that they were common. There are even suggestions of seals still living in Omani waters. It is not something that one can write-off too quickly for large areas of Oman's shoreline remain unexplored by scientists.

There are some other sections of Agatharchides that suggest identification with the Oman coastline. Immediately following the section on seals, and in a clear reference to Fish-eaters living outside of the Red Sea proper, Agatharchides describes their dwellings:

These tribes do not employ similar dwellings, but they live in ones that vary according to the peculiarities of the environment. Some inhabit caves, particularly ones that face north, in which they keep themselves cool by means of the deep shadows and the breezes that blow around this area since the caves that face south are hot like ovens and cannot be approached by man because of their excessive heat. Those, however, who lack northwards facing caves collect the ribs of whales that have been cast up on shore from the sea. As there is a great abundance of these, they intertwine the curved bones from either side, leaning them on each other, and they tie them together with fresh sea-weed. When the vaulted chamber is covered they rest in it during the worst heat.

"Some inhabit caves, particularly ones that face north" (Agatharchides).

"Numerous olive trees grow in these regions, the roots of which are washed by the sea . . ." (Agatharchides).

Intertwining these trees and creating a continuous shade, they dwell in these unusual tents. Passing their lives at the same time on land and in the sea, they live pleasantly, avoiding the sun through the shade provided by the branches and moderating the natural heat of these places through the continuous lapping of the waves and relaxing their bodies by means of the gentle breezes that blow around them.

Biological knowledge can be used here to make a likely identification with the Dhofar coastline where washed up kelp and whalebones still coincide although the demise of the whale means that there are far fewer whale skeletons. Agatharchides goes on to explain two other types of dwellings that also fit with Dhofar:

Numerous olive trees grow in these regions, the roots of which are washed by the sea. They have thick foliage and bear a fruit similar to the sweet chestnut. These are clearly mangroves and he continues as follows:

This too fits the Omani coastline although not restricted to it. But the following passage once more seems to focus on Dhofar:

... From all eternity a huge mound of sea-weed has accumulated, similar in appearance to a mountain. Compressed by the continuous pounding of the waves, this mound has become firm in texture and mixed with sand. In these mounds therefore people excavate chambers the size of a man. They leave the section at the top solid, but below they make oblong passageways and connect them to each other by tunnelling through the mound. Cooling themselves in these tunnels they remain undisturbed, but when the tide comes in they rush out and gather fish. When the tide ebbs however they retreat into the chambers to feast on their catch ... Those that die they bury at the time of the ebb tide, leaving them where they have been cast out; and when the high tide comes in, they throw the bodies into the sea.

Turtles provided easy pickings for early settlers along Oman's coastline.

Wherefore, by turning their bodies into a source of food for the fish, they follow a way of life that in striking fashion follows the same cycle throughout eternity.

The Turtle-eaters are also of great interest and could perhaps have lived on the Daymaniayat islands. The text reads as follows:

Turtle beach with inset of tracks.

There are islands in the ocean located near the mainland which are numerous, small in size, and low-lying and which bear neither domesticated nor wild fruit. Because they are close together, no waves occur in the midst of these islands since the surf expends its force on the outermost islands. Numerous sea turtles live in these places, retreating from all directions to the shelter of the calm water. They spend the night in deep water seeking food, but during the day they come into the sea that lies between the islands and sleep on the surface with their shells facing the sun, looking just like overturned boats. For they are huge in size and not smaller than the smallest fishing boat. At that time the local people, who inhabit the islands, quietly swim out to the turtles. Approaching them from both sides, one pushes down and the other lifts up until the beast is turned over. Then those on either side manoeuvre its whole bulk so that the creature may not turn over and escape...One who has a long rope, after tying its tail, swims to shore and drags the animal up onto the beach...When they have hauled it up onto the island, they first bake all the inner portions in the sun for some time, and then they feast on it. The shells, which are bowl shaped, they use to sail across to the mainland, which they do

to fetch water, and for shelter...nature seems to have granted them with one gift the satisfaction of many needs, for one and the same gift is their food, container, house and boat.

It seems likely that the turtles were large green turtles that still nest in their thousands in Oman. The following piece of text

A green turtle swims close to a nesting beach.

Whale Hall at the Natural History Museum.

At the edge of the Wahiba Sands.

also suggests that the above refers to a section of Oman's coastline for it reads:

Not far from these people the coast is inhabited by people who follow an irregular way of life, deriving their sustenance from whales that have been washed ashore. Sometimes they have an abundance of food because of the large size of the beasts they find; and sometimes because of interruptions in the occurrences of the beachings, they suffer severely from lack of food. At such times they are compelled by famine to gnaw on the cartilage of old bone and gristle that grows at the ends of the ribs.

In the above four pieces, I have introduced some personal observations on Oman's natural history. There are many other experiences I could write about, from wading through deep fast-flowing gorges to exploring the precipitous edge of thousand foot cliffs, or investigating unexpectedly green oases in the Wahiba Sands. However, Oman's fascinating natural history is the subject of many specialist studies undertaken by academic scientists, amateur naturalists and consultants acting on behalf of various government agencies. The Oman Natural History Museum has played an important role in collecting and collating information from a wide variety of sources whilst the Special Adviser on Conservation to the *Diwan Assultani*, a role fulfilled for many years by Ralph Daly, has also been of central importance in the establishment and management of several conservation programmes, including those involved with reintroduction of the Arabian oryx and conservation of the Arabian tahr and Nubian ibex. In 1992 a meeting was held in Oman under the auspices of the Minister of Regional Municipalities and Environment to discuss a National Conservation Strategy The background reports accompanying these discussions contained useful synopses of many aspects of Oman's natural history and have been of assistance in compiling the following account which is based upon a rich body of published research work.

THE GEOLOGICAL SETTING

Oman on the move

The land-mass of Oman has not always been where it is today. Even now it is on the move, gradually drifting further away from Africa at a rate of around two or three centimetres per year: not enough to be noticed except by the most accurate of surveys. The scale of geological time is, however, on a vastly grander scale than that which governs our own lives. In geological terms a thousand years is a very brief period and even a million years hardly merits a special

Al-Wajama village at
Wadi Sahtan.

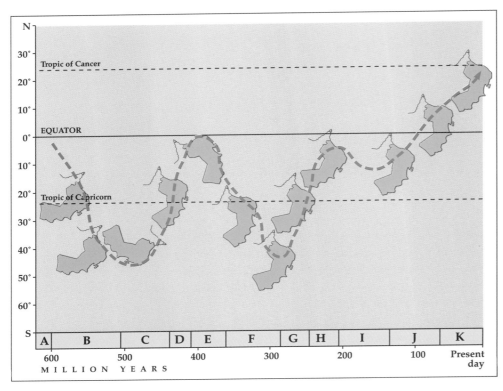

A	Pre-Cambrian
B	Cambrian
C	Ordovician
D	Silurian
E	Devonian
F	Carboniferous
G	Permian
H	Triassic
I	Jurassic
J	Cretaceous
K	Tertiary

N

30°

Tropic of Cancer

20°

10°

EQUATOR

0°

10°

20°

Tropic of Capricorn

30°

40°

50°

60°

S

A | B | C | D | E | F | G | H | I | J | K

600   500   400   300   200   100   Present day

MILLION YEARS

Movement of the land-mass of Oman over geological time. (After M. Hughes Clarke, 1990)

mention. The time-scale reads instead in hundreds of millions of years. At the beginning of the Geological Time Chart, more than six hundred million years ago the basal rock which today forms Oman lay in the southern hemisphere, astride the Tropic of Capricorn. Over the next four hundred million years it swung back and forth between sub-polar southern latitudes and the equator, remaining all the time in the southern hemisphere. This movement is

illustrated in the adjoining figure. It finally drifted over into the northern hemisphere around a hundred million years ago and continued its north-easterly movement until it reached its present location. Such dramatic shifts in crustal rocks underlying present day land-masses are by no means unique to Oman but result from global movements of the earth's plates and the attendant break-up of the mother-continent Panagaea into the super-continents Laurasia and Gondwana. Approximately sixty-five million years ago major cracks appeared in Gondwana's underlying crust and different fragments began to drift apart from one another. Oman, along with the rest of Arabia, formed part of Gondwana which included the great land-masses of Africa and India. The break from Africa probably occurred around thirty-five million years ago and resulted in the creation of a narrow trench which gave rise to the Red Sea. The Arabian Plate eventually collided with the Eurasian Plate creating zones of great pressure and upheaval manifested in the al-Hajar mountains of Oman and the opposing Zagros and Makran mountains of Iran.

Despite Oman's geological peregrinations, it is in a relatively stable zone of the earth's crust, mostly free from major earth tremors. Musandam is closest to the boundary between the Arabian and Eurasian plates and it does occasionally experience earth tremors associated with tensions along the zone of collision. The Arabian Plate abuts on to the Indian Plate deep under the Indian Ocean, to the east of Oman, along a line known as the Owen Fracture Zone and, whilst the sliding of the two plates against each other does create tremors, these are not normally noticeable inside Oman.

Flood-water erosion has gouged deep valleys through Oman's mountainous interior, such as here at Wadi Dayqah.

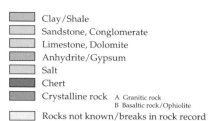

TIME SCALE: MILLIONS OF YEARS BEFORE THE PRESENT DAY

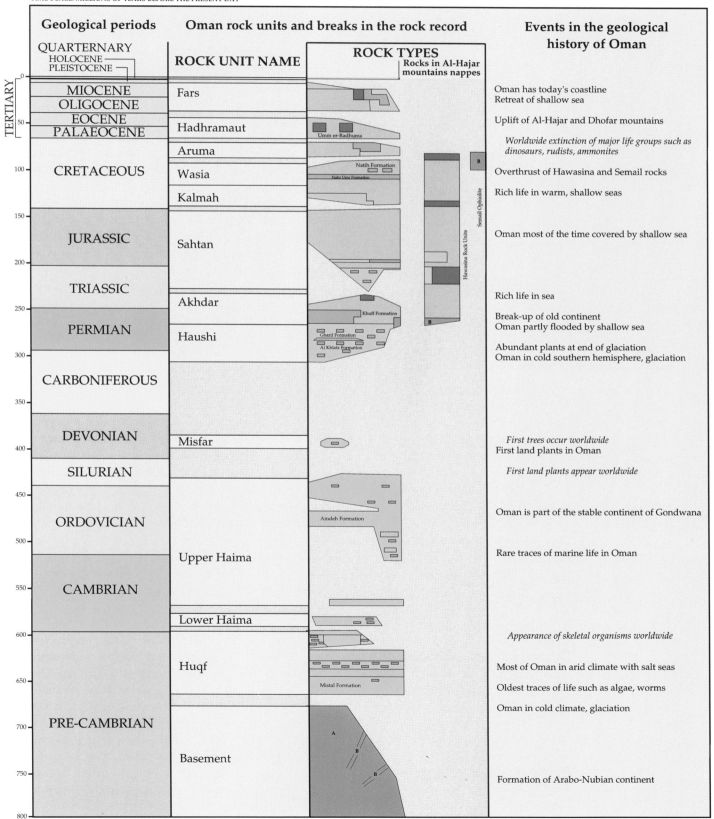

Re-drawn from diagram of A Slice Through Geological Time in Michael Hughes Clarke, 1990, with permission from Petroleum Development Oman.

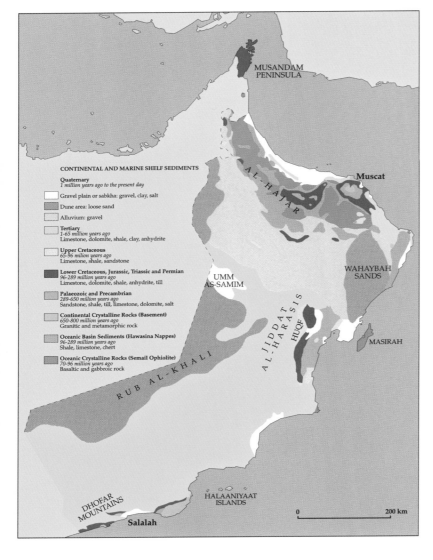

CONTINENTAL AND MARINE SHELF SEDIMENTS

Quaternary
1 million years ago to the present day

Gravel plain or sabkha: gravel, clay, salt

Dune area: loose sand

Alluvium: gravel

Tertiary
1-65 million years ago
Limestone, dolomite, shale, clay, anhydrite

Upper Cretaceous
65-96 million years ago
Limestone, shale, sandstone

Lower Cretaceous, Jurassic, Triassic and Permian
96-289 million years ago
Limestone, dolomite, shale, anhydrite, till

Palaeozoic and Precambrian
289-650 million years ago
Sandstone, shale, till, limestone, dolomite, salt

Continental Crystalline Rocks (Basement)
650-800 million years ago
Granitic and metamorphic rock

Oceanic Basin Sediments (Hawasina Nappes)
96-289 million years ago
Shale, limestone, chert

Oceanic Crystalline Rocks (Semail Ophiolite)
70-96 million years ago
Basaltic and gabbroic rock

Geological regions

Geological investigations of Oman have been promoted by the search for and discovery of valuable mineral and hydrocarbon resources. Modern research methods, including satellite imagery and remote sensing, have greatly helped to build a comprehensive picture of this vast country's structure. Basically, Oman may be divided into three distinct geological regions: i.e. the elevated escarpments and mountains of Musandam, the al-Hajar range, the Huqf and Dhofar ranges; the flat-lying young sedimentary substrates of Central Oman, such as on the Jiddat al-Harasis; and the sand-seas and dunes of the Wahiba and Rub al-Khali.

The mountainous regions, as we have indicated above, were created by upheavals in the earth's crust associated with colliding plates. Oman's major mountains were thus thrown up around thirty-five million years ago, during the Tertiary Oligocene period. Their present day form is the result of erosional forces, climatic changes and sea-level

fluctuations since that time. A classic example of this is provided by the Dhofari mountains which are formed in the main from a large inclined slab of Tertiary limestone. The slab is raised up behind Salalah and tilts northwards. Along the southern side, facing the coast, its flank is exposed as a series of dropped crustal blocks, forming in places sheer scarps, up to 1000 metres in height. Flying in to Salalah one gains an excellent view of the northern slopes of the Dhofar slab. Numerous wadis snake their way between rugged hills, eventually petering out in the arid sands of the Rub al-Khali. Erosion of wind and water are clearly evidenced in the rugged form of the land.

The mountains of al-Hajar tell a different story reflected in the varied nature of their rocks, some of which are hard and resistant to erosion whilst others are quite soft. The force of uplift was much greater than at Dhofar, heaving some of the layers into an almost vertical plain, thus exposing multi-layered edges variously susceptible to erosion. The end result is a series of quite jagged and uneven peaks. Some of the sedimentary rocks here have been deeply buried and compressed, forming quite hard rocks such as those that form the peaks of Jabal Akhdar. This range is formed from a single upfold, which has been subsequently eroded, creating a series of wide valleys or bowls.

A study of the erosional features of Oman's landscape leads one to the conclusion that there have been times when the climate must have been much wetter than today, and that the impact of water erosion at these time was far more significant than it is at present. This evidence for climatic variation during relatively recent times is also reflected in the fossil record. A major geological feature that further suggests a period, or periods, of heavy rainfall is the Omani system of limestone caves, which include some of the largest in the world.

Towards the base of the mountains the debris from erosion accumulates in low foot-hills and in impressive alluvial fans that spread out from the water-courses or wadis. The lower, more level, plains, such as that of Jiddat al-Harasis, are formed by ancient sea beds in which deposits in the form of marine sands and muds have formed limestones. The flatness of Jiddat al-Harasis, free territory for wild Arabian oryx among a host of other creatures, is a reflection of the relative stability of the terrain since these rocks were laid down. It is also here that the discerning eye may notice the slight rise around the edge of a massive, now filled-in, meteorite crater, the 'Habhab crater', a feature that is usually pointed out to visitors to Yalooni.

Deserts, in the form of the Wahiba Sands and part of the great Rub al-Khali, are among the most remarkable features of Oman's geological landscape. In the case of the Wahiba, one of the features that most fascinate first time visitors is the abruptness of the divide between the red dunes of the sands and the contrasting surrounding countryside. Studies undertaken as part of the Royal Geographical Society's Wahiba Sands Project have greatly enhanced our understanding of this complex and fascinating area, an area that has experienced cycles of cooler, wetter weather and warmer drier conditions. The Rub al-Khali or Empty Quarter has also been through these climatic shifts and there are even signs that great trees once grew in the heart of the desert. Where rains from the al-Hajar mountains drain westwards, away from the sea and into the vast dry bowl of the Empty Quarter, a salt-lake, known locally as 'Mother of Poisons', or Umm as-Samim, has been formed. It is a desolate area where driving is extremely hazardous since the salt crust is of variable thickness and ridges of salt create formidable obstacles. Elsewhere, salt has played a different role, forcing its

way to the surface from massive deposits deep underground, dragging a mixed assemblage of rocks with it until these are spilled out over the surface and left behind after the salt itself has been washed away.

Al Jabal al Akhdar, the green mountain.

Wahiba Sands, or Ramlat al Wahaybah.

Marine fossils

Ancient marinelife, trapped by limestone rocks, provided a source for oil and natural gas to be produced. Now man harvests this fossil fuel in many parts of Arabia. The project seen here is at Lekhwair camp, amid towering sand dunes of the Empty Quarter.

Signs of previous sea-levels are distinguishable at many sites along the coast and even underwater. Ancient high tide-levels are distinguished by flat wave-cut terraces, whilst lower than present levels may be observed whilst diving at sites such as Fahal Island where the wave-undercut along the rocks at tide-level is repeated deeper down, several metres underwater. Careful examination of undersea rocks may also reveal signs of their erosion by wind and rain when they were exposed during the last Ice Age when sea-level was as low as 130 metres below its present height. A striking example of a once higher sea-level is to be seen close to Muscat, where a distinctive wave-cut platform runs along the hillside between Bandar Jissa and Baushar.

Geology does not stop at sea-level and Oman's undersea geology is every bit as fascinating as its above-water features. In addition to the wave-cuts of earlier times,

seen on steep rock faces such as those at Fahal, there are undersea terraces formed by land that was once above sea-level and whose surfaces have been eroded by ancient rivers. In shallow waters corals continue to create limestone from which reefs are built in just the same way as fossil reefs that may be found among limestone outcrops on land.

From the viewpoint of today's naturalists, the aspect of Oman's geological record that is of most interest is its fossils, providing evidence of the animals and plants that lived in Oman, thousands, millions or even hundreds of millions of years ago. The sedimentary rocks in which Oman's fossils have been preserved were formed over a long period of six hundred million years - a time-frame in which the crustal rocks of Oman were dragged from the southern Tropic of Capricorn as far south as 55°S and then northwards, across the equator, to their present location. Not surprisingly, the

PDO

nature of sediments and the fossils preserved within them, varied considerably as a result of these movements, as well as the dramatic climatic changes that occurred on a global scale and the process of evolution.

The oldest sedimentary rocks that can be examined in Oman belong to the Huqf and Haima Groups and they contain stromatolites formed by aquatic algae and bacteria that lived more than six hundred million years ago, in the Pre-Cambrian period when 'Oman' was lying in temperate zones of the southern ocean. The Silurian, Devonian and Carboniferous periods are something of a closed book so far as Oman is concerned since very little rock is known from those periods. Oil drilling has revealed rare sections of the Devonian Misfar Group containing microscopic animal and plant fossils that lived in freshwater lakes. Pollen and spores from plants living on the flourishing super-continent of Gondwana during the Carboniferous have

been preserved in the Al Khlata Formation that was associated with a glacial epoch.

The earliest layer to contain abundant marine fossils is the lower portion of the Gharif Formation that was laid down in the Permian period (two hundred and fifty to three hundred million years ago). Here one can see a profusion of sea lilies and lamp shells whilst fossilized tree trunks occur in the upper layers of this formation, where soft estuarine muds preserved trunks washed down river from inland. Gondwana began to crack-up into discrete crustal plates during the Permian era and the Arabian Plate, on which Oman sits, drifted north from the southern temperate zone, towards the tropics. It was during this phase that the great mass of calcareous animal remains that later formed the limestones and dolomites of the Akhdar Group was deposited in warm, shallow, coastal waters. Impressive fossils of coral from this era can be seen in the al-Hajar mountains.

View over the Salalah coastal plain, from the crest of the escarpment of Jabal Samhan.

The subsequent Triassic (two hundred and fifty to two hundred and ten million years ago), Jurassic (two hundred and ten to ninety million years ago) and Cretaceous (ninety to sixty five million years ago) periods saw a continued drift northwards of the Arabian Plate with Oman passing through the equator, and then northwards again until by the end of the Cretaceous the region of present day Muscat lay about 10°N. Throughout much of this period Oman was alternately covered by sea or exposed as low lying land. Limey sediments, formed from the skeletal remains of plants and animals, accumulated in great abundance during the marine incursions. Quite naturally too, many sea-shells and remains of plankton or other hard remains were preserved in the sands to become fossils. Great mounds of rudists (a form of fossil marine shell) can be seen at some sites. At times this nascent territory of Oman was covered by oceanic depths and the fossils preserved in these deep muds differ from those of shallow seas. Here one may find remains of ancient molluscan forms such as the coiled shells of free-swimming ammonites and bullet-shaped internal shells of the squid-like belemnites.

Semail ophiolite

The al-Hajar mountains, that so impressively skirt Muscat represent, in geological terms, something of an aberration for they provide a unique window into the crystalline processes of layering in the oceanic crust. About seventy million years ago a vast slab of oceanic crust slid up and over the edge of the north-eastern edge of the Arabian continent and its remains are seen today in these fascinating jagged mineral rich mountains. The Semail ophiolite is probably the best example of its kind in the world, being easy to study through its exposed condition and general state of preservation. Geologists have travelled from many parts of the world to study it in order to gain a deeper understanding of the processes at work along the crustal fault lines, deep under the ocean. In his excellent book, *Oman's Geological Heritage,* author Michael Hughes Clarke writes: "It is truly the case, therefore, that in Oman scientists can picnic on rocks that formed ten or more kilometres beneath the ocean bed, on volcanic lavas that flowed out on the floor of the deep sea and on sediments that originally accumulated beneath four or five kilometres of ocean water".

CLIMATE

Moderate temperatures

Oman's climate and varied physical terrain offer many opportunities for wildlife to flourish and it is not surprising that the country contains some of Arabia's richest extant habitats for a number of endangered species. Recorded temperatures within the country range from a maximum of 50°C, recorded at Sohar in 1987, to below freezing temperatures, regularly recorded at Saiq. For a measure of just how hot it can get I particularly like the following account by a fifteenth century traveller Abdur Rezak, who was sent on a mission to Oman by the Shah of Persia in 1442. Unfortunately, his schedule landed him there in May and he was bowled over by the heat:

It was so intense that it burned the marrow in the bones, the sword in its scabbard melted like wax, and the gems that adorned the handle of the dagger were reduced to coal. In the plains the chase became a matter of perfect ease, for the desert was filled with roasted gazelles.

High drama aside, for most of the year the climate in Oman is comfortable in terms of temperatures since the cooling effects of monsoon winds help to moderate conditions. When Muscat is basking in heat with July maxima of 49°C, Salalah enjoys much cooler weather caused by the south-westerly monsoon that keeps the monthly maxima down to only 30°C. By October, Muscat has cooled down to a maximum of 41°C whilst Salalah has warmed up a few degrees to a maximum of 33°C. The effect of the monsoon is completely gone during November and the temperature gap is thus closed with Salalah overtaking Muscat in the temperature tables with a maximum of 37°C as against Muscat's 35°C. This strange dichotomy, caused by the south-west monsoon and upwelling of cooler ocean waters off the Salalah coastline, creates the strange situa-

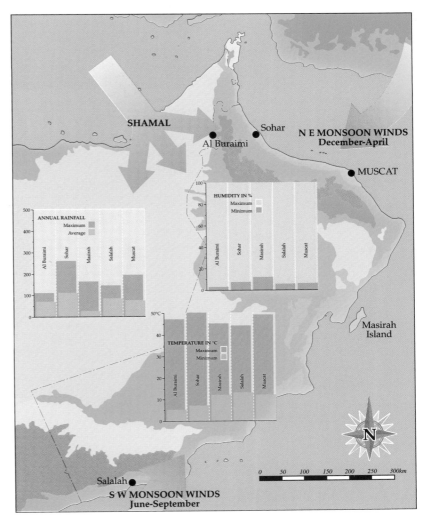

tion in which Muscat enjoys its coolest months in December and January (highs of 30°C, lows of 14°C) whilst Salalah is at its coolest from July to September when daytime highs reach the same as Muscat's winter level of 30°C. Coolest night time temperatures in Salalah do, however, occur during the winter months of December and January. The hottest place in Oman is probably Sohar where 50°C has been recorded, whilst the coolest area is near Saiq where summer highs rarely exceed 34°C and winter lows reach freezing or even below zero.

Humidity varies in most places from 100 percent to single figures, right down to one percent. As we might expect from comments made above, when Muscat's humidity is at its lowest levels with July minima of five percent, Salalah is at its most humid with maxima of 99 percent and minimum levels not falling below around 71 percent. Rainfall levels are also highly variable, depending upon one's location in Oman. The wettest place where rainfall is recorded is Saiq which averaged 299mm per year over an eight year period, whilst the driest is Masirah, averaging 27mm during the same period. Other average rainfall figures were Thumrit 60mm, Al Buraimi 68mm, Sur 72mm, Muscat 72.5mm, Salalah 83mm, Sohar 128mm, and Khasab 151mm.

Wind patterns

The wind pattern has played an important role in shaping the lives of both people and wildlife down through the ages. For thousands of years Omani sailors awaited onset of the north-east monsoon winds in December before setting sail towards India or Africa. These winds were reliable up to April when they begin to slacken. Their return trips were made on the south-west monsoon winds that affect the southerly coast of Oman and blow from June to September. It is this south-west monsoon that reverses the current pattern in the Indian Ocean and gives rise to the Somali Current. Where the strong winds blow parallel to the Salalah - Ras al Hadd coast a secondary current is established, forcing coastal surface waters offshore and replacing them with cool nutrient rich waters. Such upwellings are renowned for their productivity and are responsible for a quarter of the entire world's fish production, whilst their total area only covers 0.02 percent of the planet's sea-surface.

MARINELIFE

Coral reefs

Oman's shallow-water habitats range from tropical coral reefs to forests of a kelp weed that is normally found in the temperate waters off New Zealand. There are few places on earth where there is such a great variability of conditions, nor where there is such a profusion of sealife. Unlike the coral reefs of the Red Sea and some of the Indian Ocean islands, the marine habitats of Oman are relatively unexplored by scientific divers. Reef building corals grow best in the seas off Musandam, around the Dayma-niyat Islands, in the Muscat area and off Masira Island. They do not flourish in the sandy, less stable habitats off areas like Sur and Salalah. In the latter case they are replaced in large measure by macroalgae such as kelp and by soft corals.

A study undertaken as part of an investigation into the possible impact of the crown of thorns starfish (*Acanthaster planci*) briefly summarized the major constituents of the coral fauna in the above regions. Branching and tabular forms of *Acropora* corals predominate off Musandam where other common genera include *Pavona, Porites, Montipora, Goniopora* and *Pocillopora*. Unlike in the Red Sea where water clarity is usual-ly much better, these corals tend to be restricted to quite shallow depths, down to around 12 metres. Reef-formation is not well developed off Musandam although small fringing and patch reefs do occur. By contrast the Daymaniyat Islands have quite well developed reef structures, once more dominated by *Acropora* corals. Other common genera here include *Montipora, Pocillopora* and *Porites*. Off Muscat similar coral species occur with *Pocillopora* playing an important role in reef development off Fahal Island and in shallow waters of Muscat Bay. The west, landward facing side of Masira Island is bordered by rich coral colonies with particular emphasis on *Montipora* and *Pocillopora*. In addition *Porites, Leptoria, Acanthastrea, Platygyra, Stylophora* and *Favia* occur. Here also one encounters dense beds of the brown kelp weed, *Sargassum*. The best developed coral reefs on the west side of Masira are towards

the north where dense monospecific stands of *Montipora* form shallow reefs. Dramatic changes in seawater temperatures in this area result from current patterns and upwelling effects. Thus surface temperatures can range from 22 °C to 28 °C over a distance of only a few kilometres: a fact that has a profound bearing on distribution of marinelife.

The focus of the upwelling occurs in the Salalah area, near Marbat. Here isolated coral colonies can be found mingled with the stipes of large kelp weeds whose fronds shade the sea bed. In addition to the corals (mainly *Acropora, Favia, Favites, Turbinaria* and *Stylophora*) other common marine forms uniquely associated with these kelp beds include abalone (*Haliotis mariae*) and several sea urchin and starfish species. The kelps themselves are important as primary producers. Off California, where a somewhat similar upwelling occurs, commercial annual harvests of kelp reach 20,000 metric tons dry weight and these are used in production of alginates, agar, iodine and as a source of fertilizer. From the viewpoint of marinelife, they provide plentiful grazing for many invertebrates and fish.

Kelp forests

Oman's kelp forests are not only prolific but also unique, for they are the only place in the northern hemisphere where the southern hemisphere kelp, *Ecklonia radiata*, occurs and are also home to a recently described species, *Sargassopsis zanardinii*, peculiar to Omani waters. Like the kelp forests of south-west Africa, they are temporary features of the seascape, depending upon the seasonal upwelling of nutrient-rich colder waters for their growth and survival.

The *Ecklonia* and *Sargassopsis* communities that occur along the Marbat to Sudh coastline have been studied in some detail. They are greatly influenced by the local intensity of the upwelling current which tends to be most pronounced in those areas where deep water approaches the shoreline. It is for this reason that Ras Marbat and Sudh have much better developed kelp communities than the waters in front of Salalah where the coastal shelf extends much further offshore. Local weather conditions are also influenced by stronger coastal upwelling in the Marbat-Sudh region with cloudier weather west of Marbat.

Waves crashing against the shore-line during the south-west monsoon period create a significant splash zone where green algae such as *Ulva* coat the rocks. As the monsoon abates more stable conditions come into play and the intertidal is colonized by a range of algal species. These are grazed by limpets (*Cellana encosmia, C. karachiensis, Scutellastra exusta, Patelloida profunda* and *Siphonaria*), chitons (*Acanthopleura haddoni*), several neritid molluscs and sea urchins (*Echinometra mathaei*). Beneath tide-level during summer months one is immediately confronted by the brown alga (*Sargassopsis zanardinii*) or by a form of *Sargassum*. Towards the end of the monsoon period, as wave action decreases, *Ulva* and a filamentous alga (*Cladophoropsis*)

bloom and clog the *Sargassopsis*. The weakened kelp breaks off the rocks and the effect is like removing leaf cover in a deciduous forest, bringing light to plants that had been living in their shade. Algae such as *Sargassum* and *Cystoceira* thus gain a boost to their growth and compete against the remaining *Sargassopsis* which continue to die-back as sea temperatures rise and the seasonal upwelling effect disappears. *Ecklonia radiata* has an interesting life-cycle in Oman, differing from that which it undergoes in New Zealand where it is a perennial. In Oman it behaves like an anuual plant and apparently phases its reproductive cycle to be in harmony with the monsoon season. Although it completely disappears from sight underwater following the monsoon, its gametes lie dormant on the sea bed, ready for fertilization and subsequent development to take place again when the cooler waters return the following year. In this way the *Ecklonia* community reappears, flourishes and then disappears from view all in the space of the summer/autumn months.

As one would expect, there is a healthy population of invertebrates and fish associated with these productive kelp forests. In addition to grazing sea urchins (*Echinometra mathaei*), the abalone (*Haliotis mariae*) is present in sufficient numbers to attract a small fishery. At night crayfish (*Palinurus homarus*) emerge to feed on the urchins. The main fish grazers are rabbitfish (*Siganus oramin*), Arabian pinfish (*Diplodus noct*) and the yellow-fin bream (*Rhabdosargus sarba*), with the latter two species timing their reproduction so that their young can find shelter among the reproductive spikes of *Sargassopsis*. Another major grazer of the algae is the green turtle (*Chelonia mydas*) and it seems likely that the kelp is a major source of food for these turtles in the area during the summer months.

Sea shells

Readers interested in Oman's molluscan fauna should know that a National Shell Collection has been established at Oman Natural History Museum. The collection contains over 6000 specimens of at least 500 different species of marine, freshwater and land shells. It was established with generous donations from a number of sources, in particular Dr and Mrs Bosch. Mrs Katherine Smythe, specialist in marine shells of the Gulf and Eastern Arabia, devoted over ten years to the identification of Oman's shells and establishment of the present collection. Other 'Friends of the Museum' presently assist the Omani staff in maintaining and updating the collection. Collections made in Oman for scientific purposes have been forwarded to scientists at the British Museum and subsequently returned as identified specimens. The project has led to the discovery of several new species in Oman, including *Trochita dhofarensis*, named after the area in which it was first found.

Fish

The sea is undoubtedly one of Oman's major natural resources. It has sustained people living along the coast of Oman ever since the country was first settled. The total length of the shoreline is around 1800 kilometres and the territorial waters cover at least 300,000 square kilometres. The major commercial resources may be divided into a few main categories: i.e. small pelagics dominated in shallow-water by the Indian oil-sardine (*Sardinella longiceps*), the gold-striped sardine (*Sardinella gibbosa*), and *Coilia dussumieri*, and in deeper waters by two scad species, the Indian scad (*Decapterus russelli*), and the Arabian scad (*Trachurus indicus*); large pelagics including tuna, sailfish, and marlin; mesopelagic fish in the form of lantern fish; demersal stocks with at least 156 potentially commercial species, including rays, sharks, jacks, trevallies, scads, pompano, sweetlips, grunters, seabreams, snappers, groupers, croakers and emperors, together with the molluscan forms of squid, cuttlefish and abalone; and finally crustaceans in the form of shrimp and lobster. Expansion of fishing during the 1980's appears to have caused a sharp decline in the 1989 landings and this has been followed by efforts to establish an effective management plan.

The shallow-water marine environment along the Omani coast can be very roughly divided into two major categories, i.e. sites to the north of Ras al Hadd and those south of the prominent headland which also marks the most easterly point of the entire Arabian peninsula. To the north, coral reef associated fish are predominant at snorkel or SCUBA diving depths, whilst to the south the faunal balance shifts in favour of algal grazing or weed associated species. At the boundary, in the region of Ras al Hadd itself, there is a fascinating mixture of the two assemblages with corals, kelp and a wide variety of fish species intermingling. It is an unusual marine habitat in which new species have recently been discovered and where further new finds are likely to be made as it is more thoroughly investigated. The division at Ras al Hadd is by no means a total one however, for corals also grow quite extensively, as we have mentioned above, on the west side of Masirah. A sheltered bay on the west side of the southward facing promontory of Bar al-Hikman (the wild and remote peninsula that forms the mainland side of Masirah Channel), known as Hashish Bay (Ghubbat Hashish), was the site for discovery of a new species of butter-

Right: Gill-raker mackerel.

Far right: Carangids hunt smaller fish such as sardines along the Omani coastline.

YVES GELLIE, MINISTRY OF INFORMATION, OMAN.

flyfish, dark on the flanks with a broad vertical white stripe behind the eye and a white snout. Named *Chaetodon dialeucos*, it appears to be endemic to Oman. Described for science by Rodney Salm, who authored a major study on coastal planning in Oman, and Jonathon Mee, who helped to establish the Oman Marine Aquarium, its common name is, appropriately enough, the Oman butterflyfish.

The effect of upwelling currents along the Omani coast, generated by the south-west monsoon, are not entirely to the benefit of all species. We have seen already how the colder water associated with the upwelling promotes cooler water species and makes life difficult for tropical forms. The deeper waters that flow to the surface are rich in nutrients but low in oxygen and this also poses a problem for some species, although surface oxygen levels are actively replenished by turbulent mixing due to powerful wave action in the summer months. When the wind dies down however, after the monsoon, the sea is still laden with biomass from dying kelp and other organisms that

flourished in the monsoon. The biological oxygen demand sometimes increases to the point where so much oxygen is stripped from the shallow-water that fish cannot breathe sufficient oxygen through their gills. At such times massive fish-kills, brought about by these natural events, may result.

The unique natural conditions that influence Oman's coastal provinces have, not

Sardines are caught in vast numbers by beach seines.

Sardines are usually loaded onto pick-up trucks after they have been netted in shallow water.

The surgeonfish, Acanthurus sohal, was once thought to be a Red Sea endemic, but its distribution extends along the southern Arabian coast and into the Gulf.

Sharks are plentiful in Oman, where they are commercially fished. This shows a typical harbour scene at Marbat.

underway to record all of Oman's coastal fish and this is turning up further new, and presumably endemic, species. Conditions for fish-watching in Oman, whether by snorkel or SCUBA diving, vary according to the seasons with underwater visibility often falling far below that of the world's major coral reef diving areas. There are, however, certain periods when local conditions combine with the rich and exotic marine fauna to make undersea exploration a most rewarding pursuit. In the Muscat region the most promising months, when warm clear waters are the norm rather than the exception, are May and June. In the south, around Salalah, the best period for exploring the kelp forests is soon after the monsoon winds have abated in September.

surprisingly, fostered the development of specially adapted species that occur here and nowhere else. The Oman butterflyfish mentioned above is one such endemic, but there are others such as the pearlspotted goatfish (*Parupeneus margaritatus*) and the yellow-fin chromis (*Chromis xanthopterygia*). At the time of writing a major survey is

One option for those who do not have the opportunity to snorkel or SCUBA dive is to visit the Oman National Marine Aquarium. This fine institution, managed by the Ministry of Agriculture and Fisheries, provides a wonderful window into the richness of Oman's marine life. It also offers both scientists and the general public the chance to study fish and invertebrate behaviour under controlled conditions. Behind the scenes, the Fisheries Department staff are able to undertake applied research into Omani marinelife, utilizing the water filtration and tank holding facilities of the National Aquarium.

Turtles

Oman's marinelife includes many other treasures: apart from kelp beds, coral reefs and fish life, it is also home to five species of turtles. Anyone who has been fortunate enough to have spent a night at Ra's al Junayz, just south of Ra's al Hadd, will know how exciting it is to watch massive green turtles *(Chelonia mydas)* appearing out of the moonlit surf in order to clamber up the beach and bury their eggs. It is a sight that can be seen, most surprisingly, on almost any night of the year with up to 13,000 females laying their eggs on the beaches south of Ra's al Hadd. At least 20,000 green turtles nest along the Oman coastline each year, making it one of the most important sites in the world for preservation of the species. Loggerhead turtles *(Caretta caretta)* are even more numerous with 30,000 nesting on Masirah Island every summer (June to August) and many also nesting on the Halaniyat islands and along remote stretches of the Dhofar coastline. The hawksbill turtle *(Eretmochelys imbricata)*, usually associated with coral reefs, is less abundant, although the 300 or so nestings every year along a small section of beach on the Daymaniyat islands are highly significant in terms of the world population of this threatened species. It is an argument that has been used to justify closure of the Daymaniyat islands to visitors during the summer breeding season. The olive ridley *(Lepidochelys olivacea)* is rarer still, with only around 100 females nesting each year on Masirah and a few more choosing beaches along the Dhofar coastline. Finally, the leatherback turtle *(Dermochelys coriacea)* does not nest at all in Oman but may be seen feeding on jellyfish offshore.

The life cycle of turtles has remained something of a mystery right up to the present time. Whilst we know, for example, that female adult green turtles, 30 or more

years in age, return to beaches where they originally hatched out in order to lay their eggs, we have very little idea about what happens to them from their time of hatching to adulthood. There are very few sightings or records of young green turtles, although there are reports that shrimp trawler fishermen in the Gulf, dragging their nets over sea-grass beds, are also catching (and killing) juvenile green turtles. It is also clear that both sexes of green turtle migrate to the nesting beaches, the females to lay their eggs and both sexes to mate. Whilst males do not face the daunting task of dragging their great weights on to dry land, and are thus not so often seen, they do hang around the nesting beaches in shallow water, waiting on females as they arrive

Turtle hatchlings fall easy prey to sea-birds, foxes, feral dogs and crabs - all of which attack before they even reach the sea where many other predators await them.

The beach at Ra's al Junayz is a popular viewing place for watching green turtles nesting and returning to the sea.

Right: Turtle tracks at Ra's al Junayz.

A green turtle climbs out of its nesting place at Ra's al Junayz.

sight, although there is mounting evidence to suggest that the initial stage of their lives is planktonic, drifting on ocean currents and eating organisms they encounter in the open sea. A year or so later the young turtles return to the shallows where they feed on sea bed life and slowly grow into adults.

from offshore, and even way-laying them in the shallows soon after they have returned, exhausted, from their egg-laying. The two sexes are easy to tell apart with males having noticeably longer tails and curved claws on the elbows of their fore-flippers. Once laid in their sandy chamber and buried under a metre or more of warm dry sand, eggs take approximately two months to hatch. Hatchlings tend to emerge *en masse*, at night rather than in daytime, and flip their way down to the sea as fast as they can. It is at this point that they are at their most vulnerable to predation by foxes, feral dogs, ghost crabs and seagulls. Once in the sea they swim straight offshore, gaining their directional clues from wave movements, and they live initially on the remains of a yolk sac. They quickly vanish from

Sea snakes

Apart from turtles, Oman has another marine reptile in the form of sea snakes. The yellow-bellied sea snake *(Pelamis platurus)* is a surface feeding species that is distinguishable by its dark, variably patterned back (deep yellow, green or grey, banded or spotted) and bright yellow underside. Like other sea snakes, although it is not normally aggressive, and its poison fangs are at the back of its jaw, it is potentially deadly. This is the sea snake most often seen in the sea off Muscat.

HANNE & JENS ERIKSEN

Marine mammals

Oman's marine mammals excite great interest among the general public. They include large numbers of dolphins living in coastal waters: i.e. bottle-nose dolphin *(Tursiops truncatus)*, common dolphin *(Delphinus delphis)*, spinner dolphin *(Stenella longirostris)*, Risso's dolphin *(Grampus griseus)* and the Indo-Pacific humpback dolphin *(Sousa chinensis)*, together with nine species of whales. These are the false killer whale *(Pseudorca crassidens)*, the killer whale *(Orcinus orca)*, sperm whale *(Physeter macrocephalus)*, dwarf sperm whale *(Kogia simus)*, Cuvier's beaked whale *(Ziphius cavirostris)*, humpback whale *(Megaptera novaeangliae)*, Bryde's whale *(Balaenoptera edeni)*, the sei whale *(Balaenoptera borealis)*, minke whale *(Balaenoptera acutorostrata)*, and possibly blue and fin whales *(Balaenoptera musculus* and *B.physalus)*. The blue whale, regarded as the largest animal ever to have lived, three thousand times times as large as the smallest cetacean and the weight of two thousand people, was last seen in Oman in 1868! It is a southern ocean, greatly endangered whale. The recent addition of a Whale Hall at the Oman Natural History Museum is evidence of the presence of a variety of these wonderful creatures and of

the public's fascination with them.

If one takes a short boat-trip into Muscat Bay, between Fahal Island and the mainland, one is more than likely to encounter schools of dolphins, be they common, spinner or bottle-nose. The sight of a hundred or more spinner dolphins leaping and rotating in mid-air as they move in a dense school, often within a few metres of the boat, is a most memorable wildlife encounter. Spinners tend to live in areas of moderate to deep water and they are a common sight in the Muscat area, often swimming parallel to the shore, where they keep pace with tuna. They frequently accompany schools of common dolphin but, whilst the common dolphin simply surge forward as they take in air at the surface, the spinner puts on a spectacular performance, frequently leaping high in the air and rotating. It is a small species, less than two metres in total length with a prominent slender beak which has given rise to its alternate name: the long-snouted dolphin. Whilst males are known to have pinkish bellies, the pronounced pink colour on the Omani forms has led to the suggestion that they may belong to a previously undescribed species.

The common dolphin is among the most frequently encountered dolphins off the shores of Muscat peninsula where, as mentioned above, it intermingles with spinners. It is a pan-tropical and warm temperate species, noticeably larger than the spinner, growing to at least 2.6 metres in length. The spotted dolphin *(Stenella attenuata)* has been occasionally reported off Oman. It is an energetic, slender bodied animal of around two metres in length with a promi-

Above and left: Spinner dolphins off Muscat.

A humpback whale breaches. Humpbacks are believed to be resident in Omani waters.

nent back fin and a white-tipped beak. The pattern of spots that give it its name tends to show considerable variation between different individuals but most have a dappled camouflage pattern of large spots. Its alternative common name, the bridled dolphin, results from body markings that some possess in the form of a band from snout to eye-patch and another to the flipper. The Indo-Pacific humpback dolphin commonly swims in small groups in shallow waters along the coast of Oman. Its short stubby fin arising from a hump on its back provides an easy distinguishing mark. The bottle-nose dolphin will be familiar to many readers as the one that they have seen in oceanaria, leaping through hoops and performing other tricks. It is quite common in Oman and is a widespread species which grows to a formidable three metres in length. Bottle-nose dolphins often ride at the bows of boats and it is also the species usually associated with befriending Man. Risso's dolphin is a pale grey, even larger species, up to four metres long, with a blunt, rounded snout and furrowed forehead with body markings in the form of criss-crossing white lines that appear to be scratches or tooth marks. Adults have a tall, curved and pointed back fin. An open water species, it is found throughout warm waters of the world, and feeds on squid.

Whale-watching has not yet become a major tourist attraction in Oman, although it seems inevitable that it will do so. If one wants to see these fascinating creatures there are many different locations and opportunities to do so. Schools of dolphins are common in the waters off Muscat and during the spring months of March and April humpback, minke and Bryde's whales can be seen within the same sea-area. Humpback whales can be sighted even from the mainland as they follow sardine schools along the coast, particularly off the Batinah. They are also reported from around Masirah Island and off the Halaniyat Islands where they are present throughout the year, mating and giving birth in winter months. During this time, off their shallow-water Dhofari breeding grounds, the evocative whale-song may be heard. Whilst killer whales are rarely reported from Oman, the false killer whale, which grows to six metres in length, is fairly common. It is an energetic predator, feeding on fish, squid and small dolphins. A dwarf sperm whale, cast up near Muscat in August 1989, is exhibited at Oman Natural History, possibly the only museum in the world where this species' reconstructed skeleton can be seen.

Whales navigate along the Oman coastline, following certain depth contours, and as they skirt Arabia's easterly headland at Ra's al Hadd, their route brings them into a relatively narrow 'whale-lane', about ten kilometres offshore. It is also reported that whales gather along the south-eastern side of Masirah Island from April to June, when they can be observed prior to the main onset of south-westerly monsoon conditions. There is still a great deal to learn about whale movements and behaviour in Omani waters, but there is sufficient evidence already to confirm the country's significance for the conservation of these important marine mammals.

Mangroves

In the introduction to this chapter the subject of mangroves was briefly addressed. A study of the Qurm mangroves, undertaken over several years by keen naturalist Kathleen Smythe, resulted in a very fine small book on molluscan fauna associated with this fascinating habitat that forms part of Sultan Qaboos Public Park and Nature Reserve. In an introduction to her book the author succinctly summarises the importance of such areas.

The Qurm mangrove has been exploited for its molluscs for over 6000 years and shell middens have been found within its boundaries, complete with fragments of fish hooks and necklaces. The most common shell used by the ancient inhabitants was the large mud-snail, *Terebralia palustris*, that is still abundant in the thick mud at the head of the mangrove. In all 81 species are described and illustrated in Kathleen Smythe's attractive book, a testament to this frequently forgotten marine habitat. Her comments are reproduced below, over a picture of sunset at the Qurm mangrove.

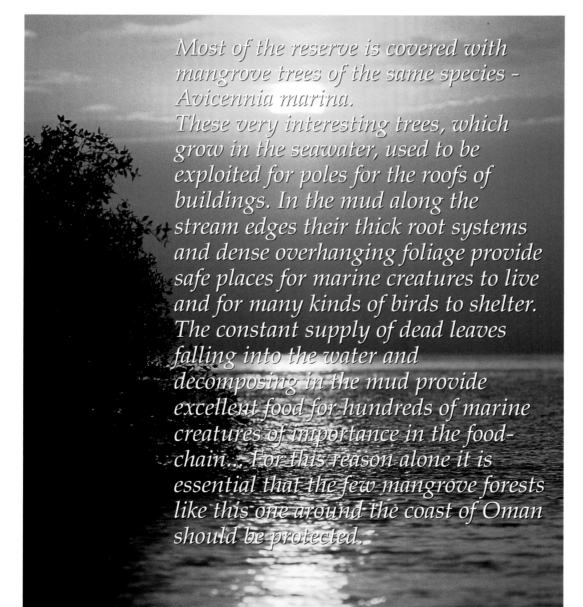

Most of the reserve is covered with mangrove trees of the same species - Avicennia marina.
These very interesting trees, which grow in the seawater, used to be exploited for poles for the roofs of buildings. In the mud along the stream edges their thick root systems and dense overhanging foliage provide safe places for marine creatures to live and for many kinds of birds to shelter. The constant supply of dead leaves falling into the water and decomposing in the mud provide excellent food for hundreds of marine creatures of importance in the food-chain... For this reason alone it is essential that the few mangrove forests like this one around the coast of Oman should be protected.

TERRESTRIAL LIFE

Survival

Oman's terrestrial life is just as varied and fascinating as its marinelif. Distribution of species is influenced by a combination of environmental factors from climate to type of substrate. Freshwater is of course vital to all forms, but some species are adapted to survive with very low intake of water. Certain desert forms, of both plants and animals, can obtain all their fresh-water needs from the morning dew. Even among the large mammals there are species that do not need to drink freshwater but which can extract sufficient moisture from the plants they eat. The Arabian oryx is one such species and it is perhaps not surprising that the last oryx observed in the wild in Arabia were on the Jiddat al-Harasis where a summer sea-mist, driven over the desert by monsoon winds, provides moisture even when there is no rainfall.

Protection of wildlife in Oman has been more successful than anywhere else on the Arabian Peninsula, thanks to the strong interest and commitment of H.M. Sultan Qaboos bin Said and the success of his policies. The account at the beginning of this chapter of a visit to Yalooni on the Jiddat al-Harasis, where Arabian oryx and gazelle roam freely, unmolested by man and protected by the Harasis rangers, gives a small personal impression of this unique wildlife habitat. Nothing can, however, really express the sheer sense of excitement and elation at seeing wild oryx, gazelle and ibex, all in significant numbers, in an unspoilt landscape that must have hardly changed since Stone Age man hunted here.

Opposite: A river flows after rain in the upper reaches of Wadi Dayqah.

The lower reaches of Wadi Halwi.

Trunk of a fossil fir tree, approximately 260 million years old, was recovered from ancient river sands in the Huqf, and now stands at the entrance of Oman Natural History Museum.

Plantlife

Standing at the entrance of Oman Natural History Museum is the trunk of a fossil fir tree, from ancient river sands in the Huqf region of Oman which have been dated to the Permian, period and it is therefore about two hundred and sixty million years old. Discovered by the PDO and brought to the capital by the SAF School of Transport, it was erected at the Museum in April 1989.

Oman's plantlife is exceptionally rich with well over a thousand recorded species. This biodiversity is promoted by the variety of habitats within the coutry's borders, including northern mountains, central plains, sandy deserts and the special conditions within Dhofar, an area that contains at least 50 endemic species. Greatest species diversity is to be found in the Dhofar mountains where, from a total listing for the entire country of 1044 species, 750 have been recorded. Least species are to be found, as one would expect, in the Rub al-Khali or Empty Quarter where less than 20 species live in the sands proper, with an additional 17 found at the edges of the desert. Regional studies have been undertaken by a number of botanists and mention

should be made of the fine work by Anthony Miller and Miranda Morrison, *The Plants of Dhofar*; a small book by James Mandaville Jr., *Wild Flowers of Northern Oman*; work carried out by the Royal Geographic Society's Wahiba Sands Project in which Cope, Laurie, Warren and Munton examined different aspects of the Wahiba's plant life; and the Oman Flora and Fauna Survey Special Reports in which Mandaville and Radcliffe-Smith have written relevant papers. In addition, Shahina Ghazanfar has produced an *Annotated Catalogue of the Vascular Plants of Oman*, and, in co-authorship with Ahmed Mohammed Ali Al-Sabahi, a paper on medicinal plants of northern and central Oman. Another paper by Shahina Ghazanfar identified a number of distinct vegetational zones and plant communities in Oman.

The latter study refers to a vegetation map of Oman produced as part of an IUCN study (J.E.Clarke, 1986). The zonal classification, based on 372 recorded plants, proposes nine major vegetational zones: i.e. northern mountain vegetation; *Acacia-Lycium-Euphorbia* scrub; a *Suaeda fruticosa* community; a *Halopeplis perfoliata* and

Cyperus conglomeratus community; an acacia community with *A.tortilis* and *A.ehrenbergiana*; a *Prosopis cineraria - Calligonum comosum* community; an *Acacia-Zygophyllum-Heliotropium* community; semi desert grassland and the southern escarpment woodland and plateau vegetation.

One tree that is of considerable importance to the desert dwelling Bedouin is *Prosopis cineraria*. It is a remarkable species that can live in what appear to be the driest of deserts, helping to stabilize blowing sand and offering vital shade for man and animals. In addition, it provides food for livestock and fuel for cooking. Its roots are exceptionally long, extending at times over 60 metres below the surface in order to reach the water-table. Its dependence upon such deep aquifer water, rather than surface rainfall, enables the tree to grow, maintain abundant foliage and produce seeds, even in periods of drought. Fears that *Prosopis* woodland in Oman is being over-exploited have led to calls for special conservation measures since the trees not only serve man but also create unique wildlife habitats and there is a considerable down-side knock-on effect when they are removed from an area of desert. The tree is now used as part of an afforestation programme in Oman. When sand dunes encroach on *Prosopis* woodland the trees keep pace with the sand accumulation by vegetative growth, both laterally and vertically. In fact, these relict woodlands are considered to be remnants of original woodlands that flourished in Oman during the last Ice Age, over 12,000 years ago. As such they do not exhibit the normal water

conservation characteristics of most desert plants but transpire freely through their leaves throughout the day, a practice that would cause most species living in these arid environments to soon dry-up. *Prosopis*, however, replenishes the lost water from the deep water-table by means of its extensive root system. The greatest danger to survival of these magnificent, if somewhat anachronistic, trees is that pumping from wells will lower the water-table to below the level of root penetration.

Plants have played an important medicinal role in the lives of Omanis for thousands of years. Herbal medicines and traditional healing methods are still regarded as having a role to play in general health care and, whilst modern medicine has removed the need for total dependence upon these natural methods, there remains a strong body of experience in, and trust of, the traditional craft of herbal healing. Studies on the subject have been written by Attib al Shaabi al Tabib (1980), Chatty (1984), Miller and Morris (1988), and Ghazanfar (1993).

Dinosaurs

Long before man ever set foot in Oman, sixty-five million years ago to be precise, dinosaurs roamed the land that now forms Oman's coastal plain. The first evidence that these giant reptiles lived here was collected by Dr Samir Hanna and Brian Clissold in November 1982, when they were climbing near Fanja. The bones that they found were the first evidence that dinosaurs ever inhabited Arabian lands. Along with the dinosaur bones they discovered bones of prehistoric turtles and crocodiles. Whilst it has not yet been possible to be certain which species of dinosaur lived in Oman, the bones found so far have been identified as belonging to the Ornithischia, perhaps members of the duck-billed hadrosaurs which were powerful runners and herbivores.

A. SPALTON

Camelus dromedarius,
*the dromedary camel,
among Dhofar
mountains.*

HANNE & JENS ERIKSEN

Terrestrial mammals

Oman's larger terrestrial wild mammals include wolf, Rüppel's sand fox, red fox, hoary fox, white-tailed mongoose, striped hyena, wild cat, sand cat, caracal, leopard, rock hyrax, common gazelle, Saudi gazelle, sand gazelle, Arabian oryx, Arabian tahr, ibex, honey badger or ratel and Indian porcupine. Sadly the lion and cheetah have gone from Arabia, whilst the leopard *Panthera pardus nimr* clings to life in its few remaining mountain strongholds on Musandam and at Jabal Samhan in Dhofar. The Arabian leopard appears to survive in Oman from hunting hyrax, hares, rodents, reptiles and birds. The caracal lynx, selected as the emblem of Oman Natural History Museum in recognition of its "fearless courage, proud bearing and its nobility as a representative of the country's rich wildlife", is known locally as *Al Wasaq* or *Ataq al Ardh* and lives in upland stony plains and higher ground where it survives by hunting rodents, birds, hares, and sometimes gazelle which are attacked at dusk. The camel has been domesticated and can no longer be regarded as a wild animal, although Oman was part of its original range. Rock hyraxes *(Procavia capensis jayakari)* are a particularly interesting member of Oman's small mammal fauna since they are the last survivors of a group of herbivorous mammals that occupied Africa and southern Eurasia 40 million years ago. The secret of the hyrax's survival, compared to the extinction of all its relatives, lies in its ability to live with no fresh drinking water and very little food. These reclusive hoof-footed ancient nocturnal mammals can be found in Oman in colonies under rock-falls at the foothills of dry mountains in the Dhofar region. As mentioned above, they are herbivores but feed on plants which in some cases are poisonous to other animals. They also supplement their meagre diet by eating insects.

Among the smaller mammals there are 14 known species of rodents in Oman and they form a particularly successful group colonizing a wide range of habitats, including deserts. Most species are nocturnal and rarely seen in daytime. The three-toed jerboa *(Jaculus jaculus)* has long hind legs that enable it to escape predators with impressive jumping skills, reminiscent of a miniature kangaroo. Its tufted feet also provide grip on loose sand. The spiny mouse *(Acomys dimidiatus)* is a desert adapted species that feeds on dried seeds. Cheesman's gerbil *(Gerbillus cheesmani)* is another desert adapted species that prefers sand-deserts where it lives in burrows,

A goat drinks at al Ansab lagoons. Unfortunately goats have been responsible for considerable habitat destruction throughout Arabia.

Donkeys near Bimmah.

a 'flying fox,' occupies high mountain caves and descends to lowland fruit orchards to feed. Oman's other bats all eat insects rather than fruit. They include the mouse-tailed bat (*Rhinopoma hardwickei*) which is found at Tawi Atair in Dhofar; the Persian leaf-nosed bat (*Triaenops persicus*), whose three-pronged nose-leaf has a sound reflecting function associated with navigation. It occurs together with the trident bat (*Asellia tridens*), in underground tunnels of the *falaj* irrigation network. Hemprich's long-eared bat (*Otonycteris hemprichi*) is a true desert species which roosts in caves or crevices on stony hills or in isolated buildings.

Other small mammals include a local sub-species of the Cape hare (*Lepus capensis*) which is quite common on stony and sandy deserts in Oman, showing a degree of variation within the species with some individuals possessing disproportionately large ears: an adaptation for dissipating heat. Those living on the sand are camouflaged by sand coloured coats and the soles of their feet are hairy, assisting with grip.

emerging only at night. Wagners gerbil (*Gerbillus dasyurus*) on the other hand lives in rocky habitats. Sundevall's jird (*Meriones crassus*) is quite a common desert rodent easily recognized by its grey-brown rat-like appearance, large eyes and tufted tail with a distinctly black tip. It prefers sandy deserts where it burrows under spiny shrubs. Insectivores include the house shrew, lesser white-toothed shrew, Somali white-toothed shrew, Ethiopian hedgehog and black hedgehog.

Oman's largest bat, the Egyptian fruit bat (*Rousettus aeyptiacus*), commonly known as

Arabian oryx

A total of 57 species of mammals live in Oman. Among these none are better adapted to desert conditions than the white or Arabian oryx whose physical, physiological and behavioural characteristics have enabled them to live in areas of Arabia where few, if any, other mammals survive. A fundamental aspect of these adaptations has to do with tolerating the very wide temperature ranges that they experience, from 50°C to almost freezing. Their coat changes with the seasons, being longer and thicker in winter when it helps to insulate against cold winds. When temperatures are low oryx stand broadside to the sun with their fur raised, thus exposing their black, heat absorbent skin. They are frequently found standing in this posture on winter mornings and afternoons. In order to avoid

192

unnecessary heat loss at night-time, they select sheltered resting places, protected from the wind, often in the lee of a sand mound or clump of bushes. Their eyes are deeply set and thus protected from the sun's glare by the shading effect of a prominent bony ridge. In addition, they possess long eye-lashes and active tear glands which help to protect their eyes from blown sand and allow them to continue feeding during sand-storms.

In hot summer temperatures oryx tend to become more active at night time, hiding from the full glare of the sun during daytime. They also have an impressive ability to survive very long periods without drinking fresh water. At such times their needs in terms of maintaining a healthy water-balance are met by moisture absorbed from feeding on green vegetation that attracts the morning dew and seasonal mists such as those that occur on the Jiddat al-Harasis. They also shed their winter coats in spring-time, as the temperature rises, becoming whiter and sleeker, enhancing their coat's heat reflectivity. The downside of this is that the oryx are highly visible in the wild, their white coats reflecting the light like beacons on a desert horizon, making them conspicuous targets for the predatory lions and cheetahs that once roamed these lands,

and, in more recent times, for Man. In addition to providing a high degree of heat reflection, their conspicuousness also helps the animals to keep together, even when ranging over several kilometres. Oryx maintain visual contact with other members of their herd during grazing, and calves that wander off are soon rounded up by the bull. This paternal protective behaviour is clearly an adaptation to reduce the dangers of predation and is not known to occur in other antelope species. At times when it is difficult to see far, such as during night-time or in sand-storms, the oryx gather closer together, often maintaining sound contact with each other by gentle 'mooing'. In the event that animals do become separated from each other, the 'lost' oryx will return to the previous feeding location, and if this does not result in it being reunited with its fellows, it will take up a prominent position such as a slight mound or piece of high ground and will thus try to see, or be seen by, the rest of the herd. In the event that this also fails to work, the 'lost' oryx then explores other areas of the herd's usual range, sometimes even tracking the foot-prints of other oryx. On long journeys oryx walk in single-file, one after the other, and they can travel great distances in search of suitable grazing.

Arabian oryx at Yalooni.

A. SPALTON

Solitary oryx at Yalooni.

Oryx reintroduction programme

A discussion of Oman's terrestrial mammals would be incomplete without a brief resume of the oryx reintroduction programme. The story will be familiar to many readers so this account restricts itself to a brief summary of the pertinent facts. It begins with the fears of conservationists that the Arabian oryx was about to disappear as one of Arabia's wild animals. By the 1960's there were probably less than 50 of these desert-adapted ungulates living in the entire Arabian peninsula and even these were under threat from hunting. An effort to establish a captive breeding herd, supported by the World Wildlife Fund and led by the Fauna Preservation Society, resulted in 1962 in the capture of two males and a female wild oryx near the border of Yemen and Oman. These were added to by a female from London Zoo that had originated in Oman; a female donated from Kuwait and four additional animals from Saudi Arabia. These nine animals, henceforth known as the 'world-herd', were eventually successfully established as a viable breeding herd at Phoenix Zoo in Arizona, USA.

While the captive breeding programme was slowly being established, with very generous assistance of the late Maurice Machris (then President of the Shikar Safari Club) the remaining wild oryx were eking out their existence. The last of these, whose presence was a jealously guarded secret of the Harasis living on the Jiddat al-Harasis, were gunned down by hunters from abroad in October 1972. For a while it seemed that Arabian oryx would never again wander freely in Arabia, but eight years after their sad demise the first animals from the captive breeding programme were returned to Oman in an ambitious attempt to reintroduce them to the wild. The unique project, forming part of a programme to assist the people living on the Jiddat al-Harasis, was the brainchild of H.M. Sultan Qaboos bin Said, and was directed, with advice from the World Wildlife Fund International's then Director General, Dr Hartmun Jungius, by Ralph Daly, Adviser for Conservation of the Environment at the Diwan of Royal Court. On January 31st 1982, the Head Ranger at the Yalooni facility that had been constructed to acclimate the reintroduced animals, opened the two heavy gates of the compound and let the first oryx run free in Arabia since their relatives had been needlessly killed ten years previously.

Since then, whilst animals have been regularly added from captive breeding efforts elsewhere, desert births gradually increased until the size of the wild population reached the one hundred mark and seemed set to keep on increasing. The dream of wild oryx once more inhabiting Arabia's expansive desert and semi-desert regions was no longer a dream but a reality. The secret of this project's unique success has been very fine management by dedicated individuals among both the Omani Harasis and the expatriate scientists and administrators and other supporting staff who have worked incredibly hard to ensure that the wild oryx herd continues to grow.

The wild oryx are protected by Harasis rangers who drive across the stony desert of the Jiddat in order to maintain visual contact with the oryx. There is no need for radio collars or satellite monitoring since the rangers have excellent tracking skills and can easily follow the herds as they freely roam across the Jiddat. Each tracking party stays away from the base camp for several days but keeps in touch with the Yalooni headquarters by radio. There are no signposts or roads but natural features of the desert plain are used to describe their whereabouts. The trackers do much more than simply report on where the herds are and can recognize many of the individual animals by physical characteristics. Each oryx is given a name and its movements are monitored. Careful observation of individual oryx allows the team to work out which is the father of a particular calf and thus a genetic picture is built-up.

Summarizing the results of the programme after ten years, field-biologist Andrew Spalton, in a paper published in the journal *Ungulates*, wrote as follows:

During the first years, 1980 to 1986, the population, comprising two very cohesive herds released in 1982 and 1984, grew at a mean annual rate of 1.22. In 1986 a three year drought was broken, supplementary feeding ceased and the two herds broke up into subgroups (Stanley Price, 1989). Later, a sterile but dominant bull was castrated and more immigrants were released in 1988 and 1989. Good rain has fallen each year since 1986. All these factors were contributory to the more rapid growth (1.39) in the wild population between 1986 and 1990.

Rain fall was very small in 1990-1991, but spring 1992 brought good rainfall and when I visited the herd towards the end of that year they were in fine condition. Each year sees the herd becoming stronger and more able to survive the inevitable set-backs that are the natural lot of such wild animals. Andrew Spalton's analytical study suggested that a wild population of 290 animals would be desirable in as soon as possible, providing the good health of the present population is not compromised. The signs are that this target will be achieved soon, but, although the oryx are back in the wild, their existence remains dependent upon our own species, both in how we respect their environment and their right to live, unharrassed by hunting and unaffected by pollution. Although Oman's government and people have shown themselves willingly committed to nature conservation, it is a sad fact that the ultimate protection of their country's wildlife depends, not just on their own conservation efforts, but on regional and global issues such as climatic change, ozone depletion and peaceful stability.

Despite the worldwide pace of change and development that has affected Oman as much as many other countries, the country retains many unspoilt areas where wildlife and man have lived for generations, and continue to live, side by side.

Nubian ibex

A visit to see the reintroduced Arabian oryx on the Jiddat al-Harasis is often accompanied by a trip towards the coast from Yalooni, to the incredible Huqf escarpment on the Jiddat's eastern flank. One such visit is briefly described at the beginning of this chapter when the author was privileged to observe around a dozen Nubian ibex within the space of an hour or so. For an animal that is firmly placed on IUCN's Red Data List, as one of the world's species most likely to face extinction, this was a particularly rewarding experience. My first encounter with this animal was in Port Sudan, where I lived for several years in the 1970's, and where the horns of *Capra ibex nubiana* were regularly offered for sale. They had come from animals hunted in the Red Sea hills on the eastern coast of Africa where their numbers seemed to be drastically low. In Oman, where they are protected from hunting, they appear to be flourishing. Agile, highly adapted mountain goats, they have narrow almost rubbery hooves enabling them to gain a grip in very rough terrain. Living in small family groups of three to five animals most of the time, they may gather in larger groups of perhaps eight to ten ibex during the rutting season, from October to December, when large males join females for mating. Ibex on the Huqf escarpment have a special liking for particular plants such as *Cadaba farinosa*, and members of the *Pluchea* genus. They are vulnerable to predation by wolves and, on Jebal Samhan in Dhofar, to leopards.

Nubian ibex (Capra ibex nubiana) *on the Huqf escarpment.*

HANNE & JENS ERIKSEN

HANNE & JENS ERIKSEN

Gazelle

The main species are the rhim gazelle *(Gazella subguttarosa marica)*, whose horns project backwards in a simple curve; and the Arabian gazelle *(Gazella gazella cora)* which possesses lyre-shaped horns. The Arabian gazelle, also known as the mountain gazelle or idmi, favours rough ground among the foothills or on stony plains. Apart from its horns it can be identified by black and white cheek markings and a distinct flank stripe, much clearer than the pallid markings of the rhim. The rhim is the larger of the two species and possesses broader feet, enabling it to run over fairly soft sand. When doing so its tail is frequently held erect. The Muscat gazelle, *Gazelle gazella muscatensis*, was the name given to a gazelle living on the coastal plain of northern Oman. In his review of Arabian gazelles, published in Wildlife Conservation and Development in Saudi Arabia,

Groves considered that this was a distinct sub-species but it may be conspecific with the mountain gazelle. The other possible species found in Oman is the Saudi gazelle, *Gazella dorcas saudiya,* which is the peninsula form of dorcas gazelle.

Legislation passed in 1976 to protect the Arabian tahr also led to protection of an endangered Arabian or mountain gazelle. Since the Wadi Sarin Reserve provided an ideal habitat for the species, a number of animals that had been found abandoned or injured, or had been kept as pets, were placed in an improvised breeding centre in the heart of the reserve at Muzra Qid. Successful breeding of these animals led, by 1987, to the release of more than 60 into the wild. Arabian gazelle from this stock can often be seen feeding alongside the foothills of the reserve, a short distance in from the coastal road.

Mountain gazelle (Gazella gazella) *at Yalooni.*

Arabian tahr

The Arabian tahr *(Hemitragus jayakari)* was first described in 1894 from two skulls of animals hunted in the Jabal al-Akhdar and bought by Lieutenant-Colonel A.S.G. Jayakar, the British medical surgeon at that time, in Muscat. Jayakar sent the skulls to Olfield Thomas in London who based his description of a new species of tahr on this evidence. Its nearest relatives, both living far to the east, were the Himalayan tahr and the Nilgiri tahr of southern India. Tahr were placed on top of the list of species requiring special protection in Oman and their special status was declared by Ministry of Diwan Affairs Ministerial decision No. 4 of 1976. The same Ministry was responsible for establishing an experimental reserve, 45 kilometres south-west of Muscat where the Wadi Sarin drains water from Jabal Aswad. A detailed study of the primitive goat-like tahr covered seven sites which were estimated to contain a total of 1293 animals. Given that this species only lives along the 600 kilometres of mountains stretching from Musandam to just south of Sur, the author of the study (Paul Munton) estimated that the total world population was around 2000 animals. He proposed that they be conserved by establishment of a traditional Islamic system of *hima* whereby the land would be laid aside as a wild habitat in which domestic livestock were not permitted to graze.

The special project established to protect this endangered species involves wildlife rangers, *mushrafin*, drawn from local people, who are responsible for keeping track of the tahr, ensuring their safety throughout the Wadi Sarin Nature Reserve. It is a task skilfully accomplished by superbly fit tribal people who were traditionally accustomed to following their own livestock in this

exceptionally rugged terrain.

Given the extremely restricted range of the tahr, the question arises as to how they came to be in Oman in the first place. Prior to the last Ice Age their ancestors ranged over a large area of Eurasia. As the ice retreated true goats were more successful in colonizing new grazing lands while *Hemitragus* (which means half-goat) only survived in a few mountainous areas. The Arabian tahr, after being described from skeletal remains in 1894, was next mentioned in written records by Wilfred Thesiger who gave an account of hunting them in 1948, in his classic account of life in southern Arabia (*Arabian Sands*) first published in 1959:

While I had been at Muwaiqih I had hunted tahr on Jabal Hafit, camping for a week under the mountain with bin Kabina and bin Ghabaisha and two of Zayid's Arabs. The Arabian tahr had never previously been seen by a European, although they had been named from two skins bought in Muscat by Dr Jayakar in 1892. They resembled goats and had very thick short horns. It was exhausting work hunting them, for the mountains rose four thousand feet above our camp, and the slopes were everywhere steep and usually sheer, without water or vegetation. The tahr fed at night round the foot of the mountain, but the only ones we saw were near the top. The Arabs shot two females and we picked up the skull of a male. We had made ourselves sandals from green hide, without which we could never have climbed these cruel limestone rocks.

The next scientific recording of the tahr still living in Arabia was made in 1973 by Michael Gallagher, whose contribution to Arabian, and particularly Omani, nature

conservation is considerable. Michael set about discovering whether the population on Jabal al-Akhdar was still viable. Local people confirmed to him that they did indeed still exist there and that they were hunted as food. A subsequent survey, however, failed to find any evidence of tahr there and it emphasizes the great difficulty in studying this secretive animal that they were missed on this occasion. In 1973 tahr were reconfirmed in the Jabal al-Aswad/Wadi Sarin area and this was therefore formed into a special tahr reserve.

Tahr live in what might be regarded as 'hostile country' from the viewpoint of any large mammal. Their territory is incredibly rough and they are adept at scaling very steep slopes over rough ground. They have a fairly catholic diet, eating most available fruit, leaves, grasses and seeds, but often displaying considerable choice with regard to which part of a particular plant they will take. They are dependent upon free water and cannot therefore be described as truly desert adapted species. This dependence has obviously been a key factor in limiting their distribution. Although the danger of being hunted by Man has been effectively removed by Oman's conservation legislation, tahr are nevertheless vulnerable to natural predators like wolf and leopard which will attack animals of any age, and eagles, raven or red fox that take young animals if the opportunity is presented.

A survey conducted in 1987 confirmed what the *mushrafin* were reporting, i.e. that the tahr seemed to be on the increase. Whilst there were reckoned to be only around 360 animals within the area of Wadi Sarin reserve in 1978, almost ten years later the population appeared to have doubled to around 700 animals, presumably as a result of hunting having ceased.

Bufo orientalis *in northern Oman.*

Amphibians

Oman has two spcies of amphibians, the toads *Bufo orientalis* and *Bufo dhofarensis.* The latter, which has a more rapid call than the oriental toad, occurs in both Dhofar and the northern mountains, whilst the former is not found in Dhofar.

Reptiles

In addition to Oman's marine reptiles in the form of turtles and sea snakes discussed above, the country is rich in terrestrial lizards, geckoes, chameleons, skinks and snakes. It also has a single amphibisnaean, *Diplometopon arudnii.* A total of 74 reptilian species are recorded from the country. The largest lizard is the grey monitor, *Varanus griseus,* which occurs on the northern plains and hunts rodents, reptiles, small birds and their eggs. (While visiting the Breeding

Centre at Seeb, I encountered one sunning itself next to the Arabian leopard breeding enclosure.) When alarmed it inflates its lungs, raises itself on its legs, hisses and lashes its whip-like tail, creating a frightening appearance. The other large lizard that one is likely to encounter is the dhub or spiny tailed lizard, *Uromastyx thomasi,* which has a yellow body colour with an orange stripe down its back and a short tail. It is more abundant than the monitor lizard and is a favourite food of the Bedouin. The spiny footed lizard, *Acanthodactylus arabicus,* lives on soft sand in northern Oman. Other quite common lizards include the yellow agama, *Agama flavimaculata,* that is often observed perched on bushes which it climbs in order to regulate body temperature, either warming up or cooling down. Males have the capacity to change their throat patch colour to blue and tail to orange. Another colour changer is *Agama sinaitica* in which males can turn their head and tail blue but females retain their brownish body colour with an orange saddle-mark. They live in boulder strewn wadis and on hill-sides. The colour changer *par excellence* is of course the chameleon, one species of which occurs in Dhofar where it lives among vegetation. It is a slow moving lizard, relying on superbly flexible camouflage, bizarre bulbous revolving eyes, and the incredibly rapid flick of its coiled tongue for protection.

Oman's land snakes, although not generally aggressive towards people, do include

Monitor lizard, Varanus griseus, *at Yalooni.*

Agama flavimaculata, *the yellow agama, can alter its body colour. It is typically found climbing in a tree.*

A. SPALTON

some that have the capacity to kill large mammals, including Man. In most cases, however, they avoid humans and would only strike in self defence if frightened. Even then the likelihood of these snakes injecting sufficient venom to cause serious conequences is relatively slim. Top of the danger list are the vipers, five species of which are found in Oman; i.e. the horned viper (*Cerastes cerastes*); the false horned viper (*Pseudocerastes persicus*) and three carpet vipers (*Echis carinatus, E. pyrimidum* and *E. coloratus.*) Of these, the carpet viper (*Echis carinatus*) is the species most likely to be encountered in Oman. It generally hides during daytime, in leaf-litter, rodent burrows or under stones, but is active at night time when it hunts toads, rodents or other reptiles such as *Stenodactylus* lizards. The horned viper is found in sandy ground and is another nocturnal hunter, feeding on small birds, rodents and lizards. It is a potential hazard when walking in sandy areas at night. The false horned viper is a relict species whose distribution in Oman is now restricted to the northern mountains. Two other dangerous species occur in Dhofar, i.e. the puff adder (*Bitis arietans*) and the burrowing asp or mole viper (*Atractaspis microlepidota*). The largest venomous snake in Oman is the Arabian cobra (*Naja haje arabica*) which lives in Dhofar's coastal mountains and wadis. It is often found associated with water, and preys on toads, small birds and mammals.

Oman's less toxic or harmless snakes include the hooded malpolon (*Malpolon moilensis*) which is found in scrub desert; the sand or tree snake (*Psammophis schokari*) that is usually found in cultivated areas where it feeds during daytime and the cat snake (*Telescopus dhara*) which is a nocturnal species usually found among the hills where it hunts for rodents, birds and bats. In addition, there are a number of completly harmless species that lack fangs or

venom. These include the thread snake (*Leptotyphlops macrorhynchus*); blind snake (*Rhamphotyphlops braminus*); Jayakar's sand boa (*Eryx jayakar*); the racer (*Coluber rhodorachis*); Thomas' snake (*Coluber thomasi*); the awl-headed snake (*Lytorhynchus diadema*) and finally the diadem snake (*Spalerosophis diadema*). Before leaving the list of snake species we should also mention a reptile that is neither snake nor lizard and is more reminiscent of a worm: *Diplometopon zarudnyi*, an amphisbaenid, commonly known as a worm-lizard, burrows in the sand where it hunts insects.

The hooded malpolon (Malpolon moilensis), *seen here on the Jiddat al-Harasis, is one of Oman's less toxic snakes.*

A. SPALTON

Insects

Seventy species of butterflies and approximately 300 moths are known to occur in Oman. As with other forms of wildlife, Oman's butterflies are dependent upon food sources and habitat preservation. This is particularly the case with these forms since the caterpillar stage tends to have quite specific plant preferences. A delightful book on the subject of Oman's butterflies, written by specialists Torben and Kiki Larsen, published for the Office of the Adviser for Conservation of the Environment, illustrates and provides notes on 72 species of butterfly known to occur in the country. They include many beautiful forms such as the swallowtails (*Papilio machaon, P. demoleus and P. demodocus*). The swallowtail (*P. machaon*) will be familiar to many readers since it has an incredibly wide distribution, being found from the USA to Asia with different colonies isolated from each other. It may be seen around Muscat and at several northern oases such as those near Rostaq where it seems to favour cultivated fennel. Distribution of swallowtails in Oman is very interesting since the two other species have

Oleander hawk moth.

HANNE & JENS ERIKSEN

either Asian or African affiliations and their ranges do not overlap. *P. demoleus*, found in eastern Arabia, Iran and most of Asia occurs in Musandam but not in the the southern province of Dhofar where, as one would expect the African affiliated species, *P. demodocus* replaces it. Both feed on cultivated citrus fruits but have never been recorded together in the same place. The swallowtail, *P. machaon*, does not occur in Dhofar but it may be seen overlapping with *P. demoleus* in northern Oman. These and other members of Oman's butterfly fauna have been used as indicators of Oman's zoogeographic affiliations, bridging Africa and Asia. A study on this subject by Torben Larsen ('The butterflies of eastern Oman and their zoogeographic composition', published in *The Scientific Results of the Oman Flora and Fauna Study*, 1975) classifies butterfly genera found in eastern Oman into a number of zoogeographic affinities with three Ethiopian; 16 Ethiopian and Oriental; six Palaearctic; three Eremic and none that are purely Oriental. A paper by the same author, dealing with zoogeographic affiliations of the butterflies of Dhofar was published in the *Journal of Oman Studies* (Special Report No.2, 1980, 153-86); and on those of Musandam in the same journal (*JOS* No.7, 1985). In the latter work Larsen comments on the effects of a tropical storm that brought large numbers of Indian butterflies to Oman; a good example of how these insects are distributed.

An insect that plays an important social role in Oman is the honey bee. In northern Oman, particularly on the Batinah where bees frequently nest in date palms, their nests are removed to more convenient sites and honey is harvested from the wild colonies. The specialist bee keepers of northern Oman have developed great skill in obtaining honey and propagating bee colonies in a sustainable

Bee keeping at Wadi Bani Auf.

manner. The larger honey bee was traditionally kept in hollowed trunks of date palms locally known as *tubl*. When beekeepers require honey they cut from the back of the *tubl*. Modern methods of beekeeping have now been introduced into Oman and honey production efficiency has been greatly improved.

An insect provided the justification for the great desert journeys of Wilfred Thesiger, whose crossings of the Empty Quarter as a field researcher for the Locust Research Centre are recounted in his classic book: *Arabian Sands*. The desert locust (*Schistocerca gregaria*) can form very large swarms on occasions in northern Oman. Although Thesiger acknowledged that from his viewpoint the locust work was an excuse for an exciting journey, he did also investigate locusts in the desert. On his first expedition he had brought back the information the centre had required, disproving

a hypothesis formulated by Dr Uvarov of the Desert Locust Research Centre who "had thought that the river beds which drained the western slopes of the 10,000 foot Jabal al-Akhdar might carry down sufficient water to the sands to produce permanent vegetation there, and that in consequence the mouths of the great wadis might be the outbreak centres for the desert locusts. I had found out that floods were rare in the lower reaches of the wadis, and that where they occurred they dispersed in the sterile salt flats of Umm al Samim, where nothing grows".

The most complete study of Oman's insects to date took place as part of the Wahiba Sands project. Concern was expressed in the reports of the project that insect fauna of Oman, and of the Wahiba in particular, should not be destroyed by unsupervised insecticide spraying or habitat destruction.

HANNE & JENS ERIKSEN

Birds

Oman's birdlife has been wonderfully portrayed by Michael Gallagher and Martin
Woodcock in *The Birds of Oman*. This work
records the presence of at least 96 species of
breeding birds, three-quarters of which are
residents. Recent reports have upped the
list of breeding species to 104, 77 of which
are residents and 27 are migrants. The main
breeding season for most species coincides
with northern spring and summer months,
but ospreys breed in winter while Socotra
cormorants breed in autumn so that their
young fledge during cooler winter weather.
One of the most interesting aspects of
Oman's avifauna relates to migration,
whether locally between lowland plains
and cooler mountains, or between different
geographic zones. Oman is privileged to be
the resting, feeding or breeding place for a
large number of migratory birds. The best
period to observe birds such as ducks and
waders migrating through Oman is the

autumn when numbers are boosted by
addition of many young birds from summer breeding, and the birds tend to be in
less of a hurry to move on compared to
their spring flights to breeding grounds. For
the smaller passerines, spring tends to be a
better viewing period. One of the spectacular migrations through Oman is the autumn
flight southwards of white storks which
have journeyed all the way from eastern
Europe. During the author's visit to Yalooni
on the Jiddat al-Harasis in December 1992,
a pair of stork that had landed next to the
base rested there for a few days before once
more taking to the skies. They generally
keep their height however, overpassing
southern Arabia *en route* to wintering sites
in East Africa. Their spring migration does
not bring them back over Oman.

A typical annual bird-watching diary for
Oman, based on that given by Gallagher
and Woodcock, is reproduced below.

Bird Watcher's
DIARY
Oman

Data derived from
Gallagher & Woodcock's Birds of Oman
with photographs by
Hanne & Jens Eriksen

JANUARY

Indian Roller

Winter visitors and passage migrants on the move, including ducks, short-toed eagle, imperial eagle, various waders, great black-backed gull, sand martin, orphean warbler and thrushes. Some Socotra cormorants arrive at Musandam from Gulf. Nesting of the following species commences: kestrel, grey francolin, palm dove, pallid swift, Indian roller, graceful warbler, purple sunbird, and great grey shrike.

FEBRUARY

Increase in northerly passage and departure of late ducks and waders. More nesting activity commences, including Egyptian vulture, long-legged buzzard, Bonnelli's eagle, moorhen, collared dove, little owl, several lark, pale crag martin, yellow-vented bulbul, Hume's wheatear, brown-necked raven, Tristram's grackle, house sparrow, Indian silverbill, and cinnamon-breasted rock bunting.

Long-legged Buzzard

MARCH

Passage migration continues.
Blue-cheeked bee-eater arrives.
The following species nest: masked
booby, little green heron, little ringed
plover, kentish plover, red-wattled
lapwing, rock dove, woodpigeon,
several owls and larks, scrub warbler,
Arabian babbler, house crow,
Ruppell's weaver.

Blue-cheeked Bee-eater

APRIL

This is the month for the main northerly migration
of many species such as red-necked phalarope, gulls,
terns, cuckoos, bee-eaters, swallows and many
passerine night migrants. In contrast there is southerly
movement of the Persian shearwater. The following
birds arrive during April: pale-footed shearwater,
Wilson's storm petrel, sooty falcon, and restricted to
Dhofar: yellow-bellied green pigeon and grey headed
kingfisher. Nesting by the following species
commences: little grebe, yellow-throated sparrow,
western reef heron, blackstart, crab plover (on
Masira), sooty gull, turtle dove and singing bush lark.

MAY

European Roller

End of the northerly passage with nightjars, rollers and rufous bush robin still on the move. Last winter visitors also depart, including kingfisher. Didric cuckoo arrives in Dhofar and nesting by the following begins: terns, bee-eaters, and, restricted to Dhofar, grey-headed kingfisher and black-headed bush shrike.

JUNE

South-west monsoon begins in Dhofar. Generally a quiet month with some migrant stragglers and the   continuation of nesting activity by breeding birds.

JULY

Shearwaters, petrels and Wilson's storm-petrel concentrate off Dhofar. Dispersal of the following after breeding: red-wattled lapwing, blue-cheeked bee-eater, sooty gulls. Arrival of early passage migrants and winter visitors including herons, greater flamingo, Egyptian vulture, waders, herring gull, whiskered tern. Socotra cormorant commences nesting in Dhofar, as do terns, sooty falcon and common noddy along coast-line.

Egyptian Vulture

AUGUST

Red-throated Pipit

This is peak month for southerly migration with major movements of waders, phalaropes, terns, pipits, wagtails. Following their breeding, crab plover and collared dove disperse. Pale-footed shearwater begins to disperse. First arrivals include white-stork, houbara and kingfisher. Ospreys return to nest sites while sooty falcons have first chicks.

SEPTEMBER

Green-winged Teal

End of the south-west monsoon.
Peak southerly migration continues,
including herons, ruff, nightjars, and
passerine night migrants.
Shearwaters disperse and early winter
visitors arrive, including great white
egret, various ducks, black-headed gull,
white wagtail, bluethroat, red-tailed
wheatear.

OCTOBER

Continuation of southerly passage, including lesser
kestrel, blue-cheeked bee-eater, desert wheatear.
More winter visitors arrive, including great cormorant,
ducks, sparrowhawk,
eagles, coot,
pheasant-tailed jacana,
black redstart and
starling. Socotra cormorant
and didric cuckoo disperse
in Dhofar.
Persian shearwater
migrates northwards.

Lesser Kestrel

NOVEMBER

The north-east monsoon begins to blow. Some late migrants may be seen such as short-eared owl. More winter visitors arrive, especially ducks and eagles. Peak numbers of Egyptian vultures observed. Dispersal of sooty falcon; grey-headed kingfisher in Dhofar and nesting by Verreaux's eagle, also in Dhofar.

Steppe Eagle

DECEMBER

Arrival of winter thrushes and occasional vagrants such as the common crane. Winter nesting by osprey and fan-tailed raven (in Dhofar).

Traditions remain strong in Oman where people are proud of their unique heritage. Here, Omani men welcome the Royal yacht, "Fulkassalamah", at Mina Qaboos on the occasion of the country's twentieth National Day.

TRADITIONS

TRADITIONAL WEAVING

Oman is a land of many differing geographical regions: mountain ranges with deep wadis, sandy deserts, green oases and 1700 kilometres of coastline. These widely varying regions have a direct bearing on the lifestyle of the people. In turn the people's lifestyles determine the crafts that they make. Although Oman is the second largest country in Arabia, its population at the census count of 1993 numbers only one and a half million. This too is an important factor when studying traditional crafts. The high birthrate of the present day now means that half of the Sultanate's population is under fifteen years old. Many of these youngsters will not have a working knowledge of the artisans' skills.

To understand why special weavings are made in particular areas it is necessary to look at the traditional structure of society. Classification of the population on a traditional basis will serve as a useful guide, but in many cases it no longer applies to modern Oman. With the change of leadership in 1970, economic conditions and social awareness have taken a dramatic leap forward.

Oman's population can be classified as urban, rural or pastoral. Townspeople and villagers, *hadher*, are settled and inhabit Muscat, the Batinah coast, the interior towns of the north and Salalah in Dhofar. The shepherds, *shawawi*, move seasonally and live either in their villages or in the hills and valleys of the mountains. They inhabit the mountainous areas such as Jabal Akhdar and the eastern Hajar range. The pastoral nomads, *bedu*, depend on rainfall for pasture and migrate with their herds in the sands or on the plains, making their encampments wherever they can find grazing; moving to their appropriate towns or villages at the date-harvesting season.

Traditionally, the settled people are cultivators, tenders of date gardens, fishermen on the coast, traders and professional craftsmen: weavers, potters, indigo dyers, jewellers, metalworkers, and *halwa* makers. Their livestock may consist of a few goats, sheep, cattle and camels. Neither the men or women spin. The male weavers, who might ply woollen yarn when necessary, work on a pit-loom full-time.

The shepherds are traditionally goat herders, tenders of gardens, collectors of firewood and honey, and carriers of goods by donkey. They are keepers of goats, some sheep, donkeys and perhaps a camel. The men and sometimes the women spin; the men weave on a ground loom but only part-time, depending on the availability of time and materials.

The *bedu* are, by tradition, herders of camels and goats and may have some sheep. The women spin on a spindle, the men on a spindle or on a stick. The women weave on a ground loom for family use, dowry and commission.

Though all these groups of people were, and still are, dependant on one another, several factors have determined major changes in their lives, such as more permanent housing, education, and transport.

To comprehend the skills of weaving the various stages of this craft must be examined, of which the livestock and the raw materials come first. Domestic goats are in evidence throughout Oman. In the Dhofar region the goats are mainly short-haired; the hair being too short to be of use. But in northern Oman the goats are long-haired and of a variety of colours, notably dark brown/black. This accounts for the fact that the traditional *bayt es-shaar*, black-haired tent is rarely seen in Oman: a few are imported and used in the south towards the Rub al-Khali. The Harasis from the Jiddat al-Harasis living at subsistence level, were without adequate shelter. However, their short-haired goats interbred with the long-haired when some households travelled north at a time of drought. These long-haired goats require more water and give

by Gigi Crocker Jones

Opposite: In the Wahiba Sands, the women make their rolags *into a* laweeyah *and spin on a spindle with the whorl at the top of the shaft.*

GIGI CROCKER JONES

Shepherds wind their rolags into a figure of eight on to a miqdaal *and support it on their left forefinger. The whorl is a pebble stone from the wadi bed and is placed at the lower end of the spindle.*

less milk. Little goat-hair is used nowadays and shorn goats are not often seen, but the hair is cut with a knife trimming down along the lie of the hair; the task done by shepherd men and usually *bedu* women. Hair is a tough, prickly fibre and is hard on the fingers to spin and weave, but the yarn makes hard-wearing ropes and cloth.

Sheep wool varies in quality, fleeces from mountainous areas being softer and less kempy than those from the plains, sands and coasts. Fleeces, mostly of dark brown but also of some soft beiges and greys, are shorn by the shepherd men and the *bedu* women. Household scissors are used for the task; the women often only able to shear two sheep a day. Abundant supplies of yarn were available in the past and some was exported to Pakistan. Camels are looked after by the men and the hair is plucked, rather than shorn, in the summer at the time of the date harvest. Goats and sheep are shorn earlier.

Cotton was grown extensively in Oman, both the white and brown variety. But, for decades, local cotton has been superseded by imports both as raw fibre in bales and skeins of yarn. Silk is imported in various sized skeins from Japan, as is metallic thread.

Hair fibres are not teased prior to spinning, but are placed in a heap with the fibres kept parallel. They are then spun from a handful, either on a stick or on a spindle. Wool, on the other hand, is teased by hand. No implements such as combs or carders are used in Oman. Handfuls of wool are pulled apart to allow unwanted particles of chaff and debris to drop down and the wool is twisted in to a roving. The rovings are wound on to various forms of distaffs, which hold the prepared wool and enable the spinner to spin with free hands. Shepherds wind their rolags into a figure of eight on a *miqdaal* supporting it on their left forefinger and spin on a spindle with the whorl (weight) at the lower end; the whorl often being a pebble from the wadi bed. The bedu make rolags into a *laweeyah*, again usually supporting it on their left forefinger. Some women near the Empty Quarter use a stick as a distaff to support their wool. The whorl is at the top of the shaft. It is usually of a rectangular shape where the *bedu* have purchased the goods in Saudi Arabia, or it may be of a round single shape as in Musandam. A hood is driven into the shaft, projecting above, and is used to suspend the yarn. The spindle is twisted by the right hand in a clockwise direction, then dropped, the fibres drawn out and the spin allowed to travel up the prepared fibres. The yarn is then unhooked and wound on to the spindle, and the process repeated. When the spindle is full the yarn is wound off into a ball. Most of the yarn is plied, which means that two strands are spun together in the opposite direction and wound into a tight ball to stabilize it.

Cotton is woven in its natural state, or dyed with indigo prior to weaving, after the cloth is woven, or even after garments are made-up. Much silk is imported already chemically dyed, though some is dyed by the weavers themselves. Of the animal fibres neither goat nor camel are dyed in dle bags are woven with an intricate pattern in the warp known as *raqum* weave. This is a 'pick-up' weave which creates striped patterns, symbols of their daily lives; the designs are traditionally passed down from mother to daughter.

Other camel trappings are made on the ground loom. The saddle pad and the U-shaped hump pad are woven either in a plain weave with decorative twining at the ends or in a pick-up weave. Girth and chest straps may be patterned too. Other trappings are woven off the loom and are made with the fingers. These include the rein, the neckband, and the loading strap.

Rugs were also woven of goat hair on ground looms. These were strong but prickly. The *bedu* women used to make long lengths of goat hair and stitch them together to form a *filli*, which protected their animals from cold winds and provided shade.

Vertical looms are used for making the robust donkey trappings of goat hair in use in rough mountainous terrain: the padded

saddle; the rump and chest straps which in some areas are beautifully decorated with tassels; girth straps and thick warm blankets. These looms are now almost obsolete.

Other miscellaneous items are made off the loom: goat hair slings for throwing stones to herd animals; shepherd's footpads of teased, layered and folded goat hair stitched firmly to form a square and worn under the ball of the foot; sandsocks, made by a looping technique, to wear in the sands to protect the feet; camel udder bags, woven between two sticks tied to a man's legs, to prevent the young from suckling; twined *kohl* bags; and, since the 1970s, vehicle trappings, especially ignition key swatches, that have been naturally and locally adapted from camel trappings.

Although the great camel caravans which once travelled throughout Arabia have disappeared with modernisation, fine trappings are still in demand from some areas of Oman, due to the encouragement of camel racing throughout the peninsula.

Bedouin of the Wahiba.

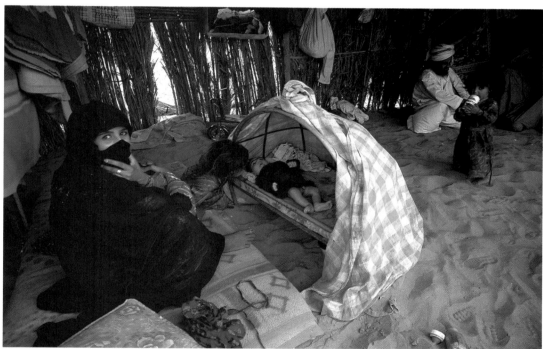

BASKETRY

by Gigi Crocker Jones

Many utilitarian objects were and still are made from the palm tree. The cultivated date palm, *Phoenix dactylifera,* has been traditionally used for many generations for numerous purposes. The same species grows in an uncultivated state in the wild, usually in coastal regions and near surface water. In the wild, it is normally sterile and appears bushy even though it may have a dominant trunk. Another wild palm *Nannorrhops ritchieana* is a large shrubby plant with distinctive fan-shaped leaves which grows in desert areas in the wadis and in sandy depressions. All the different kinds of palms, cultivated and uncultivated, are used for basketry throughout Oman.

The cultivated date palm is used by townspeople and villagers. It is also used by the *bedu* who settle outside the villages in palm frond houses in the summer at the date harvesting season. Both villagers and *bedu* may own the trees. The date palms require regular watering and though they are wind pollinated, they are mainly pollinated by hand. The tree has many uses apart from the production of dates: the trunk is used for building and especially for the beams of ceilings. It is also burnt to make charcoal, to make a local cement, *sarooj* and a white lime for painting the outside of houses. Fibre, *lif,* from the trunk has a multitude of uses from making ropes and basket handles to lining camel trappings and cleaning dishes. The ribs of the frond, *zur,* are made into fish cages, *qarkur,* bird cages or chicken coops *qafas,* clothes fumigators, *mibkhara,* or brushhandles, and it is used to reinforce and strengthen items such as the rims of food covers.

The long leaves of the cultivated palm fronds are transformed into many useful household items. Different leaves are used to make specific artefacts. In Musandam, for example, the order of preference in which these are used are: leaves from a seedling and newer leaves from the top of the tree cut when slightly yellow. These are used to make food covers, round fans *mishab* for fanning charcoal and cooling food, flag-shaped fans *marwaha* for cooling people, round cosmetic baskets *habba,* bread baskets and round mats on which to place trays of food. Other leaves, cut when green, are used to make brushes *makhama,* date sacks *khasaf,* carrying baskets of various sizes: *jebban* for picked dates, *makfa* for carrying anything in the home, *meezan* for weighing pans on a scale; mats for drying fish and dates, and prayer, sleeping and floor mats.

The fronds can be cut and gathered at any time of the year and dried in the sun for two days in the summer or three to four days in the winter. After drying they might be dyed, used in their natural colour or stored. The leaves are split whilst dry: firstly the base is snapped off, the two sides of the leaf pressed together so that the leaf peels in half lengthways, then with a bundle

This fine Kumazi braiding is made into a food cover. To make the rim firm it is reinforced with palm frond ribs.

GIGI CROCKER JONES

223

GIGI CROCKER JONES

Shamsa, from the Central Area, is making a small basket using the coiling technique. The shredded fronds for stitching are kept damp in a little airtight basket in her lap. She uses the pointed implement to make a hole through which the stitching element is passed.

of leaves in one hand the opposite thumb nail is inserted into the leaf near the base and several strands are then shredded.

In some areas, especially Dhofar, plants were used for dyeing the palm frond fibres, for example, *Aloe inermis* which gave the traditional blue-black colour. In other areas, such as Musandam, the dye plants were not indigenous, and therefore chemical dyes were used, as they are everywhere nowadays for practical reasons. The chemical dye powder is added to the dyebath and stirred, dampened fibres added and simmered for ten minutes, lifted out and placed flat on the ground in the shade to dry.

The dampened fibres are braided, usually by women, with the braider working the elements in her fingers with a bundle of fibres by her side. A new element is added on top of an already working element before that element is finished. New elements are added from the right hand side, except in the making of patterns when colours may be added from either side. Elements may be braided over one and under one, or over and under two depending on the item being made. Likewise the thickness may vary by using one or several elements on top of each other.

When the rewired length of braid is worked, it is wound and stitched in a circular movement from the centre for round items, or stitched together in vertical strips for rectangular mats. Generally women do the stitching though men stitch the date sacks. The fine stitching cord is also tradi-

tionally made from palm elements, though nowadays nylon thread is often used. The finest work using this species of palm has been undertaken in Kumzar in Musandam.

Another technique of basketry using the cultivated palm is that of coiling. The core of coiled baskets is made from the axis of the stem from which the dates have been harvested. It is finely split and bundled to form the core which is sewn in a spiral from the centre of the base. Split date palm leaves are used as the stitching material; the stitching element is wrapped around the core and stitched into the previous layer, as is each successive layer.

Many ropes, *habl*, are made for local uses from the fibre, *lif*, of the date palm trunk. A piece of fibre is pulled from the trunk, wetted and teased keeping the fibres parallel; a small piece of this is pulled out and twisted in the fingers. This is repeated until a heap of rolags are prepared. The spinner places two rolags together lying parallel and holds them with a big toe. With the rolags between his hands he twists them separately away from himself; then giving a single twist in the same direction they are rolled together. This is repeated using more rolags until the required length is reached. Various folds and twists are made to achieve the diameter required.

The wild date palm grows mostly along the coastal regions from where it was collected and used for braiding. These fronds are split, dyed and braided in much the same way as the cultivated date palm. As with all crafts the quality of the artefact varies between makers and from area to area. Although work with this palm is not considered to be as skilful as with the fan-shaped palm, there is some fine work produced in Dhofar, especially of bread baskets, water container tops, food mats and prayer mats. Braiders in this area preferred to use the leaves from the more northern date palm, but of course it was difficult to obtain. Dhofar was notable for the use of dye-plants.

The wild palm, *Nannorrhops ritchieana,* is considered to be the best quality palm material to work with. The leaves can be split into the finest fibres and the women are particularly skilled at this work.

In the Central Area *bedu* would travel by donkey or camel to the wadis below the escarpment; perhaps twice a month in the winter time, and spend the day there. Generally men would do the cutting and collecting, cutting individual fronds with a knife when a quarter to a half open; taking four or five fronds from a bush, and tying up the bundles with palm cord made whilst there. The men braided camel muzzles, camel udder bags to prevent the young from suckling, sling-shots for herding animals, and corded lizard snares (loops that tightened); often using the palm fibres whilst green. Camel and donkey panniers were braided as were mats that were placed under the acacia trees for collecting the pods for animal fodder.

The women dry the fronds in the sun for a week, but bring them inside at night to prevent the dew from wetting them and turning them black. They finely shred the fronds and use the coiling technique to make milking bowls, lidded baskets, *fatia* and *kerma,* and a woman's storage container, *duri.* The shredded fronds are kept damp in a little woven pot and pulled out as needed, the basket is built up with each coiled row stitched into the previous one with a stitching element aided by a pointed implement to make a hole through which the element is passed.

Where the wild palm was available some pastoral *bedu* braided the split leaves into long strips and stitched them together to form *simah* mats to cover the roofs of their houses; while the fishing bedu still make *simah* for the exterior walls of their *barasti* dwellings. These mats can be rolled up to

GIGI CROCKER JONES

let in the breeze or let down for warmth depending on wind and weather.

Dhofar is renowned for the quality of its milking bowls. This superior workmanship comes mainly from the mountain and desert areas to the north. The bowls are made for cows and goats milk; a wider one for camel milk. The undyed fibres are first soaked in milk to strengthen them; though for the tourist market they must be soaked in water, which is almost as lubricative, to avoid the pungent smell. The exterior of the bowls is covered with a piece of prepared, tanned and stretched goat skin and further embroidered with strips of leather. Other small baskets and containers are also decorated with leather, like in other areas. Milking bowls are now sometimes made from coconut, *Cocos nucifera,* fibre for the tourist market, though these are far less durable.

Another important fibre worthy of mention is the reed, *rasal.* There were many reed weavers on the Batinah and at Fanjah. Two weavers remaining at Fanjah make mats, *naqsh,* using the reeds in their natural colours or dyeing them a variety of colours using chemical dyes. The reeds are beaten for mats and prayer mats, *sada*; but unbeaten reeds are used for weaving the mats, *talqi,* used for carrying the dead to the grave. These can be washed; the ones made from beaten reeds cannot.

Basketry is surviving longer than most other crafts in the Sultanate. The raw material is still available and in some cases more accessible due to modern transport. Some of the artifacts have disappeared, but some are still very much in evidence and continue to perform a functional role.

Fish cages are now made of wire, though this one is of traditional materials; the ribs of the fronds from the cultivated date palm. This traditional fish cage maker is perhaps the last in Khasab.

FURTHER READING

In addition to numerous papers in the Journal of Oman Studies and other specialist publications, and more popular articles of interest in PDO News and a variety of periodicals, the following books are recommended.

Anon. (multi author) *Scientific Results of the Oman Flora and Fauna Survey 1975, Journal of Oman Studies, Special Report No. 1.* Ministry of Information and Culture.

Anon, (multi-author), *Oman Flora and Fauna Survey 1977 (Dhofar) Journal of Oman Studies, Special Report No.2.* Office of the Government Advisor for Conservation of the Environment.

Anon, 1992, *Discovering Oman,* Apex Exlorer's Guide 1. Apex.

Burstein, S.M. (translator), 1989, *Agatharchides of Cnidos: On the Erythraean Sea.* Haklyut Society, London.

Costa, P., 1991. *Musandam, Architecture and material culture of a little known region of Oman.* Immel Publishing.

Dipper, F., and T. Woodward, 1989, *The Living Seas, Marine Life of the Southern Gulf.* Motivate.

Directorate General of National Statistics. *Statistical Year Books.*

Doe, B.,1992, *Socotra: Island of Tranquillity,* Immel Publishing, .

Facey, W., *Oman: A Seafaring Nation.*

Fiennes, R., 1992, *Atlantis of the Sands: The Search for the Lost City of Ubar.* Bloomsbury.

Gallagher, M. and M. Woodcock, 1980, *The Birds of Oman,* Quartet Books.

Ghazanfar, S. *Annotated Catalogue of the Vascular Plants of Oman.*

Hawley,D., 1977 *Oman and its Renaissance.* Stacey International, UK.

Hourani, A., 1991, *A History of the Arab Peoples.* Faber and Faber.

Hughes Clarke, M., 1992, *Oman's Geological Heritage,* PDO.

Kay, S., 1992, *Seafarers of the Gulf,* Motivate.

Kay, S., 1992, *Enchanting Oman,* Motivate.

Klein, H. and R. Brickson, 1992, *Off Road in Oman,* Motivate.

Larsen, T. and K., 1980, *Butterflies of Oman,* Bartholomew.

Mandaville, J. Jr.,1978, *Wild Flowers of Northern Oman,* Bartholomew.

McKinnon, M. 1990, *Arabia: Sand, Sea, Sky.* BBC Books and Immel Publishing

Miller, A. and M. Morris, 1988, *Plants of Dhofar. The Souther Region of Oman. Traditional, Economic and Medicinal Uses.* Office of the Advisor for Conservation of the Environment, Diwan of Royal Court, Sultanate of Oman.

Miller, D.R., 1991 *Economic Development Planning in the Sultanate of Oman.* United Media Services, Sultanate of Oman.

Ministry of Information, *Oman '92, Oman '93* and other publications.

Ministry of Regional Municipalities and Environment, *National Conservation Strategy.*

Potts, D.T. , 1990. *The Arabian Gulf in Antiquity. Vols 1 and 2.* Clarendon Press, Oxford.

Risso, P., 1986, *Oman and Muscat, an early modern history,* Croom Helm.

Salm, R. and R. Baldwin, 1991, *Snorkelling and Diving in Oman,* Motivate.

Sheppard, C., A.Price and C. Roberts, 1992, *Marine Ecology of the Arabian Region: Patterns and processes in extreme tropical environments.* Academic Press.

Stevens, A., 1990, *Oman : Citadels between sand and sea.* Terra Incognita.

Sultan Al Qasimi, 1986, *The Myth of Arab Piracy in the Gulf,* Croom Helm

Thesiger, W., 1959, *Arabian Sands* (available in Penguin Travel Library series)

Vine, P.J., 1986, *Pearls in Arabian Waters, The Heritage of Bahrain.* Immel Publishing.

Vine, P.J. and M. McKinnon, 1991, *Tides of War.* Boxtree and Immel Publishing.

Vine, P.J., and P.Casey, 1992, *United Arab Emirates,* Immel Publishing.

Vine, P.J., 1992, *The Heritage of Qatar,* Immel Publishing.

ACKNOWLEDGEMENTS

First and foremost I feel that I must thank the very many people I met in Oman, during the course of my research for this book, who offered me friendship, hospitality and kindness. They made my work entirely pleasurable and helped greatly to make me feel "at home" despite my lengthy trips away from my family. Those who know Oman will understand these comments well for it would be hard to find a more delightful people than the Omanis. I could not possibly list here all the people who, in one way or another, helped on my way. More than anything, I appreciated the high esteem in which traditional values are held. The hospitality and dignity of the welcome I received from people living among the Wahiba Sands, or in the Jiddat al-Harasis, for example, has made a deep impression that I shall treasure for the rest of my life.

Turning now to the logistics and practicalities of working on such a task as this book, I must pay tribute to the trust and confidence placed in me by His Excellency Abdulla bin Mohammed Al-Thahab, previously Ambassador for the Sultanate of Oman in London and presently serving as Oman's Ambassador in Washington, with whom I first discussed this project and who encouraged me to undertake the task. Once in Oman I was warmly greeted by H.E. Abdul Aziz bin Muhammed Al Rowas, Minister of Information, who kindly offered extensive support facilities and who was consistently encouraging and interested in progress with the book over the following two years during which I carried out my research. Without this level of support I should have found it impossible to complete the work. The Minister's personal interest extended also to that of his colleagues andstaff within the Ministry of Information, all of whom were ready to help with my numerous requests. H.E. Hamad bin Mohamed bin Mohsin Al Rashdi, Undersecretary for Information Affairs, liaised closely with me during the book's production and I wish to thank him for his kindness and cooperation, as well as the high level of professionalism and attention to detail that he applied to this task. I also wish to thank Nasser Al Saybani, Abdullah bin Nasser Al Rhabi, Amin Al-Riyami, Souad Al-Harthi together with Anthony Ashworth, Consultant to H.E. the Minister of Information, for their assistance and encouragement throughout the project. In addition I wish to mention Zuhoor Hameed Al Saleh, Shekka Al Kindy, Nasr Al Wahaibi, Amour Saif Al Abri, Abdullah bin Mohamed Al Amri all of whom assisted me with my work. It is a pleasure to also acknowledge the assistance and advice of Rosemary Hector who, in addition to efficiently liaising with me from Anthony Ashworth's office, also introduced me to the Oman Historical Society. I also wish to acknowledge the cooperation of Lucy O'Flaherty within the same office. For assistance with my work in Oman's museums I should like to thank the Director of Museums, Mrs Leila bint Mohamed bin Suleiman Al Lamki; the curator of the Qurm Museum, Mrs Fatma Mohamed Mousa and the Director of the Omani French Museum Dhia Jawad Hassan Ali Al Lawati.

I also wish to thank H.E.Shaikh Amer bin Shuwain Al Hosni, Minister of Regional Municipalities and Environment for assistance with aspects of researching Oman's natural history and for access to the conference on a National Conservation Strategy. H.E. Said bin Ahmed Al-Shanfari, Minister of Petroleum and Minerals was kind enough to give his time to my work, both by granting me an interview, and by making arrangements for me to receive further practical assistance from his Ministry, and from Petroleum Development Oman (PDO). I also wish to thank H.E. Mallalah Habib for graciously granting me an interview.

The chapters on Oman's ancient and more recent history could not have been written without the research efforts of many people who have worked in this field over the years. I am particularly grateful for the access I was granted to the various museums situated in Muscat. In addition, I delved deeply into The Journal of Oman Studies and many papers contained within its pages. In this regard I should especially like to thank Dr Paolo Costa who played an important role in respect to the journal, and whose book on Musandam is such a valuable reference source. As a modern resumé of Oman's archaeological record, Dr D.T.Potts: The Arabian Gulf in Antiquity, published by Clarendon Press, was of considerable assistance, as were the papers and letters of Dr Paul Yule from the German Archaeological Mission to Oman. I am also grateful to Paul Yule for providing photographs from his own collection as well as those from Dr Gerhard Weisgerber. I should also like to mention the books by Donald Hawley (Oman & its Renaissance) and William Facey (Oman: A Seafaring Nation) as providing both inspiration and valuable information. Additional guidance was provided by Dr Jeffery Orchard from the School of Antiquity,

Birmingham University; and Dr Barri Jones from the Department of Archaeology at the University of Manchester.

Lesley Forbes, Keeper of Oriental Books from the University Library, University of Durham also provided help with reference sources. The Oman Historical Society was a most valuable meeting place and its work on preserving an interest in, and love for, Oman's history, culture and natural history is to be highly commended. The expertise within the society itself far exceeds any knowledge of my own and it was therefore with more than a little trepidation that I faced into writing this account, I must thank the Society for their interest in my work and for some very valuable assistance. I take full responsibility however for the many inadequacies that they will inevitably discover in this abbreviated version of Oman's past.

Oman's traditions are rich and varied and deserve a book in their own right. It was not possible to cover the whole field in this volume but I am deeply indebted to Gigi Crocker Jones, who is an expert on Omani weaving and basketry, for her fascinating contribution on these subjects. Readers who wish to discover more are referred to Gigi's own book, and to other specialist publications dealing with a wide range of themes, from cooking to silver work.

The natural history of Oman is also a vast subject and one that has been covered in a number of specialist publications such as The Birds of Oman by Michael Gallagher and Martin Woodcock, The Plants of Dhofar by Anthony Miller and Miranda Morris, the Oman Flora and Fauna Surveys and a number of other books, reports and specialist journals. It was partly for this reason that my account in this book draws heavily upon my own personal experiences in Oman and attempts to impart something of the flavour of Oman's fascinating wildlife, as well as some of the more important facts. I am especially grateful to Ian McLeish for taking me on some of his own trips into "the field"; both among the mountains of Salalah and the countryside of northern Oman. Ian's sharp botanical eye, and his interest in, and knowledge of, Oman's natural history, provided a great source of pleasure as well as very practical assistance. I must pay special tribute to Ralph Daly, Adviser on Conservation to the Diwan Assultani. Ralph has nurtured and guided various conservation programmes in Oman. The work of preserving Oman's wildlife is now competently handled by a dedicated and enthusiastic Omani task-force, under the leadership of His Excellency Shaikh Amer bin Shuwain Al Hosni, Minister of Regional Municipalities and Environment. I also wish to pay tribute to their efforts to ensure that Oman maintains its high standards of nature conservation. In particular, I would like to thank Ali Al Kiyumi, Director of Nature Conservation Strategy, from the Ministry of the Regional Municipalities and Environment for his special interest in my work and for his introduction to Oman's turtles. Also from the same Ministry, Dr Mehdi bin Ahmed bin Jaaffar was both helpful and encouraging. Many others helped with various aspects of my research into Oman's natural history and I should like to mention Michael Gallagher MBE; Dr Barry Jupp; Roddy Jones; Andrew Spalton; Shahina Ghazinfar, Hanne and Jens Eriksen; Rodney Salm, Robert Baldwin and the Oman Diving Centre.

Research for the chapter on Modern Oman took me along many different avenues of exploration and discovery, from flights with Oman Aviation to visits to modern petrochemical facilities. I am especially grateful to Mansour N. El-Amry, Public Affairs and Information Manager of Petroleum Development Oman, for his, and, and PDO's, assistance with information, references and photographs. There are many more people whom I should mention for their help with this book. I hope that they will forgive me if they do not find their names listed above. They should know how much I appreciated their kindness. I hope that they will feel that their efforts were worthwhile.

INDEX

Abbasid Influence, 67
Abdul Aziz ibn Said, 106
Abdur Rezak, 69, 173
acacia, 144, 189, 225
Acanthodactylus arabicus, 200
Achaemenid, 38, 46
Admiral Ruy Freire de Andrade, 78, 80
aflaj, 41-42
Agama sinaitica, 200
Agatharchides, 159-162, 226
AGCC, 139
agricultural production, 122, 156
agriculture, 42, 67, 121-122, 126, 131,
        133, 180
Ahmad ibn Said, 91-97, 99-100
Akkadian Empire, 25-26
Al Azd, 55
Al bu Said Dynasty, 91-92
Al bu Said Dynasty, founder of, 90-91
Al Hazm, 76
Al-Fath al-Mubeen, 80, 95
Al Sayyid Sultan ibn Ahmad, 98-100
Al Sultan Al Sayyid Faisal ibn Turki,
        107
Al Sultan Al Sayyid Said ibn Sultan Al
        Busaidy, 102-103
Al Sultan Al Sayyid Salim ibn
        Thuwani, 105
Al Sultan Al Sayyid Thuwani ibn Said,
        104
Al Sultan Al Sayyid Turki ibn Said,
        106
Al Sayyid Sultan ibn Ahmad, 98-101
al-Hajar, 166-169, 171-172
al-Muhabbar, 60
al-Rostaq, 59, 96
al-Tabaqat al-kubra, 65
Alarms and Excursions in Arabia, 108-
        109
Alexander the Great, 46, 48, 89
Alfonso de Albuquerque, 71, 73
Alfonso de Noronha, 71
Aliya Faisal, 107
Aloe inermis, 224
amphibians, 200
amphisbaenian, 200
anchovy, 124
ancient copper mining, 30
ancient history, 5, 11, 13, 15, 17, 19, 21,
        23, 25, 27, 29, 31, 33, 35, 37,
        39, 41, 43, 45, 47, 49, 51, 53,
        55, 57, 59, 61
Andrew Spalton, 6, 145, 195
Animal Resource Research Stations,
        123
aquaculture, 125
Arab Gulf Cooperation Council, 139
Arab League, 111, 139
Arabia Petrea, 75
Arabian Gulf in Antiquity, 15-16, 59,
        67, 226
Arabian horses, 77
Arabian oryx, 15, 144, 146-147, 150,
        164, 169, 187, 191-194, 196
Arabian Plate, 166, 171-172
Arabian tahr, 150, 164, 191, 197-199

Ardashir, 59
Artisinal fishing, 124
Asabon, 56, 58
Assurbanipal, 41
Atlantis of the Sands, 39, 226
Babylon, 27
Bahla, 25, 30, 40, 67, 78, 84, 90-91, 100
Bahrain, 15, 28-29, 35-37, 46, 90, 100-
        101, 111, 139, 144, 159, 226
Baldwin, Robert, 153
Baluchistan, 16, 24, 28, 100
Barkaa, 90, 93, 97, 100, 105
barley, 21, 27, 29, 68
Baron R. C.Keun de Hoogerwoerd, 16
basketry, 6, 222-225
baskets, 223-225
Basra, 77, 90, 96-101
Bat, 20-23, 29, 40, 192
Batinah, 17, 40, 42, 59-60, 101, 121, 184,
        202, 215, 2225
bedu, 215-216, 218-219, 223, 225
Bel'arab ibn Hamyar, 90-91, 93-94
Bir Khasfa, 15
Birba, 129
Bird-watcher's Diary, 205
birdlife, 158, 204
birds, 11, 29, 151, 157, 185, 191, 200-201,
        204-205, 207-208, 226
Birds of Oman, 204, 226
Biri Pasha, 77
black hedgehog, 192
blue whale, 183
boat-building, 36, 134
Bogle, Archibald, 100
Boswellia sacra, 47
bottle-nosed dolphin, 183-184
braid looms, 218
bridled dolphin, 184
British India Steam Navigation
        Company, 104
Bryde's whale, 183
burial structures, 21
burials, 21, 40, 55
bustard, 143
butterflies, 202, 226
butterfly fish, 151, 152, 179-180
Buweyhids, 68
Byzantine emperors, 60
Calaei islands, 56-57
Cambyses, 46
camels, 25, 28-29, 39, 66, 75,108, 123, 136,
        144-145, 147-148, 191, 215-216,
        218-219, 223, 225
camel caravans, 39, 219
cape hare, 192
captive breeding centre, 144
caracal, 147, 191
Carter, 18, 31
cattle, 20, 29, 156, 215
central area, 224-225
chameleons, 200
cheetah, 191
child health, 118
child mortality rates, 118
China, 56, 60, 68
chlorite, 25, 29

Christianity, 60
Christians, 60, 71, 75, 80, 82
chromite, 133
chromium, 133
city wall, 78
Claudius Ptolemy, 58
climate, 15, 136, 156, 167-168, 173, 187
coal, 133, 173
coffee, 97, 145, 148
commercial mining, 133
common dolphin, 183
copper cathodes, 30, 133
copper, 13, 20, 22-33, 35, 37, 57, 133, 135
coral reefs, 175, 181
corals, 151-152, 170, 175-176, 178
cotton, 19, 216-217
crayfish, 124, 151, 153, 177
Crocker Jones, Gigi, 6, 214-218, 223-225
crocodiles, 190
culture, 25, 29, 35, 39, 59, 115-116, 121, 136,
        226
cuneiform tablets, 33
Cutler, Nathaniel, 90
Cuvier's beaked whale, 153, 183
Daly, Ralph, 164, 194
Darius I, 46
date palm, 29, 223-225
date palm trunk, 224
dates, 13, 21, 38, 52, 55, 57, 98, 120, 122-
        123, 145, 148, 223-224
Daymaniyat islands, 57
desalination, 137
desert fox, 147
desert shrimp, 150
development plan, 131
development programmes, 118, 131-132
Dhofar Cattle Feed Company, 156
Dhofar, 15-16, 23, 47-48, 57, 69-70, 111,
        121, 151, 155-156, 162,167-168,
        181, 188, 191-192, 196, 200-202,
        207-211, 215, 224-226
Dilmun, 23-28, 33, 35, 37, 159
Dilmun, rise of, 35
dinosaur bones, 190
dinosaurs, 67, 190
Diplometopon arudnii, 200
diving, 56, 151, 153-154, 170, 178, 180, 226
doctors, 119
dolphin, 17, 153, 183-184
drinking water, 122, 191
dwarf sperm whale, 209, 211-212
dwarf spinner, 153
dye plant, 217
dyeing, 224-225
earliest settlers, 11
early Christians, 60
East Africa, 67, 95, 100, 102, 204
East India Company, 96, 98-100
Ecklonia, 176-177
economy, 115, 122, 125, 131-132, 134
education, 89, 115-118, 120-121, 128, 135,
        146, 215
Egypt, 23-24, 29, 39, 41, 46, 49, 51, 53, 56,
        87, 99
Egyptian fruit bat, 192
Elf, 127, 129

emmer, 21
Empty Quarter, 39, 126, 129, 169-170, 188, 203, 216,
environmental issues, 137
erosional features, 168
Ethiopian hedgehog, 192
Ethiopian kingdom of Axum, 60
Eudaemon Arabia, 51
Fahal, 77, 151, 153, 170, 175, 183
Fahud, 111, 126, 128
Falaj, 40-43, 45, 122, 192
false horned viper, 201
false killer whale, 153, 183-184
Fauna Preservation Society, 194
female education, 116
Fiennes, Sir Ranulph, 39
fin whales, 183
fish, 11, 13, 16-19, 21, 27, 124-124, 151, 153, 157-158, 160-163, 174, 176-181, 184-185, 223, 225
fishermen, 12-13, 15-20, 23, 29, 124-125, 151, 153, 157-158, 161, 181, 215
fishing methods, 18, 124
fishing settlements, 17
Five Year Plan, 132-133
flying fox, 192
food sector, 122
fossil fir tree, 188
fossil reefs, 170
fox, 147, 191-192, 199
frankincense, 13, 39, 41, 46-53, 55, 57, 77, 122, 155-156
frankincense tree, 47-49
French, 15, 31-32, 96-100, 102, 107, 127, 161
Frere, Sir Bartle, 106
fresh water, 83, 137, 193
funerary ware, 29, 36
Futuh al-Buldan, 66
Gaifar, 65-67
Gallagher, Michael, 199, 204
gas, 126-134, 170
Gazelle gazella muscatensis, 197
gazelle, 11, 13, 17-18, 29, 143-144, 147, 187, 191, 197
GDP, 132, 134
geckoes, 200
geological record, 170
geological regions, 168
gerbil, 191-192
Gilgamesh, 159
goats, 20, 123, 145-146, 192, 196, 199, 215-216, 225
gold, 26, 47, 50, 57, 67-68, 74, 133
government subsidies, 124
graves, 16-18, 21-22, 25, 28-29, 36, 40, 55, 60-61
Greek, 38-39, 46-50, 53, 77
Greek Interest in Oman, 46
green turtles, 18, 57, 163, 181-182
grey monitor, 200
Griffith, Julius, 98
gross domestic product, 120, 132, 135
ground loom, 215, 217-219
Guti, 26-27

Guti Upheaval, 26-27
H.E. Said bin Ahmed Al-Shanfari, 127
H.M. Sultan Qaboos bin Said, 114-115, 139, 187, 194
Habarut, 15
Hafit graves, 21-22
Haima, 145-146, 167, 171
Halaaniyaat, 57
Halaniyyah, 70
Hamad ibn Jahafi, 107
Hamad ibn Thuwaini, 107
hammerhead shark, 153
Harasis, 15, 143-148, 150, 187, 194-195, 215
hawksbill turtle, 181
Hawley, Donald, 103, 190
H.E. Abdul Aziz bin Muhammed Al Rowas, 227
health care, 118, 121, 205
health, 22, 116, 118-121, 128, 137, 190, 195
heat, 69, 161-162, 173, 192-193
H.E. Hamad bin Mohamed bin Mohsin Al Rashdi, 227
Hemitragus jayakari, 198
Hemprich's long-eared bat, 192
herbal healing, 190
herbal medicines, 190
Hili, 21-22
historic forts, 136
Holy Koran, 39, 55
honey badger, 191
honey bee, 202-203
Hormuz, 68-69, 73, 75, 78-79, 100-101
horned viper, 201
hospitals, 111, 118-120
houbara, 143, 209
Hudhaifah ibn Mihsan al-Makhzumi, 67
Humaid ibn Muhammad ibn Razik, 30, 80, 87, 95
humidity, 174
humpback whale, 183-184
Huqf, 12, 148-149, 167-168, 171, 188, 196
Ibadi religion, 67
ibex, 12, 29, 143, 147-150, 164, 187, 191, 196
Ibn Batuta, 70
Ibn Habib, 60
Ibrahim ibn Qais, 106
Ibri, 21, 36, 40, 57
Ice Age, 170, 189, 199
Ichthyophagi, 15
Ikrimah ibn Abi Jahl, 67
Imam Ahmad ibn Said Al Busaidy, 92, 99
Imam Azzan ibn Qais, 105
Imam Bil'arub ibn Sultan, 89
Imam Ghalib ibn Ali, 110
Imam Muhanna ibn Sultan, 90
Imam Nasir ibn Murshid, 80
Imam Said ibn Ahmad, 97
Imam Saif ibn Sultan, 75, 89-93
Imam Salim ibn Rashid al Kharusi, 108
Imam Sultan ibn Murshid, 90, 92
Imam Sultan ibn Saif, 80, 83, 87, 89-90
Imam Ya'rub ibn Bil'arub, 90

Indian porcupine, 191
indigo dyers, 215
Indo-Pacific humpback dolphin, 183-184
Indus Valley, 25, 29, 46
industrial estates, 134
industries, 121, 128, 134
infrastructure, 120, 132, 134, 136
Intercontinental Hotel, 16, 157
international relations, 138-139
Iran, 24, 26, 28, 59, 139, 166, 202
Irem, 39
Iron Age, 35, 39-40, 55
iron, 35, 39-40, 49, 55, 68, 76, 81, 133
irrigation, 41-42, 45, 123, 156, 192
Islam, 59-60, 65-67
Islamic Era, 5, 65-111
Islamic preparatory institutes, 116
IUCN, 188, 196
Jabal Hafit, 21, 199
Jalali, 76
Jamdat Nasr, 22, 24
Japex, 127, 129
jerboa, 191
Jericho, 24
Jiddat al-Harasis Development Project Part B, 145
Jiddat al-Harasis, 143-148, 168-169, 187, 193-196, 201, 204, 215
Jones, Roddy, 148, 227
Julanda, 59-60, 65-66
Jungius, Hartmun, 194
Kelb Ali Khan, 91-92
kelp forests, 176-177, 180
key swatches, 219
Khalaf ibn Mubarak, 90
Khalfan, 100
Khamis ibn Salim, 93-94
Khasab, 58, 79-80, 108, 174, 225
Khashf al-Gumma, 59, 66
Khor Jeramah, 58, 71
Khusraw Anosirwan, 59
killer whale, 153, 183-184
King Mannium, 26
King Suleiman, 41
kingfish, 124
kingfishers, 157
Kish, 25
Kuria Muria islands, 57, 70, 103
Laqit ibn Malik Dhu at-Tag, 67
Late fourth and third millennia, 15, 17
Late Wadi Suq Period, 38
Latif Khan, 90
leatherback turtle, 181
Lekhwair field, 126, 129
Lekhwair, 126, 129-130, 170
Lekhwair Waterflood Development, 129
leopard, 191, 199-200
lion, 57, 191
livestock, 189, 198, 215
Liwa, 39
lizards, 200-201
Lizq, 39-40, 43
Lizq period, 39-40
loggerhead turtles, 57, 181
looms, 212, 217-219
Louti, 144, 148-150

Machris, Maurice, 194
Magan, 23, 25-30, 33, 35, 37-38, 41
magnesium, 133
Majid ibn Said, 104
Majid ibn Sultan, 93
Malik ibn Faham, 55
manganese, 133
mangroves, 11, 12, 16, 157-158, 162, 185
Marib, 39
Marine Aquarium, 179-180
marine environment, 124, 159, 178
Masira, 31, 57, 175, 207
Maysar, 22, 24-25, 29, 32-33, 40, 43
Mazin-ibn-Ghadhubah, 66
Mecca, 39, 65, 69, 101
Mediterranean, 46-47, 53, 161
Meluhha, 25-27, 41
Mercantile Developments, 68
Mesopotamia, 12-13, 23-26, 28, 32-33,
        36-37, 159
metalworkers, 133
mineral deposits., 217
Mining, 4, 20, 22, 24-25, 30-37, 40, 55-57,
        60-61, 131, 133
Minister of Information, 227
Minister of Petroleum and Minerals,
        127, 227
Ministry of Agriculture and Fisheries,
        122,180
Ministry of Commerce and Industry,
        135
Ministry of Petroleum and Minerals,
        126
minke whale, 183
Mirani, 76
Modern Oman, 7, 115-140
modern society, 116
molluscs, 16-18, 57, 176, 185
monsoon, 47, 52-53, 156, 173-174, 176-
        177, 179-180, 184, 187, 208,
        210-211
Moscha, 50-52, 56-57
moths, 202
mouse-tailed bat, 192
mud-snail, 185
Muhammad ibn Abdulla al Khalili, 108
Muhammad ibn Nasir al Ghafiri, 90
Muhammad Ibn Sa'ad, 65
Muhanna ibn Sultan, 90
Mundhir, 59
Munton, Paul, 198
Musandam, 23, 46, 52, 58, 60, 67, 74, 79-
        80, 91, 108-109, 121, 166, 168,
        175, 191, 198, 202, 206, 216
        223-224, 226
Muscat, 15-16, 22, 40, 58, 68, 73-80, 83,
        87, 89-101, 105-110, 121, 131,
        134-139, 145, 151, 153-154,
        170, 172-175, 180, 182-184,
        197-199, 202, 215, 226.
Muttrah, 76, 80, 92-93, 105
myrrh, 39, 47-49, 53, 55, 73, 77
Mysore, 96, 98
Nadir Shah, 90-93, 95
Nannorrhops ritchieana, 223, 225
Naram-Sin, 26, 33

national economy, 131-132
National Health Programme, 118
Natural History Museum, 153, 164,
        177, 183, 188, 191
Natural history, 7, 141-212
Navy, 69, 73, 79-80, 87, 89, 91, 95-96,
        101-102, 104, 109
Nearchus, 46
Nestorian Church, 60
nickel, 32, 133
Niebuhr, Carsten, 30
Nineveh, 41
Nizwa, 30-31, 55, 58, 67, 73, 82, 85, 87,
        89-91, 97, 100
non-oil sector, 120, 133-134
Nubian ibex, 147-148, 164, 196
Occidental Oman, 127, 129
oil discoveries, 111
oil exploration, 111, 126-127
oil, 27, 32, 51, 111, 120, 126-135, 138,
        151, 170-171
oil price, 129
oil production, 120, 127, 129-130, 132
oil sector, 120
Oligocene period, 168
olive ridley, 181
Oman Aviation, 155
Oman Chromite Company, 133
Oman Development Bank, 135
Oman Mining Company, 30, 133
Oman Refinery Company, 129
Oman's Geological Heritage, 172, 226
Omanisation, 128-129
open cast mines, 31
oryx, 14-15, 18, 29, 143-148, 150, 164,
        169, 187, 191-196
oryx reintroduction programme, 194
Ottoman, 96, 101
palm, 29, 56, 206, 223-225
palm tree, 223
PDO, 8, 42, 62, 64, 78, 112, 126-131, 135,
        155,
pearl-oyster, 16, 56
Periplus of the Erythraen Sea, 51, 56-57,
        159
Persian leaf-nosed bat, 192
Persian siege of Basra, 96
Persian siege of Sohar, 91, 93
Persians, 16, 41, 55, 59-60, 66-67, 69, 78,
        90-93, 96, 101, 105, 138
Phillips, Wendell, 50
Phoenicians, 38
Phoenix dactylifera, 223
Phoenix, 49, 194, 223
pit-loom, 217-218
plantlife, 147, 188
Plants of Dhofar, 216
Pliny, 48-49, 51-53, 57-58, 159
Political Resident in Oman, 100
population growth, 121
population, 32, 41, 118, 121, 131, 144,
        146, 158, 177, 181, 195, 198-
        199, 215
Portuguese boat building, 76
Portuguese, 63, 68-69, 71, 73-85, 87, 89,
        138, 151

Portuguese strongholds, 80
Portuguese supremacy in the Indian
        Ocean, 78
potters, 36, 215
pottery, 13, 17, 22, 25, 29, 36-40, 45, 50, 60
Potts, D.T., 12, 15-16, 20-22, 25-26, 35, 37,
        39-40, 59, 67, 226
Pre-Cambrian Period, 171
primary schools, 115-116
prism seal, 29
private sector, 132, 134
Prosopis cineraria, 189
Protection of wildlife, 187
Ptolemy, 40, 53, 58
Ptolemy's map, 40, 58
Qaboos, 99, 110-111,114-116, 118, 131,
        137-139, 185, 187, 194, 213
Qade, 41
Qais ibn Azzan, 104
Qais ibn Zuhair, 60
Qalhat, 55, 68, 70-71, 75
Qatar B, 15
Qawasim, 96, 100-102
Queen Sheba, 156
Queen Victoria, 103
Quriyat, 30, 71, 73-75, 80, 92
Qurm mangrove, 158, 185
Ra's al Hadd, 174, 178
Ra's al-Hamra, 16-17, 157
Ra's al-Junayz, 25, 38
Ra's al-Khaimah, 96
Ra's Jibsh, 18
radio-carbon dating, 16
rainfall, 47, 122, 147, 168, 174, 187, 189,
        195, 215
Ramlat Fasad, 15
rasal, 225
ratel, 191
Red Sea, 38-39, 46, 51, 56, 75, 77, 97, 107,
        160-161, 166, 175, 180, 196
reed, 225
reptiles, 159, 190-191, 200-201
resources, 30, 36, 120, 124, 128, 131-135,
        137, 168, 178
rhim gazelle, 197
Rim-Sin, 37
Risso's dolphin, 183-184
rock hyrax, 191
rolags, 215-216, 224
Roman, 38-39, 47-49, 51-53, 58, 77
Romans, 46, 51, 56, 70, 151
Rostaq, 58-59, 79, 89, 91, 94-95, 97, 104,
        202
Royal Geographic Society's Wahiba
        Sands Project, 188
Royal Geographical Society, 169
Rub al-Khali, 168-169, 188, 215
rugs, 218-219
Said ibn Sultan, 96, 102-104
Saif ibn Himyar, 91-92
Saif ibn Sultan, 75, 89-93
Salalah, 50, 52, 57, 137,145, 155-156, 168,
        172-176, 180, 215
Salih ibn Ali, 106-107
Salim ibn Rashid al Kharusi, 108
Salim ibn Thuwaini, 105

Salm, Rodney, 6, 153, 179
Samad Period, 55-56, 61
Samaram, 50 (see also Samhuram)
Samhar, 50 (see also Samhuram)
Samhuram, 47, 50-53, 57
sand cat, 191
sand fox, 191
sardines, 19, 124, 178-179, 184
Sargassum, 175-177
Sargon, 25, 33
Saruq, 15
Sasanian Empire, 59
Sasanians, 59
Saudi Arabia, 15-16, 23, 111, 139,144, 194, 197, 216
Sayyid Said ibn Sultan, 102-104
SCUBA, 151, 178, 180
sea snakes, 159, 182, 200
sea-fogs, 145
seals of Umm an-Nar Period, 29
seamen, 38, 56
sea routes, control of 56
secondary schools, 116-117
Seeb International Airport, 136
sei whale, 183
Seljuk dynasty, 68
Seljuks, 68
settlements & cultivation skills, 17, 20-22, 35, 37-39, 56, 59, 75
Seven Year War, 96
Shah Alam, 102
Shaikh Muhammad ibn Sulaiman, 109
sharks, 151, 160, 178, 180
Sharqiyah, 25
sheep, 20, 29, 123, 215-217
shepherds, 215-218
Shikar Safari Club, 194
Shisr, 39-40
shoreline, 11-12,124, 153, 159-161, 176, 178
silk, 68, 216-218
Siya, 21
skinks, 200
slaves, 47, 57, 89, 97, 100, 110
smelting, 20, 22, 31-32, 135
Smythe, Kathleen, 185
snakes, 159, 182, 200-201
snorkel, 178, 180
Socotra cormorants, 204, 206
Socotra, 70-71, 75, 204, 206, 209-210, 226
soft-stone vessels, 37
Sohar, 30, 32, 36, 40, 42, 52, 55, 60, 66-68, 75, 78, 80, 90-94, 96, 100-101, 104-105, 133, 173-174
Somali Current, 174
Somali white-toothed shrew, 192
sorghum, 16, 21-22, 29
sperm whale, 153, 183-184

spinner dolphin, 183
spiny tailed lizard, 200
spotted dolphin, 183
Statistical Yearbook, 120-121
Steatite, 18, 36, 40
Stone Age, 11, 13, 187
stone arrowheads, 13
stone implements, 13, 16
stone tools, 13, 15
Stone-Age man, 158
striped hyaena, 219
students, 115-117, 120
Sulaiman ibn Himyar, 110
Sultan Al Qasimi, 102, 226
Sultan ibn Murshid, 90-92
Sultan ibn Saif II, 89-90
Sultan Sayyid Faisal ibn Turki, 107
Sultan Sayyid Said ibn Taimur, 106, 110-111
Sultan Sayyid Taimur ibn Faisal, 108-110
Sultan Sayyid Thuwani ibn Said, 104
Sultan Sayyid Turki ibn Said, 105-106
Suma Oriental, 75
Sumer, 25, 27
Sumeria, 13, 20, 24, 26, 36-37
Sumerian, 25, 35
Sumerians, 13, 23, 31-33
Sumhuram, 50 (see also Samhuram)
Syagrus, 51-52
Tabari, 65
tahr, 150,,164, 191, 197-199
Taqi Khan, 90-91
Tarikh al-rusul wa-al-muluk, 65
Tawi Sa'id, 38
Tawi Silaim, 21
teachers, 116, 120
temperatures, 47, 173, 176-177, 192-193
terrestrial life, 187
Theophrastus, 48-49
Thesiger, Wilfred, 199, 203
Thomas, Bertram, 108-109
Thuwani, 99, 104-107
Tiwi, 71
Tome Pires, 68-69, 71, 75
tortoise-shell, 56-57
tourism, 112, 136, 147
Trade, 23-25, 27-28, 31, 35-38, 41, 47, 50-53, 56, 67-68, 71, 76-77, 87, 89, 93, 96-98, 100, 102, 106, 120-122, 134, 138
Trade with Magan, 27
Travels in Arabia, 30
Tribulus, 149
trident bat, 192
Triops, 206
Tristan da Cunha, 71
tuna, 124, 178, 183
Turkestan, 24

Turkey versus the Portuguese, 77
turtle-eaters, 163
turtles, 17-18, 29, 38, 57, 162-163, 177, 181-182, 190, 200
Ubar, 39-40, 226
Umm an-Nar period, 22, 24-25, 29, 32-33, 36, 40
Umm an-Nar, 21-25, 27-40
United Nations, 111, 137, 139
Ur-Nammu, 27
Varanus griseus, 200
vegetational zones, 188
visitor centres, 136
Wadi Andam, 25
Wadi Bahla, 25, 40
Wadi Batha, 25
Wadi Far, 25
Wadi Halfayn, 25
Wadi Ibra, 25
Wadi Ithli, 25
Wadi Jizzi, 21,25, 30, 32, 36,
Wadi Samad, 21, 25, 29, 32, 39-40
Wadi Sarin Nature Reserve, 198
Wadi Sarin, 197-199
Wadi Sunaysil, 36
Wadi Suq Period, 32-33, 35-38
Wadi Suq, 21, 32-33, 35-38, 55
Wahhabi, 101, 104-105
Wahiba Sands, 15, 148, 164, 169, 188, 203, 215, 218
Wakidi, 65
Wali Ahmad ibn Said, 92-93
weavers, 215-218, 225
weaving, 4, 215-218, 225
Wellstead, J.R., 31, 103
Whale Hall, 153, 164, 183
whale sharks, 153
whales, 17, 153, 161, 164, 183-184
wheat, 21, 29, 51, 68, 83, 98, 122
White Oryx Project, 200, 203-204
white-tailed mongoose, 191
wild cat, 191
Wild Flowers of Northern Oman, 188
wild palm, 223, 225
wind, 151, 168, 170, 174, 179, 193
wool, 27, 214, 216-217
World Wildlife Fund, 194
Ya'aruba rulers, 87
Yalooni, 13, 16, 143, 146, 148, 150, 169, 187, 193-197, 200, 204,
Yarubi rulers, 42
Yemen, 39, 59-60, 139, 194
Yibal, 111, 126, 129
Zanzibar, 98-100, 102-105, 107
Zarins, Juris, 39
Zenobian islands, 56-57
Zenobians, 70
Zubara, 96, 101